LINCOLN'S QUEST FOR UNION

shifting field of vision   p. 154

a public arena of political rhetoric   p. 154
   that he domesticated

largest trial practice   p. 172

supremely honest   p. 176

Lincoln's sense of the outrageous   p. 178

consolidate his political career   p. 179

HE TRIED FLEETINGLY TO FIND A PUBLIC SELF TOO SOON   p 206

The rhetorical difficulty Lincoln faced   p. 218
was to express the meaning of the spread of slavery.

Cimmerian darkness - p 225

"no one's laugh was heartier than his"   p 237

LINCOLN'S QUEST FOR UNION

A PSYCHOLOGICAL PORTRAIT

Charles B. Strozier

SECOND EDITION, REVISED
FOREWORD BY GEOFFREY C. WARD

Philadelphia 2001
PAUL DRY BOOKS

First Paul Dry Books Edition, 2001

Paul Dry Books, Inc.
Philadelphia, Pennsylvania
www.pauldrybooks.com

Text type: Monotype Bembo
Display type: Bauer Bodoni
Composed by Duke & Company
Designed by Adrianne Onderdonk Dudden

1 3 5 7 9 10 8 6 4 2
Printed in the United States of America

Library of Congress Cataloging-in-Publication Data

Strozier, Charles B.
    Lincoln's quest for union : a psychological portrait / Charles B. Strozier ; foreword
by Geoffrey C. Ward.— 2nd ed., rev.
        p. cm.
    Includes bibliographical references and index.
    ISBN 0-9679675-1-1 (alk. paper)
        1. Lincoln, Abraham, 1809–1865. 2. Lincoln, Abraham, 1809–1865—Psychology. 3.
Presidents—United States—Biography. I. Title.

E457 .S897 2001
973.7'092—dc21
[B]
                                                                                00-068086

Frontispiece: *Abraham Lincoln in 1858. Courtesy of Arthur P. Dudden.*

For Trevor, Jay, and Carolyn

Contents

Illustrations

———•———

Foreword

Lincoln's Quest for Union is one of the most important—and most provocative—books about Abraham Lincoln to have been published in the past quarter of a century. It seeks in the grim facts of its subject's boyhood the causes of the depressions that wracked him all his life, shrewdly probes the complexity of his marriage (and the conflicted personality of his wife), and boldly posits that before he could become the implacable champion of the American Union, Lincoln first had to heal deep divisions within himself.

Yet when Charles Strozier first published *Lincoln's Quest for Union* in 1982, several of his eminent predecessors in the field dismissed his efforts to unravel the mysteries of Lincoln's personality—through insights derived from Freud, Erik Erikson, and Heinz Kohut—as something roughly akin to voodoo. Psychobiography was in bad odor then, in part because of the grandiose claims being made for it by its least supple practitioners, partly because of the evident terror the merest whiff of psychological speculation struck in the hearts of many traditional historians. And at its worst, psychobiography was everything its enemies charged—jargon-ridden, reductive, ahistorical.

Strozier's work was different, however. He wrote with vigor and clarity and narrative power, for one thing, and he imposed no theoretical templates on the facts of Lincoln's life, never forced his subject to run a gauntlet of preordained "stages of life." His goal was to be "both careful and psychological," the result being that, since this book's first appearance, no one writing about the private Lincoln has been able to do so without dealing seriously with the ideas Strozier explores.

One needn't agree with all of the author's speculations to enjoy this new edition. Strozier is clearly comfortable with the notion that history and biography are endless arguments. His critics were not sparing in their initial reaction to his book, and this time around he takes obvious pleasure, both in his revised text and the footnotes that accompany it, in giving as good as he got. But he also listened: new ideas have been inserted, old ones discarded.

Eighteen years after it first appeared, *Lincoln's Quest for Union* still does what only the very best books about Lincoln do: It makes us think afresh about how so great a man could have grown from such meager beginnings.

Geoffrey C. Ward

Preface

Lincoln continues to be the subject of fast-moving research and spirited debate. So much of his story has become legend that we are probably better informed about the trivial anecdotes and more confused about the significant events of his formative years than about those of any other figure in American history. Most of us know—or think we know—a good deal more about his rail splitting or his absentmindedness than we do about the shape of his personality, especially the sources of his periodic, paralyzing bouts of depression; what gave meaning to his relationship with his wife and his children (and what difference it makes); and what made him a leader uniquely fitted for a nation rent by discord. In suggesting some tentative answers to these and related questions, I have drawn upon a considerable body of documentary evidence. Throughout my approach is avowedly psychohistorical: that is, I have attempted to apply concepts from psychoanalytic theory critically and unobtrusively to bring the evidence alive in some new ways.

This new edition has given me the welcome opportunity to revise some sections in the light of recent scholarship and to correct some minor errors in the original. I have not altered the argument in any significant way; that has stood the test of time rather well since I first published this book in 1982. But in a number of places in the text and notes, I have incorporated the results of insights of colleagues, and in other places I argue with the conclusions of those who have been criticizing me for, lo, these many years. I also have deleted a chapter on what I called then the "group self of the 1850s," which at best represented something of a digression. I would like to think of this new edition as a more perfect version of the original. This is a book of my youth, conceived before I turned thirty, and published well before I turned forty. I have not tried to tinker with it excessively from the vantage of middle age.

No one can tell the completely "true" story of any piece of the past. In the case of Lincoln it is particularly difficult to sort out fact from legend. For his childhood, there are no contemporary records, except indirect and relatively insignificant documents such as bills of sale. Both of Lincoln's parents were illiterate, so the tapestry of letters one often finds in educated families is absent. Mythmakers have found great material in Lincoln's early years because of the paucity of evidence about them and because of the idealizing needs of a country newly reunited after a terrible civil war.

Lincoln's years of youth and maturity, though better documented, also have been blurred by exaggeration and legend. None of us can remain totally free from the legends of Abraham Lincoln, for they are too deeply embedded in the American consciousness. We learn them too early. The stories come to us as fairy tales, and we in turn embellish them with unconscious fantasy. Often as adults we turn against such idealized images of our childhood; a figure like Lincoln easily attracts debunkers who search relentlessly for warts that will turn heroes into antiheroes. Psychologically, however, debunking and idealizing represent two sides of our ambivalent attitude toward parental figures. Both are rooted in the needs and confusions of childhood, and both carry the burden of irrational distortion.

Probably every biographer identifies with his subject to some extent and is likely to distort the subject if he fails to acknowledge this. In this book I make no naive claim of being above this dilemma. The "real" Lincoln remains obscure to me. However, I have been acutely sensitive to the issue of my own involvement with Lincoln. I have analyzed my dreams of him and noted rather precisely the way he fits into my imagination. I have tried to gain insight into the point of convergence between his life and my own. Such self-examination is not frivolous self-absorption but an attempt to go beyond mere idealization or debunking to the critical subjectivity that defines the working method of psychohistory.[1]

To a large extent this book is theoretically eclectic; there is nothing to be gained by forcing historical materials into any Procrustean bed. I have tried to become familiar with the essence of psychoanalytic theory since Freud and to use it to shape my questions of the sources. Many competing "schools," for example, have shed light on the intricacies of the mourning process. I have tried to read widely and deeply in this literature. Nevertheless, as a close student of Heinz Kohut and as a product of the Chicago Institute for Psychoanalysis, I owe a special intellectual debt to psychoanalytic self psychology.[2]

★★★

For the most part this book relies on sources familiar to historians. There is no way anyone could read everything that has been written on Lincoln, nor would anyone of intelligence want to. Most is trivial or legendary or derivative. As James G. Randall once put it wryly: "The vastness of Lincoln literature is a bit misleading."[3] One learns after some time in the field which books are reliable, and these are dutifully mentioned in my notes. But the essential source for the book is Lincoln himself: his letters, speeches, poetry, and miscellaneous writing that make up *The Collected Works.* I have also consulted the letters, diaries, and comments of those contemporaries who knew or worked with Lincoln. This book is biography, not social history, but I have tried to paint as rich a picture as possible of Lincoln's world.

One Lincoln document I use extensively deserves special mention. On the brink of his election as President, Lincoln wrote a very brief autobiographical sketch. This document lacks the expansive quality of Gandhi's *My Experiments with Truth,* the bombastic fervor of Hitler's *Mein Kampf,* or the relentlessly introspective vigor of Freud's *The Interpretation of Dreams.* Still, it is important for an understanding of Lincoln. In it, he looked back on his childhood, youth, and rise to prominence at that critical juncture before accomplishing his major work. Certainly political ambition motivated his reflections. Few people outside Illinois knew much about him, and in those days it was regarded as unseemly for a candidate to campaign on his own behalf. His story, as prepared for John L. Scripps in the early summer of 1860, brought before the public the politically relevant facts of his life. But the effort of recalling his past also brought forth a number of psychologically significant memories filtered through a half century of experience. Telling that story was not an easy chore for Lincoln, whom his law partner, William Herndon, once characterized as "the most shut-mouthed man" he had ever known. "There was something about his origin he never cared to dwell on," Herndon wrote. In talking with Lincoln, Scripps at first faced considerable difficulty in getting him to communicate "the homely facts of his youth." Lincoln protested to Scripps that it was "a great piece of folly to attempt to make anything out of my early life. It can all be condensed into a simple sentence, and that sentence you will find in Gray's *Elegy*, 'The short and simple annals of the poor.' That's my life, and that's all you or anyone else can make out of it."[4]

Anyone working on Lincoln has to deal with William Herndon. The devoted law partner decided from the moment of Lincoln's death that he would spend the rest of his life researching and writing a biography. He spent many years jotting down his own thoughts and collecting the thoughts of others. But the book itself languished. Herndon, in need of money, allowed Ward Hill Lamon and his ghostwriter, Chauncey Black, to use, for a fee, his materials for their 1872 *Life*. Herndon's book did finally appear in 1889, but only with the help of a competent young journalist, Jesse Weik. What emerged from this collaboration was an extensive correspondence between the two coauthors and the most controversial book ever written on Lincoln. Bound in "three ridiculous little volumes," as Herndon's biographer, David Donald, comments, Herndon's and Weik's *Life of Lincoln* "has been absorbed into the stream of American folklore. It is usually safe to wager that any well-known anecdote about Lincoln derives from Herndon's writings."[5]

But there is more than folklore to Herndon's *Lincoln*. Herndon knew Lincoln longer and saw him in more varied public, private, and work situations than did any other man or woman except for Lincoln's wife, Mary, who left no such full record. Herndon had a rich fund of experience on which to draw, and in his own curious way he was committed to the truth. He created virtually every important myth about Lincoln, and yet his book made him our most important source on the pre-presidential man. The key to truth or falsehood in Herndon lies in attention to his own sources and understanding a few important characteristics of his personality. He was an outgoing, flamboyant, young man who seemed to become instantly and uncritically loyal to Lincoln when he joined him as a law partner in 1844. Herndon jealously rivaled Mary for Lincoln's attention. The proud owner of an impressive library, he was well read and informed on current intellectual developments. He served actively in Whig, and later Republican, circles, and even won election for one term as Springfield's mayor. He was a highly competent lawyer whom Lincoln was able to entrust with an equal share of the business and even, during Lincoln's frequent spells of campaigning, all of it.

Yet Herndon, when he later attempted to analyze Lincoln, lacked a sense of humor and seemed constitutionally deficient in compassion or empathy. His mind was always rushing forward, frantically searching for a new idea before digesting the last one. He loved to pile on adjectives with breathless haste. Lincoln was thus "tough-solid-knotty-gnarly, more or less like his body." Dashes also expressed the flurry and confusion in Herndon's mind: "The *whole* of the man objectively and subjectively, should be truthfully and fully, without suppression, suggestion—or evasion —or other form of falsehood, stated—generously written out."[6]

Herndon never consciously lied. In fact he attempted (at times with a kind of naive passion) to tell the truth. David Donald was struck by the fact that no letter or manuscript of Herndon's "reveals a desire or willingness to tell an untruth about Lincoln."[7] This is in marked contrast to Lincoln's secretaries, John G. Nicolay and John Hay, for example, who deliberately skewed their story of Lincoln to keep Robert Lincoln happy, for he controlled the papers on which their book was based. But Herndon was a terrible historian, a gullible listener, and a pretentious generalizer. When he relied on someone else as a source—that is, when he acted as a historian organizing and interpreting the evidence rather than providing it from personal experience—he was usually wrong. Thus most of Herndon's portrait of Lincoln that falls outside their period of extended contact (1837 to 1861) can be discarded.

There are also problems with what Herndon reports about Lincoln in the years when he knew him in Springfield. Paul Angle, who wrote a preface to Herndon's republished book in 1930, felt that "when Herndon relates a fact of his own observation it may generally be accepted without question."[8] But even in dealing with those years when he was closest to Lincoln, Herndon often got things muddled, his memory sometimes blurred, and his own idealization of Lincoln helped give a mythical edge to his story. For example, he claimed to know some surprising things about Lincoln's sexual activities.[9] Most of these statements require corroboration before they can even tentatively be accepted. Finally, Herndon tended to overstate his own importance and, on many issues, to misunderstand Lincoln's subtle irony.

A different kind of problem is presented by Herndon's portrait of Mary and his account of Lincoln's domestic life. Herndon's view of Mary was distinctly uncharitable, and he characterized Lincoln's home life as a "domestic hell." We know from other sources that Mary always detested Herndon for his vulgarity and drunkenness and, perhaps, because she cherished an exclusive love for Lincoln that Herndon's abject devotion seemed to threaten. The fact that Herndon never entered the Lincoln home might cast some doubt on his account of their domestic relations. However, Herndon worked daily with Lincoln not four blocks from that home, saw him interact with his children at the offices on Sunday, and was himself a member of the same small (perhaps "tight" would be more accurate) Springfield community as Lincoln for his entire adult life. Therefore, his views on Lincoln's domestic life, though indirect, merit serious, if cautious, consideration.

The material Herndon collected for his book presents even more complex problems than his personal memories of events. After Lincoln's death, he wrote to everyone he could who had known Lincoln and asked them to write down their memories.

He also interviewed former acquaintances throughout Kentucky, Indiana, and central Illinois and, with the illiterate, wrote down what they told him. This was one of the first extensive oral history projects in American history and, until technology facilitated interviewing, one of the most important. These fascinating materials, recently published in a book superbly edited by Douglas Wilson and Rodney Davis, *Herndon's Informants* (University of Illinois Press, 1998), have only begun to be used thoroughly. Ward Hill Lamon and Chauncey Black, lacking sympathy for Lincoln, insensitive to nuance, and unable to evaluate this material critically, abused the material in their 1872 *Life*. The same can be said for most writers, including Herndon himself, until Carl Sandburg, whose 1920s *Abraham Lincoln* was sympathetic and sensitive but, alas, not very critical. In fact, Sandburg's lyrical success turned subsequent writers against the Herndon material altogether.

Around the time of Sandburg, Albert Beveridge, a relentless researcher, presented a marvelously detailed picture of Lincoln's early days and log cabin life. His description, to my mind, remains the best available for detail and accuracy. But Beveridge's account has its limitations. He took a harsh view of Lincoln's father, Thomas, was disgusted with rural life in general, and seemed to be ambivalent about Lincoln himself. Beveridge's most significant failing was that he had no sensitivity to important psychological issues. Thus his only comment on the effect of the death of Lincoln's mother restricts the possibility of interpretation: "Abraham was now nine years old, and there is no evidence that his emotions were unlike those of other children of similar age and in that situation."[10]

The most important Lincoln biographer of our generation, David Donald, uses the Herndon documents well but sparingly.[11] There is, of course, need for extreme caution in using this material. Memories fade, and with Lincoln, many factors in play after 1865 distorted dimly recalled antebellum scenes. By then any early association with the martyred president, even a fantasized one, was treasured. One can make a good case that the best approach to these documents is to use in them only what can be corroborated elsewhere in the written record.

That approach, however, shortchanges the value of Herndon's vast records. Oral history is now regarded with much more respect than before. Roy Basler, who helped turn subsequent writers away from the Herndon material with his comments on Sandburg in 1935, subsequently changed his mind. "When I was writing *The Lincoln Legend*," he once said, "I was a young man and saw the people Herndon talked to as old fools. I'm now almost a half century older and read this material differently." Basler also noted that, although it is unlikely the interpretation of Lincoln's war years would change much, the complete story of Lincoln's childhood and youth—indeed, the whole story before 1860—has yet to be written.[12]

LINCOLN'S QUEST FOR UNION

I have found that people who know that they are preferred or favored by their mother[s] give evidence in their lives of a peculiar self-reliance and an unshakeable optimism which often seem like heroic attributes and bring actual success to their possessors.

Sigmund Freud, *The Interpretation of Dreams*

1

CHILDHOOD ON THE FRONTIER

"God bless my mother," Lincoln told his law partner, William Herndon, in 1850. "All that I am or ever hope to be I owe to her." This simple, direct, and perhaps eternal human sentiment had particular poignancy for Lincoln because he believed his mother was illegitimate. This statement to Herndon was one of the few times Lincoln mentioned his mother. He and Herndon were riding in a buggy to court in Menard County to handle a suit that raised the issue of hereditary traits. Lincoln said his mother, Nancy, was the illegitimate daughter of Lucy Hanks and a well-bred Virginia farmer or planter. From this Virginian, Herndon remembered Lincoln saying, came all the traits—his power of analysis, logic, mental activity, and ambition—that distinguished him from the Hanks family. He even appeared to believe that "illegitimate children are often-times sturdier and brighter than those born in lawful wedlock." Having unburdened himself, Lincoln became quiet and was "sad and absorbed." The buggy moved on but not a word was spoken. "He drew round him a barrier which I feared to penetrate. His words and melancholy tone made a deep impression on me. It was an experience I can never forget."[1]

There are a variety of ways to interpret Herndon's account of this experience. One is to dismiss it as improbable. To do so, however, is to reject Herndon as a source in the one area where all thoughtful observers agree his word is valid: where he recounts an actual experience he had with Lincoln. The episode, of course, proves nothing about Lincoln's genealogy. It only suggests that Lincoln doubted his mother's legitimacy. A more interesting question that could be asked is which mother Lincoln had in mind when he spoke of his gratitude, for he deeply loved his stepmother, Sarah Lincoln, and yet undoubtedly had a residue of feelings for his biological mother, Nancy Hanks Lincoln. This question would seem an open one if Lincoln had only credited his "angel mother" for all that he was. Lincoln, however, went beyond that somewhat stereotyped praise to dwell on the issue that really concerned him—his mother's legitimacy. No one, not even any of the people Herndon interviewed in Kentucky or Indiana, ever questioned Sarah Lincoln's legitimacy. Many questioned the legitimacy of Nancy Lincoln. Furthermore, in his autobiography, Lincoln described Nancy as his "mother" and Sarah, though she "proved to be a good and kind mother," as his "stepmother." Lincoln also told his friend Leonard Swett that he had only faint recollections of his mother, for he was so young when she died, but, Swett concluded, "he spoke most kindly of her and of his stepmother, and of her [Sarah's] care for him in providing for his wants."[2] The distinctions in these statements implied a quality of caretaking (mothering) that Lincoln attributed to the kind and gentle Sarah. Sarah could thus be a "mother" and yet clearly be distinguished in Lincoln's mind as stepmother. Lincoln used words carefully.

The issue of Nancy Hank's illegitimacy may seem trivial, but few aspects of the Lincoln story have been more exhaustively investigated. During the 1920s two formidable genealogists—Louis A. Warren and William E. Barton—debated the Hanks ancestry. They tramped through graveyards, combed Virginia and Kentucky archives, and pulled together every scrap of relevant and irrelevant information. Ideally, this kind of basic research produces general agreement on the facts; in this case, however, passionate disagreement resulted. Both Warren and Barton were serious, honest, diligent, informed; yet they came to opposite conclusions. Warren felt he had demonstrated the legitimacy of Nancy Hanks; Barton persuaded himself of the opposite. Nor is the issue in this debate one of sentimentality versus realism. Many rigorous scholars accept Warren, while Barton's research influenced the misty-eyed Carl Sandburg:

> The mother of Nancy was nineteen years old when she made this trip [from Virginia to Kentucky] leaving Nancy's father, who had not married her, back in Virginia. She could croon in the moist evening twilight to the shining face in the sweet bundle. "Hush thee, hush thee, thy father's a gentleman." She could toss the bundle into the air against a far, hazy line of blue mountains, catch it in her two hands as it came down, let it snuggle to her breast, and feed, while she asked, "Here we come—where from?"[3]

There is little to be gained by rehearsing the endlessly complex details that support each side of the argument over the legitimacy of Lincoln's mother. All of the "hard" evidence needed to settle such a discussion is absent.[4] Nevertheless, as David Donald has pointed out, Lucy was once charged with fornication in Mercer County, Kentucky; no marriage license has come to light to show that Lucy was wed before the birth of her daughter; the Kentucky and Illinois settlers whom Herndon interviewed agreed on the illegitimacy of Nancy; and Lincoln in his autobiography said his mother was "of the name of Hanks" (Lucy's maiden name). On the other side of the argument, the position of Louis Warren is quite strong, and Donald feels that "there is room for honest difference of opinion." Still, as Donald concludes, there seems to be a "slight preponderance of testimony favoring the Herndon theory of illegitimacy," and most scholars now accept the fact of Nancy's illegitimacy.[5]

Illegitimacy has always been a common but sensitive aspect of American family life. Our religious and social traditions place a heavy weight on those who are, or believe they are, born out of wedlock. The precise meaning of illegitimacy, however, has varied enormously over time for different individuals in various parts of the country. African Americans in slavery, for example, out of necessity developed a much more accommodating attitude toward bastard children than their hypocritical white masters who often sired these children.[6] And in white society itself there was a great deal of difference between the sentimentalized domesticity of the urban middle class and the raw reality of life on the frontier. The "cult of domesticity" in the first half of the nineteenth century extolled the virtues of a benevolent, wise father, as idealized in the figure of George Washington, and a devoted, present, capable mother, as described in Catherine Beecher's *Treatise on Domestic Economy*.[7] There were, of course, variations in this picture, and recent work on the history of women has noted several competing "styles" of domestic adaptation during the period.[8] Still, idealized family life in the antebellum days glorified paternal values of moral authority and maternal values of acquiescent warmth and devotion to the hearth. A generation of American statesmen credited their "angel mothers"—exalted, pure, pious—for all they became. The ideal carried with it an implicit condemnation of illegitimacy.

Lincoln's experience with and attitudes toward illegitimacy departed sharply from this middle-class, urban ideal. For the Lincoln family, and probably for the frontier community at large, illegitimacy formed an integral and accepted part of life. Charles Friend, who had grown up with Lincoln in Kentucky, told Herndon, "In this country all bastard children are taught to call their mothers 'aunt' . . . ," which is what Nancy apparently called her mother, Lucy.[9] For a number of years after the move to Indiana, Nancy's illegitimate first cousin, Dennis Hanks, lived with the family, and Sophie Hanks, who resided in the area, was one of six illegitimate children of a Sarah or Polly Hanks.[10]

Even Lincoln may have doubted his own paternity: At least there is *some* evidence that the painstakingly honest Herndon *thought* Lincoln implied as much. "From what Lincoln has casually and indirectly said," Herndon wrote Ward Hill Lamon on February 25, 1870, "I was convinced that his illegitimacy was thrown up to him when a boy."[11] When Lamon balked at this information, he drew forth Herndon's wrathful reply: "If I thought Mr. Lincoln an illegitimate I should state it. . . . He was born into the social world with a curse on him, a millstone tied to his neck."[12] In 1886 Herndon spelled out his elaborate theory in a long letter to his coauthor, Jesse W. Weik: Thomas Lincoln was sterile; he married the pregnant Nancy because his first love, Sarah Bush, had rejected him; Nancy had been made pregnant by Abraham Enloe, who continued to live in Kentucky and who later fathered two more children by Nancy (including Abraham); sometime in 1815 Thomas found Nancy and Enloe together, and a terrible fight resulted in which Thomas bit off Enloe's nose; Thomas then left Kentucky for Indiana; and Nancy never again became pregnant, nor did Thomas's second wife, his first love, the widowed Sarah Bush Johnston. However, there is not much evidence to recommend Herndon's theory. William E. Barton

*William Herndon in old age, when he wrote his classic biography of
Lincoln with the help of the younger and more disciplined Jesse Weik.
Courtesy of Meserve-Kunhardt Collection.*

and Louis A. Warren have effectively discredited the Enloe thesis, and David Donald has remarked that the notion of Lincoln's
illegitimacy is "utterly groundless."[13]

Herndon seemed to feel that Lincoln carried "a millstone
tied to his neck" with the knowledge of his mother's illegitimacy
and whatever murky misgivings he carried about his own paternity. But here Herndon went beyond reporting, which he did
well, and turned to interpretation, which he usually botched.
Rather than shame, Lincoln felt a secret pride in his clouded past.

On the confessional buggy ride, after telling Herndon of Nancy's illegitimacy, Lincoln continued: "Did you ever notice that bastards are generally smarter, shrewder, and more intellectual than others? Is it because it is stolen?"[14] The distant and mysterious "Virginia planter" thus gave Lincoln a genetic explanation for the profound differences between him and his crude, illiterate, low-born family. "He told me," Herndon reported at another point, "that his relations were *lascivious, lecherous,* not to be trusted."[15] The workings of fantasy seldom follow the rules of logic. Thus, Lincoln failed to question his implicit distinction between his angelic, genetically "high-born" but illegitimate mother and the rest of his crude, lascivious, and lecherous—but legitimate—relations (except for Dennis Hanks). It seems that, as a child, Lincoln had worked out a rather elaborate genetic myth that both explained and nourished his separateness from his family and environment. It may well be that Lincoln in the core of his being harbored the idea that he was a grandson of Thomas Jefferson or George Washington.

Little else is known about Lincoln's mother. Because she is so obscure, Nancy has inspired poetry that has become, for better or worse, part of the record. "She believed in God," wrote Sandburg, "in the Bible, in mankind, in the past and future, in babies, people, animals, flowers, fishes, in foundations and roofs, in time and the eternities outside of time; she was a believer in keeping in silence behind her gray eyes more beliefs than she spoke."[16] Lincoln's account of Nancy in his autobiography is sparse indeed. "Getting back into Kentucky, and having reached his twenty-eighth year, he [Thomas] married Nancy Hanks—mother of the present subject—in the year 1806." Lincoln added simply that his mother was from Virginia and that relatives of hers "of the name of Hanks, and of other names, now reside in Coles, in Macon, and in Adams counties, Illinois, and also in Iowa."[17]

The accounts of Nancy by those who knew her differ in detail but are remarkably consistent in tone and overall impression. "She was a tall slender woman," wrote Lincoln's cousin, John Hanks, "dark-skinned, black hair and eyes, her face was sharp and angular, forehead big. She was beyond all doubts an intellectual woman, rather extraordinary if anything." A neighbor in Indiana, William Woods, who knew Nancy for a year and a half before her death in 1818, also noted how "very smart, intelligent, and intellectual" Nancy was. Dennis Hanks, probably the best source, confirmed the picture painted by others who knew her but added some important details:

> Mrs. Lincoln, Abraham's mother, was five feet eight inches high, spare made, affectionate—the most affectionate I ever saw—never knew her to be out of temper, and thought strong of it. She seemed to be immovably calm; she was keen, shrewd, smart, and I do say highly intellectual by nature. Her memory was strong, her perception was quick, judgment was acute almost. She was spiritually and ideally inclined, not dull, not material, not heavy in thought, feeling, or action. Her hair was dark hair, eyes bluish green— keen and loving. Her weight was one hundred thirty.[18]

There is no question that Nancy could only sign a mark for her name. But she seemed to have a quality of mind that distinguished her in the frontier settings in which she lived. Lincoln himself, interestingly enough, told Herndon that his mother was "an intellectual woman, sensitive and somewhat sad."[19] Many of the contemporary observers whom Herndon interviewed also called her "intellectual." All this has influenced people like Sandburg who would have her reading the Bible to young Abraham.[20] That seems unlikely though not impossible. Many children on the frontier learned to read but not to write. Even some slaves, who almost never wrote anything, learned to read. This quiet, strong woman who never had any opportunity to get an education absorbed readily and thoroughly the oral culture of her environment, a culture that was based much more than today's on the Bible.[21] A smart, receptive person on the frontier could "know" the Bible and still sign with a mark. Nancy must have shared this knowledge with her special son, who in turn was deeply influenced by Biblical phrasing, style, and content. He was also, in his style of intellectuality and creativity, much more a listener and speaker than a reader and writer. Most of his important and memorable prose was written to be read aloud.

Nancy's character can never be fully known. Contemporary observers tended to remember distantly that "Nancy Hanks was as above Thomas Lincoln as an angel is above mud." There is so little to go on that "her face and figure waver through the mists of time and rumor." For Dennis Hanks she was warmly affectionate, never out of temper, and immovably calm. Another theme in the sources notes Nancy's "habitual sadness" that may have some connection with her primitive Baptist faith.[22] It would seem that Nancy was a remarkably intelligent woman who responded warmly and empathically to Lincoln during his earliest years, nourishing him with rich emotional supplies into his late infancy. This is the psychological message one gets from people like Dennis and John Hanks, and it was implied in Lincoln's own memory of his mother when he told Herndon of her angelic quality. Certainly, one suspects that Lincoln's adult strengths—his flexibility, empathy, humor, and creativity—derived from a close, loving relationship with his mother.[23]

But ambivalence affects any relationship. As a young man of twenty-nine, Lincoln wrote a humorous letter on April Fool's Day 1838 to his good friend and maternal figure, Mrs. Orville Browning. The letter mocks his recent unsuccessful courtship of

Mary Owens, whom he could not behold without "thinking of my mother; and this, not from her withered features, for her skin was too full of fat, to permit its contracting into wrinkles; but from her want of teeth, weather-beaten appearance in general, and from a kind of notion that ran in my head, that *nothing* could have commenced at the size of infancy, and reached her present bulk in less than thirty-five or forty years."[24] In this letter Lincoln used the image of his mother as a kind of baseline for ugliness. It is true, of course, that Lincoln called Sarah Lincoln "mother," as he was later to refer to Mary after they had children. But unconsciously "mother" for Lincoln also had to mean Nancy. Perhaps she had become that ugly. Certainly the only form of dentistry in those days was extraction, and on her deathbed she may have looked suddenly old and withered to her young son. The endurance of this image in Lincoln suggests that it carried some sense of childhood disappointment with his mother. In a part of himself he seemed not to trust her.

★★★

Lincoln's father was slightly less obscure than his mother, but he too is a source of endless controversy. The major questions center generally on his competence and possible impotence. These were causally related for Herndon: Thomas was hopelessly incompetent because at some point for some reason he had lost his potency. Herndon was at his worst in handling the primary sources on this question, but he did not invent the story out of wholecloth. Dennis Hanks reported that Thomas and Nancy had no other children after Abraham's birth. The cause was said to be "a private matter."[25] (Hanks was wrong about dates here, for a third child, Thomas, was born in 1811 or 1812; he died within a few days.) Herndon variously gathered reports that Thomas had castrated himself, had one testicle the size of a pea, had two testicles the size of peas, had always been sterile, or had the mumps and then became sterile.[26] Herndon pondered to himself: "But you say that Thomas Lincoln went in swimming and that people saw his manhood was taken out; grant it, and yet no witness fixed the date." Herndon never wavered from the idea that Thomas at some point became sterile. In 1886 he told his coworker Jesse Weik to be sure to confirm this issue with Dennis Hanks: "When you see him, ask him, in a roundabout way, if Thomas Lincoln was not castrated because of the mumps when young. Dennis told me this often and repeated it."[27] For Herndon, Thomas Lincoln's sterility became a crucial factor in his theory of Abraham's illegitimacy as well as a useful explanation for the physiological basis of Thomas's "utter laziness and want of energy." The problem, Herndon wrote, "is due to the fact of fixing."[28]

All the talk to Herndon of Thomas's emasculated or sterile condition carried a decidedly derogatory view of Thomas. A neighbor of Thomas's, Nat Grigsby, told Herndon that Thomas was not "a lazy man, but . . . a piddler, always doing but doing nothing great, was happy, lived easy and contented."[29] This image of Thomas as lazy and inert long held sway in the literature. Josiah G. Holland, who published a book on Lincoln in 1866 after a conversation with Herndon, first introduced the theme of the shiftless, irresponsible Thomas whom Lincoln thoroughly disliked. Ward Hill Lamon, in his 1872 ghostwritten *Life*—also based on the Herndon documents—so disliked Thomas that he wrote of his own "great pleasure" when he could leave him behind in the biography. In 1889 Herndon and Weik arrived at their own characterization of Thomas as "roving and shiftless," "proverbially slow of movement, mentally and physically"; "careless, inert and dull." Thomas could never pay for the parcels of land he purchased, because he never "fell in with the routine of labor." Various writers echoed the main lines of this view of Thomas, especially

Albert Beveridge, whose 1928 book on Lincoln characterized Thomas as "improvident," "slow," and "plodding," "a carpenter of sorts" who farmed in a "desultory way." He could sign his name, according to Beveridge, but preferred to use his mark, even on important documents.[30]

Research in the early twentieth century, however, uncovered some new information on Thomas Lincoln. He always owned one or more horses after he was twenty-one and generally enjoyed credit with no unpaid accounts. An Indiana tax book for 1814 ranked him fifteenth out of ninety-eight in terms of property values for those listed in the local county records. Thomas left Kentucky because of difficulties over title to his land, but many of his contemporaries also suffered from insecurity over land tenure. In post-revolutionary Kentucky, unscrupulous lawyers and speculators exploited the original settlers. In Thomas's case, faulty surveys and title disputes reduced holdings of 238 acres to 200.[31] Thomas brought several pieces of property in Illinois after 1830, though he had to sell some of these to cover his debts.

Thomas was a respected member of the various communities in which he lived. The cabins he built were adequate for his needs. He was a responsible neighbor, a trustworthy citizen, and, with some exceptions as he aged, a good farmer and carpenter. He helped construct local churches and seemed to participate in other community activities.[32] Dennis Hanks noted that Thomas "didn't drink an' cuss none."[33] He was definitely illiterate, able to write only his name, but then educational deficiencies were the rule, not the exception, on the American frontier. Thomas was also a devoted husband to his two wives. He always got along well with Sarah's children, especially John D. Johnston. Dennis Hanks remained a close friend of Thomas's through his later years. And, finally, Thomas was a perfectly good father to his own children by any criteria relevant for early-nineteenth-century frontier life.

Sarah testified to his determination to see his talented son acquire skills he himself lacked. The two quarreled at times, but nothing suggests an open antagonism; Thomas occasionally whipped young Lincoln but hardly brutalized him. Apparently, Thomas was able to handle easily enough the competitive thrust of his son.

Louis A. Warren concluded in 1926 that "We must now bury the traditional Thomas Lincoln in the 'stagnant, putrid pool' discovered by William Herndon, and introduce to future biographers the historical Thomas Lincoln of Hardin County." Paul Angle, in his 1930 edition of Herndon's *Life of Lincoln,* reflected this view of Thomas when he felt obliged to interject an entire paragraph on the "real" Thomas following Herndon's disparaging characterization. Benjamin Thomas agreed with Angle's revised picture of Thomas Lincoln, though he noted: "In the father, Thomas, there seemed to be a falling off in the general level of Abraham's ancestry."[34] After Herndon, in other words, scholars revised the image of Thomas from that of a lazy ne'er-do-well into that of sober, hardworking carpenter and farmer who won the respect of his neighbors.

This revisionist work on Thomas Lincoln has effectively stripped away the myths surrounding the despicable figure created by the early commentators. Thomas was not improvident, slow, terribly lazy, incompetent, dull, or dumb. He was interesting enough, among other things, to attract two apparently outstanding women to be mothers to his children. The revisionist research, however, has been fundamentally misplaced. It has assumed that a grasp of what Thomas was actually like will clarify our understanding of his infinitely more important son. Ironically, Lincoln's mental picture of his father was a good deal closer to Herndon's characterization than observers have wanted to acknowledge. There is little congruence between the three-dimensional figure of the "real" Thomas and Lincoln's psychological conception of him. All the evidence suggests that Lincoln retained some admiration and love for his father but basically grew up with an abiding sense of disappointment with and alienation from him. He struggled mightily with his inner picture of his father, a picture shaped by the distortions of unconscious wishes and fantasies.

The concrete evidence that Lincoln loved his father and dutifully molded his character after him is scant, though not altogether absent. There is no evidence that Lincoln ever openly rebelled against him. As an adolescent, he worked hard at the farming and diverse needs of survival on the frontier. He stayed with the family through its long move to Illinois in 1830 and helped it survive the devastating winter of 1830–31 on the banks of the Sangamon River near Decatur. As an adult, Lincoln often provided financial assistance to his father. Lincoln even named his fourth son Thomas, which at least suggests some degree of affection. In personality, there seems to be a certain line of continuity between father and son. Each had a rich sense of humor and was remembered by neighbors for his friendliness. Both were physically strong and able wrestlers. Both seemed moderate in their habits. At one critical juncture in his own life, Lincoln referred to his father's old saying, "If you make a bad bargain, hug it the tighter."[35] William E. Barton, in 1929, noted that "some of the qualities which made Abraham Lincoln great, his patience, his good humor, his kindliness, his love of fun, he inherited from his father."[36] Such a genial picture of Thomas is questionable, but to the extent that it is true, Lincoln's most memorable personality traits derived in part from his positive identification with his father. It may also be that the source for Lincoln's adult interest in the law, and particularly his frequent handling of land cases, lay in Thomas's difficulty in establishing clear title to his land.

But Lincoln's own picture of his father was painted in many

hues. Most of the hard evidence indicates that in Lincoln's mind Thomas *was* illiterate and irresponsible, a man who chased rainbows but never managed to find any pots of gold, a typical low-born product of the frontier that Lincoln worked hard to escape and to which, once he had escaped, he never returned. Nowhere does Lincoln ever say anything good about Thomas—a reticence that contrasts strikingly with his openly expressed idealization of Nancy and his deep affection for Sarah. Benjamin Thomas came up with an interesting (if strained) interpretation of this aloofness: it reflected Lincoln's "fundamental honesty"; he disliked his father and therefore remained aloof, the only "honest" position to assume.[37]

In fact, Lincoln made clear his negative feeling toward his father, who never quite came up to his own standards. Thus Lincoln, in his 1860 autobiographical statement, described Thomas as a "wandering laboring boy" who grew up "literally without education. He never did more in the way of writing than to bunglingly sign his own name." Some twelve years earlier, in response to a question from a relative, Lincoln also stressed his father's ignorance: "Owing to my father being left an orphan at the age of six years, in poverty, and in a new country, he became a wholly uneducated man; which I suppose is the reason why I know so little of our family history. I believe I can say nothing more that would at all interest you." It seemed to pain Lincoln to realize how dull his father was, which tells more about Lincoln's driving ambition than it does about Thomas's character.[38] As a boy, Lincoln had aspirations beyond his grasp.

Lincoln's style of intellectuality and his interest in books created frequent conflict with his father. Dennis Hanks noted that Thomas sometimes had "to slash him for neglecting his work by reading." His inquisitiveness also irritated Thomas: "When strangers would ride along and up to his father's fence, Abe always, through pride and to tease his father, would be sure to ask the stranger the first question, for which his father would sometimes knock him a rod." This teasing seemed calculated to displace Thomas, who could only respond with anger. Sarah, however, who was undoubtedly more understanding of Thomas, provides a different perspective. "As a usual thing, Mr. Lincoln never made Abe quit reading to do anything if he could avoid it. He would do it himself first." Thomas was sensitive to his own educational deficiencies and wanted "his boy Abraham to learn, and he encouraged him to do it in all ways he could." Lincoln, one suspects, understood these ambitions in his father and played on them. He was "rude and forward" as Dennis noted, teasing, testing, provoking his father by continuing to read when he knew he should be working. Up to a point, Thomas tolerated, even encouraged, his son's independence, but young Lincoln often seemed to push him too far. Then came a whipping, and in Dennis Hanks's phrase, Lincoln would drop "a kind of silent unwelcome tear."[39]

★★★

The homes Thomas built for his family, as they moved west from Kentucky to Indiana and finally to Illinois, were simple log cabins. The cabin in which Lincoln was born had an earthen floor and a roof made of slabs held in place by poles or stones. A small opening in each of the side walls, perhaps covered by greased paper, let in light. Two broad pieces of wood fastened together were hung by hinges to an opening high enough for a man to pass through. A stone fireplace with a chimney of sticks and clay stood at one end of the single room. Everything in the simple structure was made of wood since there was no iron available. The family crowded into the cabin with its one large bed when the children were young; later a smaller bed would serve the children. "The sense of modesty was embryonic," noted Beveridge of log cabins in general, "and men took off their clothes before women without a thought by either of any impropriety."[40]

The first cabin Thomas built in Indiana in the fall of 1816 was a simple lean-to that kept out the wild animals, some of the rain, and hardly any cold. The next spring he built an enclosed structure of rough rather than hewed logs with no window and with

Lincoln's second cousins Dennis Hanks (left) and John Hanks standing beside the old Lincoln home. Dennis married Lincoln's stepsister, Elizabeth. Both Dennis and John Hanks were important, if controversial, contributors to the oral historical record on Lincoln. Courtesy of Lloyd Ostendorf.

a roof that was not yet finished when winter came. This crude building, about four miles from Gentryville, stood on a round hill or "knob." For his growing family Thomas created some additional space by putting in a loft. Sarah Lincoln, who arrived in 1819 as Thomas's second wife, commented later that this was "a good log cabin, tolerably comfortable. . . . Abe slept upstairs, went up on pins stuck in the logs, like a ladder."[41] Years later Thomas built a larger, two-room cabin, which the family never lived in because they left to seek a new home in Illinois. By then Lincoln was a young man.

As we think back to this period in American history, so distant in experience if not in time, it is easy either to romanticize the simple joys of the rugged outdoor life or to shrink back in disgust at the dirt, the smells, the hardships. The allocation of social and sexual roles on the frontier followed the "natural" order of things. Thomas cleared the land, farmed during the season, did all the heavy work with animals, and worked as a carpenter in the off-season. Nancy, and later Sarah, took responsibility for all the chores inside and near the house: cooking, gardening, cleaning, child-rearing. As de Tocqueville was to note somewhat later, special attitudes in America gave women independence and self-reliance in carrying out duties that elsewhere were part of an overall pattern of degradation and inferiority. There were hardships to be sure, but a pervasive equality defined the style of life.[42] Children, too, could acquire certain qualities from the strenuous frontier life—if, however, they were not numbed by the experience. In Lincoln's case, the frontier, it seems, gave him certain strengths such as self-reliance, patience, and understanding. Survival itself demanded them. Yet Lincoln never retained any attachment to the log cabins of his childhood; indeed, he strove relentlessly to rise socially into the comfortable, even genteel, upper middle class. That he later exploited his humble origins for political purposes should not obscure his essential impulse to escape his own past. Ironically, the cabin in which he may have been born rests now within a marble temple in Kentucky. Thus do we idealize our heroes.

Nancy bore three children in rapid succession. Sarah, her firstborn, came in 1807; she would die in 1828 in childbirth as a young woman. Abraham, born in 1809, grew up with her. Two or three years after Abraham's birth (there is no way to be more precise), his brother Thomas arrived and "died in infancy," as Lincoln was to say.[43] The baby was buried in a small grave within sight of the cabin. Many years later, after his father died in 1851, Lincoln filled in his genealogy in the front of the family Bible, but for some reason did not enter the birth of the short-lived boy.[44] After Thomas's birth in 1811 or 1812, Nancy bore no more children, though she lived until 1818. Nancy's childbearing pattern departed from that of the typical frontier woman, who bore a child every two years or so. We do not know whether the limited size of Nancy's family was due to Thomas's alleged sterility, some physical problem of Nancy's, marital indifference, or control. But the family's small size apparently influenced Lincoln; he and Mary rigorously controlled the size of their family.

The Lincolns stayed only briefly at Abraham's birth site near Hodgenville, Kentucky, then moved some two miles to Knob-Creek. Here Lincoln lived until he was seven, growing rapidly, absorbing the culture of his environment. He and his sister attended for short periods two "A–B–C schools" kept by Zachariah Riney and Caleb Hazel. Of his education Lincoln had a somewhat deprecatory view (which tended to put his self-made success in a better light): "There were some schools, so called," he told Jesse Fell. "But no qualification was ever required of a teacher, beyond *'readin, writin, and cipherin,'* to the Rule of Three. If a straggler supposed to understand Latin, happened to sojourn in the neighborhood, he was looked upon as a wizzard. There was absolutely nothing to excite ambition for education."[45]

In 1816 Thomas decided to move to Indiana. "This removal," Lincoln commented, "was partly on account of slavery; but chiefly on account of the difficulty in land titles in Kentucky." Thomas genuinely opposed slavery and had broken from his local Baptist church during a debate over that institution. The antislavery group Thomas was associated with established a separatist church, "which not only renounced human bondage but eschewed all written creeds and official church organizations, relying on the Bible as the sole rule of faith." In 1816, Thomas and Nancy Lincoln joined the separatist church and prayed with its antislavery ministers. However, the more important reason for the move to Indiana was, as Lincoln himself said, the confusion over land titles. Dennis Hanks said it was untrue that the existence of slavery in Kentucky had anything to do with the move to Indiana. He felt Thomas wanted to better his material condition by buying land at $1.25 per acre.[46]

So the Lincolns moved west after packing up their few belongings in an old wagon. At first life went well in Indiana. Lincoln, "though very young, was large of his age, and had an axe put into his hands at once." The household soon expanded with the addition of Thomas and Elizabeth Sparrow, two of Nancy's relatives, and Dennis Hanks, the illegitimate eighteen-year-old son of another aunt. Lincoln and Sarah occasionally attended more A-B-C or "blab" schools, the sum total of which "did not amount to one year." Lincoln went to school, he said, "by littles," but what he acquired he held onto with pride. "He was never in a college or academy as a student," Lincoln wrote of himself, "and never inside of a college or academy building til since he had a law license." After he left home in 1831 he studied English grammar, and later, as a United States congressman from 1847 to

*Lincoln's stepmother, Sarah, in old age. She was
"good and kind" to Lincoln, whose biological mother died
when he was nine years old. Courtesy of
Illinois State Historical Library.*

1849, began to read and master the six books of Euclid. He regretted his "want of education," but the pride of the self-made
man shines through when the Presidential candidate, who was
soon to write some of this country's best prose, noted how "imperfectly" he knew English grammar and that "What he has in
the way of education, he has picked up."[47]

Before moving from Kentucky at the age of seven, Lincoln
apparently could not read, but very soon he got "hungry for
books, reading everything he could lay his hands on." He was,

Dennis Hanks reported, "a constant and I may say stubborn reader." His "library" included the King James Bible, Noah Webster's old spelling book, the *Life of Henry Clay, Robinson Crusoe,* Parson Weems's *Life of Washington,* Aesop's *Fables,* and Bunyan's *Pilgrim's Progress.*[48] In Indiana, Lincoln encountered a number of very good grammar books, as well as *Arabian Nights,* David Ramsey's *Life of Washington,* and William Grimshaw's *History of the United States.*[49] John Hanks, his cousin, reported young Lincoln's devotion to reading and noted that he had made a kind of bookshelf out of two pins on the wall with a clapboard on them. "Lincoln got it of Crawford, told Crawford and paid it in pulling fodder by two or three days' work."

Lincoln's stepmother, Sarah, described him as "the best boy I ever saw. He read all the books he could lay his hands on." Sarah added that he read the Bible some, "though not as much as said," and turned eagerly to newspapers, especially in the later 1820s.[50]

> He read diligently, studied in the daytime, didn't after night much, went to bed early, got up early, and then read, ate his breakfast, got to work in the field with the men. Abe read all the books he could lay his hands on. And when he came across a passage that struck him, he would write it down on boards if he had no paper and keep it there til he did get paper, then he would rewrite it, look at it, repeat. He had a copy book, a kind of scrapbook, in which he put down all things and then preserved them. He ciphered on boards when he had no paper or no slate, and when the board would get too black, he would shave it off with a drawing knife, and go on again. When he had paper, he put his lines down on it.[51]

John Romine, a childhood acquaintance and early employer, remembered how Lincoln was always reading and thinking. In fact, Romine, who wanted his chores done, used to get mad at Lincoln and thought he was "awful lazy." He would, said Romine, "laugh & talk and crack jokes & tell stories all the time, didn't love work but did dearly love his pay. He worked for me frequently—a few days only at a time. His breeches didn't & socks didn't meet by 12 inches—Shin bones Sharp—blue & narrow. Lincoln said to me one day that his father taught him to work but never learned him to love it."[52] This delightful memory expresses the ambivalence of the frontier toward any learning and suggests how determined Lincoln must have been to acquire knowledge (and at the same time to gently tease his self-righteous employer).

Lincoln's early fascination for newspapers absorbed much of his intellectual curiosity and in turn helped feed his interest in politics. According to Herndon, "Politics were his life, newspapers his food, and his great ambition his motive power." Nevertheless, he added that Lincoln sometimes dipped into Herndon's own re-markable library, which may have been one of the best private collections in Illinois in the 1840s and 1850s.[53]

Lincoln listened with the same energy that sparked his interest in books. As a child, he occasionally went to church, and when he did, he listened closely to the sermon. At home, later, to the delight of the children, he would mount a stump or log and hu-morously repeat the sermon almost word for word. Sarah noted how young Abe "was a silent and attentive observer" who never spoke or asked questions until the person he was listening to left. Then he had to understand everything, "even to the smallest thing, minutely and exactly; he would repeat it over to himself again and again, sometimes in one form and then in another, and when it was fixed in his mind to suit him, he became easy and he never lost that fact or his understanding of it." The intensity here is remarkable. Lincoln seemed driven, and his listening, like his reading, had a certain compulsive quality to it. Not to grasp something was impossible. Indeed, "Sometimes he seemed perturbed to give expression to his ideas and go mad, almost, at one who couldn't explain plainly what he wanted to convey." Herndon later encountered the same intensity in the adult Lincoln, whom he once described as "persistent, fearless and tireless in thinking." Herndon would greet Lincoln on the street, for example, but Lincoln, lost in thought, would appear not even to notice his friend. Some hours later, he might say: "Billy, what did you say to me on the other side of the square this morning as we passed?"[54]

In the fall of 1818 there were tears to shed. Lincoln's mother, Nancy, and Thomas and Elizabeth Sparrow died of the "milk sickness," a disease cows periodically caught from poisonous roots and then transmitted through their milk. The deaths left Thomas Lincoln alone to care for his nine-year-old son and eleven-year-old daughter. Within a year, in 1819, he married Mrs. Sarah Bush Johnston of Elizabeth-Town, Kentucky, a widow with three children: Elizabeth, twelve, John D., ten, and Matilda, eight. Now the Lincoln household was much larger than ever before: two adults, three boys (counting Dennis Hanks), and three girls. The parents and girls occupied two beds on the first floor and the boys slept in the loft. There is some suggestion of temptation and sexual excitement in this household menagerie, for within a year the twenty-one-year-old Dennis Hanks married Elizabeth Johnston and moved to a cabin a short distance away.[55]

Lincoln also seemed to feel some of the same pressures as the children grew into adolescence. Sarah's daughter Matilda was responsible for taking lunch to Lincoln when he went deep into the woods to cut trees. As Matilda later reported to Herndon, when he was eighteen and she was sixteen, tongues apparently began to wag in the neighborhood about the two young people running wild and alone in the forest together. Sarah ordered Matilda to prepare Lincoln's dinner *before* he left for his day's work. All worked well, except that in time Matilda grew tired of the restraint. She decided secretly to follow Lincoln into the woods for a "good long chat and a wild romp." Matilda sneaked up behind Lincoln and jumped on his back to surprise him. In the resulting fall Lincoln's ax cut a gaping wound in Matilda's thigh near an artery. Both were frightened. Lincoln tore off the "tail of his undergarment" to staunch the wound. The issue then became what to tell Sarah. Matilda was inclined to lie but Lincoln urged her to tell the truth. "Tell the whole truth, 'Tilda, and trust your good mother for the rest."[56] This ruthless honesty is ostensibly the point of the story; Herndon thus labeled it in his notes, "Honest Abe—A Story of Lincoln's Youth." However, the sexual play and excitement between adolescent siblings unrelated by blood, living in a one-room cabin, seem the deeper meaning of the anecdote.

Sarah was a gentle woman who helped young Lincoln adjust to the painful loss of Nancy. Dennis reported that Sarah "had been raised in Elizabeth-Town in somewhat a high life," but adapted easily to the rugged life near Little Pigeon Creek in Indiana. The year or so between Nancy's death and Sarah's arrival was difficult for the Lincoln household. The speed with which Thomas found a second wife suggests his loneliness. Dennis reported that when Sarah arrived, "Abe and his sister were wild, ragged and dirty . . . she soaped, rubbed and washed the children clean, so that they looked pretty, neat, well, and clean. She sewed and mended their clothes, and the children once more looked human as their own good mother left them."[57] On Friday, September 8, 1865, Herndon visited Sarah and recorded her memories of Lincoln. Her account is honest and informative, warm and yet free of sentimentality. "His mind and mine, what little I had," she said, "seemed to run together, more in the same channel." Herndon recalled that as he was leaving, "she arose, took me by the hand, wept, and bade me good-bye, saying: 'I shall never see you again, and if you see Mrs. Abraham Lincoln and family, tell them I sent them my best and tenderest love. Good-bye, my good son's friend, farewell.'"[58]

Lincoln loved his stepmother. As a lawyer in Springfield, he occasionally visited Sarah, who lived about ninety miles away, near Charleston, Illinois. "I saw him every year or two," she told Herndon. The most emotional visit to his stepmother was the one Lincoln made just before leaving Springfield for Washington in 1861. According to Ward Hill Lamon, who made the trip with him, "The meeting between him and the old lady was of a most affectionate and tender character. She fondled him as her own 'Abe,' and he her as his own mother." Joshua Speed, Lincoln's close friend in the late 1830s and early 1840s, later spoke of Lincoln's great fondness for Sarah. Lincoln's wife, Mary, echoed this sentiment in a letter of December 19, 1867, to Sarah: "In memory of the dearly loved one, who always remembered you with so much affection, will you not do me the favor of accepting these few trifles?" In Sandburg's evocative terms, Sarah became "one of the rich, silent forces" in Lincoln's life.[59]

★★★

It is usually difficult to identify the central events of childhood. Even in clinical psychoanalysis, as Freud discovered, what is remembered as experience may have originated entirely in fantasy.[60] Even when "real," early memories function primarily as condensed representations of psychological relationships.[61] In this sense, life indeed seems to be a stage—or, perhaps, a dream. But some events, particularly if they occur early enough, do seem capable of significantly distorting all else that follows. Early parent loss is such an event.[62] The problem with the theoretical literature on this subject is its failure to identify any clear *necessary and sufficient outcomes* for a child who loses a parent. One may hypothesize a desperate and continuing need for archaic substitutes following childhood parent loss, but one often encounters the same need in a person whose parents have both been alive and well throughout his childhood. Furthermore, there may be a loss without death, for example, divorce or serious illness, that may or may not have similar effects as death, or there my be relative emotional health despite childhood traumas that should make the best of us schizophrenic. When all is said and done, however, there is one universal observation about childhood parent loss that anyone would agree with: It is a significant event that may be central in shaping development. One can only know for sure by a close examination of the facts in each case.

In his autobiography, Lincoln tells a curious story of killing a wild turkey just before his eighth birthday. The story, which he told in the third person and placed in parentheses, goes:

> (A few days before the completion of his eighth year, in the absence of his father, a flock of wild turkeys approached the new log cabin, and A. with a rifle gun, standing inside, shot through a crack, and killed one of them. He has never since pulled a trigger on any larger game.)[63]

The turkey story follows a brief description of the move to Indiana in 1816, when Thomas settled "in an unbroken forest" and Lincoln "had an axe put in his hands at once." But then the first sentence after the turkey story relates both the death of his mother and his father's remarriage: "In the autumn of 1818, his mother died; and a year afterwards his father married Mrs. Sally Johnston." Such a juxtaposition of memories suggests an association between the wild turkey and his dead mother. Both are helpless, and both die. The odd insertion of the turkey scene in parentheses between the description of Indiana and the report of Nancy's death seems a symbolic way of communicating unconscious feelings about his mother's death. The most important detail in the turkey story is Lincoln's responsibility for killing the bird. This apparently left deep remorse—guilt in our terms—and makes it impossible for Lincoln to pull "a trigger on any larger game." This guilt, one suspects, has been displaced from his mother onto the wild bird. Thus it seems he felt somehow responsible for causing his mother's death.

It would appear from the story that renounced infantile sexual longings toward the mother prompted the sense of guilt Lincoln felt after her death. This sexual theme enters the story by proxy, for Lincoln killed the turkey "in the absence of his father" and with a "rifle gun" that probably belonged to his father and that, according to Dennis Hanks, may have been loaded by his mother.[64] If we take the appropriation of the father's gun as a wish—and the story itself seems dreamlike—then the meaning of the condensed memories expressed in the story becomes more apparent. Lincoln unconsciously wished his father away because he wanted to possess his mother. He could only realize the wish, however, by appropriating the magical power of the father's gun as he struggled to beat out his father in competition for the mother. At some point, he must have felt victorious in that struggle, but the gun he appropriated proved more deadly than anticipated, for with it he killed the helpless turkey. Punishment must be extracted: "He has never since pulled a trigger on any larger game." In the confusion of mourning his mother's death, Lincoln thus seemed to construct an unconscious explanation for her loss that "explained" her death in terms of punishment for his own earlier forbidden sexual wishes. As punishment for his love, she died.[65]

One indirect, if curiously confirming, piece of evidence for this interpretation is Lincoln's lifelong sympathy for animals. Such a sentiment was hardly the norm for the frontier. By his report he was reluctant to hunt large game. He also seemed to have had bad experiences with animals; when he was ten he was kicked in the head by a horse, and in his words, "apparently killed for a time."[66] Several reports later testified he was sensitive "almost to a fault" about animals. Mary S. Vineyard (whom Lincoln courted as Mary Owens) reported Lincoln's story of helping a mired shoat (young pig) because "the poor thing seemed to say so wistfully: There now! my last hope is gone." J. D. Wickizer reported Lincoln's furious anger on once finding an old sow eating her young ones: Lincoln heard the squeals of the little pigs and leaped out of his buggy to break up such an "unnatural" scene.[67] There is also the story about how Lincoln helped his frightened little dog across an icy bridge on the trip from Indiana to Illinois in 1830. The grateful dog, when safe on dry land, "cut up such antics as no dog ever did before."[68] This otherwise innocuous story became a staple Lincoln tale and, apparently, something of a family legend.

But such things are seldom simple. Dennis Hanks reported hunting often with Lincoln in Indiana, and Sarah Lincoln noted that Lincoln disliked hunting but "sometimes went coon hunting and turkey hunting at nights." Lincoln himself reported the "ludicrous" incident of sewing up the eyes of some hogs. It was 1831 and Lincoln was working for Denton Offutt, who thought of the scheme to make his thirty hogs more manageable. Lincoln did the actual sewing and seemed glad to report that the whole idea was a complete failure. Nor were animals free from Lincoln's absorbing rivalry with his father. Lincoln often repeated for Herndon the odd story of the way he and John Johnston handled Thomas's cussed little yellow dog who always gave away their attempts to sneak out late and go coon hunting. One night they took the dog with them and sewed around it the skin of a dead coon. The terrified dog ran for home, but his powerful scent attracted a host of neighborhood dogs who proceeded to kill him. "Father was much incensed at his death," Lincoln reported to Herndon.[69]

The turkey scene from his autobiography suggests in highly condensed form Lincoln's particular oedipal tensions as they emerged in connection with his mother's death: a competitive sense of regretful victory over his father; a deep and abiding love for his mother that was powerfully libidinal; guilt for feeling forbidden sexual desires which became, in the irrational but psychologically comprehensive mind of the child confronted with parent loss, responsibility for death; and, finally, an unconscious connection between loving and killing that was to severely affect Lincoln's intimate relations as an adult. The rumpled, even dirty appearance of nine-year-old Abraham and eleven-year-old Sarah after their mother's death, and the disarray of their home suggest not only the severe impact of the loss but also that Nancy was being profoundly if crudely mourned. The arrival of the "new" mother, Sarah Lincoln, with her gentle, loving, understanding qualities, may have cut short Lincoln's mourning process, encapsulating his guilt and areas of conflict behind a defensive wall. This is, of course, speculation, but just as Sarah meliorated the pain of Nancy's death for Lincoln, she may have aggravated the unconscious guilt he felt for having somehow caused her death; and as she provided desperately needed continuity to allow Lincoln's further development, she may also have helped create a major discontinuity for young Lincoln that took him a lifetime to work through.

If such an approach to one story deeply embedded in the autobiography seems fanciful, there is other evidence that the wrenching loss of Nancy was the critical point in Lincoln's childhood.[70] In the fall of 1844 Lincoln, then a rising young Whig lawyer-politician, took a campaign swing through Indiana in behalf of Henry Clay. On the way he visited "the neighborhood in that state in which I was raised, where my mother and only sister were buried." The visit "aroused feelings in me which were certainly poetry," Lincoln told a newspaper editor at the time, "though whether my expression of those feelings is poetry is quite another question."[71] Lincoln wrote two lyrical poems after the trip, both of which express the exquisite pain he felt on visiting his "childhood's home." The dating of the poems, their internal structure, and even whether they should be considered one rather long poem are unclear. The answer to these confusions may lie in the dreamlike quality that his childhood memories seem to have aroused in Lincoln.[72]

> *My childhood's home I see again,*
> *And sadden with the view;*
> *And still, as memory crowds my brain,*
> *There's pleasure in it too.*
> *O Memory! Thou midway world*
> *'Twixt earth and paradise,*
> *Where things decayed and loved ones lost*
> *In dreamy shadows rise,*

Out of these "dreamy shadows" from the past Lincoln retrospectively isolated several emotionally laden memories. One was:

> *When first my father settled here,*
> *'Twas then the frontier line:*
> *The panther's scream, filled with fear*
> *And bears preyed on the swine.*

A stroke of disaster seemed imminent in the move to Indiana, a "panther's scream" filling the night with fear.

This part of Indiana in 1816 was, in fact, wild country full of animals. Albert Beveridge, using twelve different accounts of settlers and travelers, described the "raccoon, squirrel, opossum, skunk, deer, bear, wolf, wildcat, panther."

> Wild turkeys ran through underbrush filled with grouse and
> quail; wild ducks and geese flew overhead. Incredible num-

bers of pigeons hid the sun, darkening the air like a thick passing cloud, and, when settling for the night, broke down stout branches of trees. Swarms of mosquitoes rose from dank, stagnant pools and noisome swamps; large black and poisonous yellow flies abounded. Innumerable frogs rasped the stillness.[73]

Psychologically, however, Lincoln's fear of the panther's scream and of the bear preying on the swine suggests that he may well have experienced the move from Kentucky as a painful separation and even trembled as a child in anticipatory anxiety at what awaited him in Indiana. Death occurs in these few lines when helpless animals are destroyed by wild and brutal bears and panthers. This, indeed, is the theme of the entire poem, though it takes an ironic twist at the end.[74]

But the poem even more clearly suggests that, at some point, Lincoln invested certain relatively incidental memories from before his mother's death with the predictive power of what was to come. The animals may or may not have been frightening at the point of his moving to Indiana. Probably there was some fear, though nothing beyond a young boy's normal dread of the unknown, of strange and potentially dangerous sounds. After Nancy's death, however, and Lincoln's apparent association between her and helpless wild animals, these earlier memories assumed new significance as Lincoln worked over his confused, conflicted feelings during mourning.

Death is also the central theme of the earlier canto (or separate poem) that begins "My childhood's home I see again." Here he describes the memories and sights of his youth that were so poignantly real: "Now twenty years have passed away" since he last saw his playmates from childhood. "And half of all are dead."

I hear the loved survivors tell
How nought from death could save,
Till every sound appears a knell,
And every spot a grave.

I range the fields with pensive tread,
And pace the hollow rooms,
And feel (companions of the dead)
I'm living in the tombs.

The feelings of seeing his mother's grave and his childhood home flooded Lincoln with memories of her death and everyone else's from that era. He felt himself to be a companion of the dead and thus separated from the present and reunited with the past through his own death. Such depersonalization at seeing his "childhood's home" suggests incomplete mourning and a repressed encapsulation of everything associated with his mother. This was to play an important role in shaping his personality.

I tell you, Speed, our forebodings, *for which you and I are rather peculiar, are all the worst sort of nonsense.*

A. Lincoln to Joshua Speed, February 25, 1842

2

YOUNG MAN LINCOLN

As a young man in his twenties, from 1831 to 1837, Lincoln lived in New Salem, Illinois. This small, bustling community with a buoyant sense of its own importance had been staked out as an entrepreneurial venture to rival Cincinnati and St. Louis. It included many artisans; John Allen, a physician and graduate of Dartmouth; the loquacious Mentor Graham; and a slick businessman, William Greene. At its founding in 1829 New Salem had as much apparent urban potential as the larger town of Springfield (which contained five hundred people in 1830). Men—and women—gathered in a debating society to discuss the range of human affairs within their horizons;[1] and the moody figure of Lincoln reading on a woodpile, though regarded as unusual, was left alone.[2] As it turned out, New Salem failed economically, and in 1836 the post office was moved to Petersburg, which became the seat of the newly formed Menard County in 1839.[3]

Lincoln arrived in New Salem in July 1831, having just taken a load of produce down the Mississippi to New Orleans on Denton Offutt's flatboat. He had left home some five months before.[4] Lincoln's first job in the village was as a clerk in Offutt's store, work which he carried out affably but without commitment. He left this job in April 1832 for service in the Black Hawk War. He was immediately elected captain by his company, an honor that for Lincoln was a source of enormous satisfaction. When in May his term ended, he reenlisted for twenty more days in the service of Captain Elijah Iles, and then in June he signed on for thirty more days in Captain Jacob M. Early's company. This extended service was not a result of military need; Lincoln later ridiculed his "bloody encounters" with mosquitoes and told William Herndon that the only reason he served so long was that he had no other work.[5]

So Lincoln drifted back to New Salem. He toyed with the idea of "learning the black-smith trade" and considered the study of law, but he "rather thought he could not succeed at [the law] . . . without a better education." Even before his first arrival in the village, he had announced his intention to run for office. Shortly after his return from the war, he sought election to the state legislature. He lost the election, though he carried his own precinct—New Salem—by 277 to 7. Surviving on odd jobs, he next stumbled onto the purchase of a store with William Berry. With the store he assumed a heavy mortgage and responsibilities. These he did not seem prepared to handle, and he got little help from Berry, who proceeded to drink himself to death. As Lincoln later commented, "Of course they [Lincoln and Berry] did nothing but get deeper and deeper in debt." In no time, "The store winked out."[6]

Lincoln also tried surveying during the New Salem period. John Calhoun, the country surveyor, had befriended him and recommended him as his assistant. As Lincoln described it: "He

[Lincoln] accepted, procured a compass and chain, studied Flint, and Gibson a little, and went at it. This procured bread, and kept soul and body together."[7] In his attempt to master the necessary mathematics for surveying, Lincoln had enlisted the help of Mentor Graham. As Benjamin P. Thomas writes: "Often he and Graham stayed awake until midnight, interrupting their calculations only when Mrs. Graham ordered them out for a fresh supply of wood for the fire."[8] But this new venture was as ill-fated as the investment in the store. In order to begin surveying, Lincoln had purchased on credit from William Watkins a horse, saddle, and bridle for $57.86. Lincoln failed to make the payments for these items, and on April 26, 1834, Watkins got a judgment in the Sangamon County Circuit Court on Lincoln's personal possessions.[9] Though a competent surveyor, Lincoln was hardly dedicated enough to become a successful one.

Lincoln also served as village postmaster, a position to which he was appointed on May 7, 1833. Though a Whig, he served during the Jackson administration because, in his own words, "the office . . . [was] too insignificant, to make his politics an objection."[10] The mail arrived once each week. Postage was determined by the number of pages and the distance the letter traveled. Thus a single sheet cost six cents for the first thirty miles, ten cents for thirty to eighty miles, and so on. There were no stamps or envelopes. Letters were simply folded and sealed, and the postage charge, written in the upper right-hand corner, was paid by the person receiving the letter. For Lincoln, the best part of being postmaster was the opportunity it gave him to read all the newspapers. But during his tenure in office, which lasted until May 30, 1836, Lincoln was neither conscientious nor competent. On September 17, 1835, New Salem settler Matthew S. Marsh wrote his brother: "The Post Master is very careless about leaving his office open and unlocked during the day—half the time I go in and get my papers, etc., without anyone being there as was the case yesterday. The letter was only marked twenty-five [cents] and even if he had been there and known it was double, he would not have charged me any more." Marsh may have been something of a busybody, but Lincoln also had trouble with George C. Spears, to whom he wrote on July 1, 1834: "At your request I send you a receipt for the postage on your paper. I am some what surprised at your request. I will however comply with it. The law requires News paper postage to be paid in advance and now that I have waited a full year you choose to wound my feelings by insinuating that unless you get a receipt I will probably make you pay it again."[11]

All of these New Salem activities of Lincoln's were necessarily part-time affairs. And they were supplemented by occasional stints at splitting rails, working at the mill, harvesting, and tending store for Samuel Hill. After December 1834, Lincoln served as the local agent for the *Sangamo Journal* and regularly clerked at the polls on election days. He even spent the better part of one winter working at Isaac Burner's still.[12] Between these diverse and not particularly demanding duties, he only gradually came to make creative use of his free time. Until 1834 he was too intimidated by his lack of education to begin the study of law. Even after John T. Stuart encouraged him to start reading law, he did it selectively, though carefully. He had access to the law books of Stuart and H. E. Drummer and could have delved into Stuart's fine personal library. The books were available, but he was not ready for them.[13]

Only after joining the Illinois legislature did Lincoln achieve any consistent success. He was elected in 1834, 1836, 1838, and 1840. His service in the legislature, it should be noted, also was a part-time activity. Each regular session met in Vandalia before 1837 and after that in Springfield, the new capital, from late November in the year of election until February or March of the next year. Frequently there were special sessions, such as the one in the summer of 1837 to deal with the financial panic. Lincoln the legislator developed slowly. He gradually won respect from his colleagues in the ranks of the Whig minority, and in his last term he became minority leader. He was one of the nine legislators instrumental in moving the state capital in 1837.

As a legislator, Lincoln was always diligent and earnest but not always wise and responsible. Paul Simon, who has thoroughly investigated Lincoln's legislative career, chastises him for his ambiguous stand on education. But Simon is most critical of Lincoln's unequivocal support of the Illinois Internal Improvement Act, which nearly ruined the state by burdening it with an overwhelming debt for the next four decades. The act began as a ridiculously optimistic venture to encourage economic development by a program of improvements costing $10,250,000. Hardly any improvements were actually made and most of the funds ended up in speculators' pockets. By 1857 the debt stood at $17,000,000; not until 1882 were the bonds finally paid off. Simon concludes quite sensibly that Lincoln learned a great deal about the operation of government and politics during his years in the legislature. This education, however, nearly bankrupted the state.[14]

During the New Salem period Lincoln was, in short, undirected and unfocused, charming and well liked by his neighbors, but singularly unsuccessful in most ventures he undertook. He had failed in a series of enterprises and had faced two lawsuits on account of his personal debts. He fell into surveying as he did splitting rails or delivering the mail or working at the still—by chance, as opportunity beckoned and the need to survive demanded. Even in his most rewarding activity in these years, serving in the legislature, he felt his way cautiously and with some serious errors in judgment.

Lincoln's long, stumbling search for satisfying work with which to supplement his political career may in part have been simply a reflection of his lack of a formal education. But his experimentation may also have been part of a larger search for personal coherence and integrity, a search that theoretically makes sense in terms of psychoanalytic concepts of identity. Sigmund Freud, as an old man, was apparently asked what defines normality. He replied with the terseness characteristic of his old age: "lieben und arbeiten" (to love and to work). Each person must discover for himself or herself how to love and to work. An inability to love precludes working that is free from compulsive fastidiousness; and the commitment to professional activity that realizes one's potential and risks failure flows from a firm sense of sexual identity. The youth is challenged from many directions. There is a forward movement that must meet the needs of society. There are as well inner expectations that draw on enduring childhood issues of self-cohesion. Work and career focus a large part of these concerns; love, social relating, and sexual identity constitute other important aspects of the emerging self.[15]

Lincoln's earliest romantic involvement was with Ann Rutledge in New Salem.[16] She was eighteen when it seems he fell in love with her in 1832, at the age of twenty-three. Ann was generally regarded in the village as quite beautiful, even exquisite, but she was betrothed to a John McNamar, who left the village for New York to retrieve his family just as Lincoln returned from his stint in the Black Hawk War. For the next three years Lincoln and Ann chastely courted, because marriage hinged on whether she could escape her commitment to McNamar. Almost all of Herndon's informants testify to an engagement between the two, a private arrangement that was widely assumed but not formally proclaimed. Douglas Wilson argues tenuously that their engagement became more formal in 1835, but the point is moot. That summer was hot and wet; disease spread across the prairie, and on August 25 Ann died of what was probably typhoid.[17]

The death of Ann Rutledge left Lincoln bereft. He was, as New Salemites variously reported, "plunged into despair," "much distressed," "very disponding [*sic*]," and "his reason was in danger." To those who knew him he seemed changed, withdrawn, indifferent to things, lost in thought, fixated on Ann's grave. He may even have become suicidal.[18] Once dismissed as absurd, the oral history evidence of Lincoln's old friends and neighbors should be taken seriously indeed, though Herndon's further notions that the memory of Ann created Lincoln's life-long depression *and* polluted his marriage with Mary Todd is a psychological stretch without basis in fact or logic.[19] It is enough that Lincoln loved Ann Rutledge and was devastated by her death. It would seem that Lincoln's unconsummated love for Ann brought him hope that he could love and find intimacy. Her sudden death was tragic in its own right, but it was certainly doubly painful for Lincoln because it evoked the loss of his mother, including his inchoate and only partly conscious sense of responsibility for her death: Those he most loved died.

After Ann, Lincoln became involved in a very curious relationship with Mary Owens, "an amiable, attractive Kentucky girl of considerable culture" who was already in her late twenties and of considerable bulk.[20] The complicated way Lincoln dealt with Owens is perhaps most important in the way it foreshadows his tortured courting of Mary Todd. Lincoln first met Owens in 1833 when she visited her sister, Mrs. Bennett Abell, in New Salem. After she returned to the village in 1836, Lincoln began to court her. There never appeared to be much passion on either side; nevertheless, by May 1837, the two were clearly discussing marriage. Lincoln was curiously ambiguous in the proposal he made in a letter:

Whatever woman may cast her lot with mine, should any ever do so, it is my intention to do all in my power to make her happy and contented; and there is nothing I can immagine [*sic*], that would make me more unhappy than to fail in the effort. I know I should be much happier with you than the way I am, provided I saw no signs of discontent in you. . . . What I have said I will most positively abide by, provided you wish it. My opinion is that you had better not do it.[21]

A little over three months later, Lincoln broke off his relationship with Mary Owens in a confused fashion. He wrote: "I can not see you, or think of you, with entire indifference," a phrasing that cast his supposedly affectionate feeling into a double negative. He continued: "I want in all cases to do right, and most particularly so, in all cases with women." Doing right in this case, Lincoln suggested, probably meant leaving her alone. If that was her desire, he urged her simply not to answer the letter. Such a solution to their "romance" forced her to act and made Lincoln the passive recipient of her decision. He then made the same point again with greater emphasis: "Do not understand by this, that I wish to cut your acquaintance. I mean no such thing. What I do wish is, that our further acquaintance shall depend upon yourself. . . . If you feel yourself in any degree bound to me, I am now willing to release you, provided you wish it; while, on the other hand, I am willing, and even anxious to bind you faster, if I can be convinced that it will, in any considerable degree, add to your happiness."[22]

Lincoln, with apparent disregard for himself, desperately feared hurting Mary. At all costs he sought to make her happy, and if his actions hurt her, he was hurt even more himself. He loved ambivalently, and at the point of marriage, with its potential of intimacy, he withdrew in a clumsy, if genuine, expression of sympathy for Mary's feelings. As she later wrote to Herndon, "Mr.

Views to the west and east of the Springfield, Illinois, town square in the late 1830s. Courtesy of Illinois State Historical Library.

Lincoln was deficient in those little links which make up the chain of a woman's happiness—at least it was so in my case."[23]

In a letter to his friend, Mrs. Orville Hickman Browning, the wife of a state senator from Quincy, Lincoln dismissed the love affairs in a most casual way. He recounted that he had first seen Mary in 1833 and had not been displeased; that in 1836 his New Salem acquaintance, Mrs. Abell, had played matchmaker for a willing swain; but that when he saw Mary again he was aghast at how fat she had gotten—"a fair match for Falstaff." Yet Lincoln confessed his suffering and mortification at Mary's turning him down: "She whom I had taught myself to believe no body else would have, had actually rejected me with all my fancied greatness; and to cap the whole, I then, for the first time, began to suspect that I was really a little in love with her."[24]

Lincoln's courtship of Mary Todd was something altogether different. He first met and was captivated by the sprightly, well-educated, and charming Mary Todd in 1839 in Springfield. James C. Conkling, a young lawyer from the East and a graduate of Princeton, described Mary as "the very creature of excitement," and Lincoln courted her vigorously and successfully throughout 1839 and 1840.[25] Each of Mary's three extant letters from these two years mentions him, and the third one dwells at some length on marriage.[26] Apparently, before the end of 1840 Lincoln and Mary were engaged. Lincoln was then thirty-one. He had some useful experience as a lawyer behind him and was making a respectable income. He had made a mark in the legislature and was generally esteemed by friends and colleagues throughout Springfield. Still, he was something of a social upstart in Mary's snobbish circle, which centered on the home of her sister, Elizabeth Edwards, and Elizabeth's husband, Ninian Wirt Edwards, the kind of people whom, in Lincoln's first impression of Springfield in 1837, he had referred to as "flourishing about in carriages here."[27] His fiancée was probably the most desirable unmarried woman in Springfield. Yet suddenly, in a move that perplexed all his friends—and was to baffle historians and biographers—he broke off the engagement on January 1, 1841.

Herndon's fanciful account of that event—to the effect that the wedding was scheduled for that date and that Lincoln failed to appear—was first proven false by the masterful detective work of Ruth Painter Randall in ways that have persuaded later historians. Randall notes that both Mary's guardian, Ninian Edwards, and her father opposed her marriage to young Lincoln. Yet Lincoln loved her. Randall hypothesizes that in the end Lincoln respected the feelings of the Todd family: "How could he marry the girl when her family thought he would make her unhappy? He had so few things upon which to pride himself, but among these things was his integrity. Yet no course of action was open to a man with his torturing conscience that left that integrity unviolated."[28] Randall speaks of Lincoln and Mary's "appealing love story," one Herndon obscured with "belittling distortions and fabrications," but one that the nation can be proud of as an "American romance" in which an aristocratic girl and her "lover of log-cabin origin" triumph over family opposition.[29] This drama of Romeo and Juliet, American style, posits an external force to explain Lincoln's breaking the engagement. The snobbish Todds, so the narrative goes, intimidated the fragile young man, though he eventually was to win the hand of his beloved.

Lincoln, to be sure, was uneasy in social situations during these years. As a newcomer to Springfield, he felt out of place. Throughout his life he often joked about his homeliness and excessive height. He felt somewhat embarrassed by his humble origins, though in time he became aware of the political value of having been raised in a log cabin. Nevertheless, he was not easily intimidated by anyone, not even the lordly Todds ("God," he once said, "only required one d"[30]). His natural assumption of intellectual superiority and his vigorous ambition were always sources of great strength. John Hay, Lincoln's private secretary during the war, believed that it was "absurd to call him a modest man. No great man is ever modest. It was his intellectual arrogance and unconscious assumption of superiority that men like Chase and Sumner could never forgive." For Herndon, Lincoln's ambition was "a little engine that knew no rest," and "The sober truth is that Lincoln was inordinately ambitious." The first visible expression of this ambition occurred "in the year 1840 *exactly.*" But Mary's sister, Elizabeth Edwards, provided in 1887 a different but also interesting explanation of the broken engagement. Mrs. Edwards, an important member of the family opposing the marriage, said Lincoln "doubted his ability and capacity to please and support a wife."[31]

Elizabeth Edwards dimly perceived Lincoln's excruciating ambivalence. For, as with Mary Owens, he broke off a fully developed romance just at the point of marriage and sexual union. In both relationships Lincoln feared intimacy with a woman. His natural exuberance and virility led him toward both encounters, but in each his ambivalence led to agonizing retreat before consummation. At least it would appear that Lincoln's ambivalence is at the heart of a psychologically sophisticated explanation for the broken engagement. There are, however, other ways of seeing the evidence.

It may be that Mary broke the engagement. Such is the tenuous theory of Jean Baker in her 1987 biography, *Mary Todd Lincoln.* Baker begins by accepting as fact the idea that Stephen Douglas seriously courted and proposed to Mary, who rejected him in favor of Lincoln. Few scholars regard this story as anything but unsubstantiated myth, based as it is solely on accounts from two second-hand witnesses, one in the 1880s, a former maid in the Lincoln home, and the second Mary's former White House seamstress.[32] Both may well have reported accurately on what they heard from Mary in distraught states, but rejection of an actual marriage proposal from Stephen Douglas would have left other evidence in gossipy Springfield. Already on thin ice, Baker proceeds to make up a chronology that has Lincoln arriving late to a dance on New Year's Eve 1940, preoccupied with law business, and Mary, to get his goat, flirting with Edwin Webb. They argue and Mary sends Lincoln off, ending the engagement.

There is almost nothing to recommend Baker's narrative of events. To be sure, Webb was a suitor, but not one taken seriously by Mary ("I love him not," she wrote[33]). There is no source that describes Baker's imagined party, no testimony to Lincoln's mood, and no one, even decades later, who describes Mary arguing with her lover and airily dispatching him. Baker's only concrete piece of evidence that Mary broke the engagement is a stray note in Herndon's oral history documents—a piece of second-hand testimony that contradicts a number of other, more direct accounts.[34] Baker also misinterprets a letter Mary wrote in June 1841 to her friend, Mercy Ann Levering:

> The June Court is in Session & many distinguished strangers grace the gay capital, we have an unusual number of agreeable visitors, some pleasant acquaintances of last winter, but in their midst the *winning widower* [Edwin Webb] *is not, rumor* says he with some others will attend the Supreme Court next month, in your last, you appeared impressed with the prevalent idea that we were *dearer* to each other than friends, the idea was neither new nor strange, dear Merce, the know-

ing world have coupled our names together for months past, merely through the folly & belief of *another* [Lincoln?], who strangely imagined we were attached to each other, in your friendly & confiding ear allow me to whisper that my *heart can never be his,* I have deeply *regretted that his constant visits, attentions &&* should have given room for remarks, which were to me unpleasant, there being a slight difference of some eighteen or twenty summers in our years, would preclude the possibility of congeneality [*sic*] of feeling, without which I should never feel justifiable in resigning my happiness into the safe keeping of another, even should that other be far too worthy for me, with his two *sweet little objections.*[35]

All one can reasonably conclude from this passage is that in the early summer of 1841 (which is, of course, six months after her engagement with Lincoln was broken), Edwin Webb was trying unsuccessfully to court Mary, and that someone suggested to her that Lincoln believed she was taking Webb seriously, which to her is so ludicrous ("a slight difference of some eighteen or twenty summers in our years" and the widower's "two *sweet little objections*") that she seems not to be greatly bothered, though she is concerned to set the record straight with her friend. Baker amazingly concludes, however, that this letter proves that Mary's "dalliance" with Webb in late 1840 "disrupted" the courtship and that Mary broke the engagement.[36]

Douglas Wilson's explanation for the courtship, on the other hand, solidly based as it is on the available evidence, is a different matter. It is impossible to do full justice to Wilson's account in this space, but it is worth noting that his radically revisionist account hinges on the argument that Lincoln broke his engagement with Mary because he was so taken with Matilda Edwards. The idea is not without foundation, as Joshua Speed, James Matheny, and Orville Browning all told Herndon about Matilda.[37]

On this issue, however, Speed and Matheny were second-hand witnesses, and Browning not only hedges his statement with a crucial "perhaps" but also was not at this point particularly close to Lincoln nor was ever an intimate part of the Todd family circle.[38] It seems much safer to rely on the crystal clear testimony of Mary's sister, Elizabeth Edwards, with whom Mary was living when the courtship drama unfolded. Elizabeth specifically said in her 1866 interview with Herndon that Matilda had nothing to do with the break-up and that she had even investigated the matter prior to the interview ("I asked Miss Edwards—Subsequently Mrs. Strong —if Mr. Lincoln Ever Mentioned the subject of his love to her. Miss Edwards Said—'On my word he never mentioned Such a Subject to me: he never even Stooped to pay me a Compliment.'"). Elizabeth also reaffirmed her strong conviction that Matilda had nothing to do with the broken engagement in her later, joint interview with her husband, Ninian.[39] It is instructive, as well, that Herndon himself, who knew all the players in the story extremely well, basically ignored what amounted to the well-fed Springfield rumors about Matilda and accepted the testimony of Elizabeth Edwards (though of course he added his own glosses that are suspect).[40] Matilda, who was apparently beautiful, occasioned much gossip. In the tight world of Springfield society, it seems some imagined she must have been the reason for the strange behavior of Lincoln, and those rumors filtered down to Herndon and have become the centerpiece of Wilson's narrative. In building the story around Matilda, Wilson normalizes Lincoln and makes him seemingly rational, if a little flighty.[41] In fact, the story is much more psychologically complicated. Matilda Edwards, it would seem, never figured in the emotional life of Abraham Lincoln in late 1840. Joshua Speed did.

There is one final issue to deal with in trying to understand Lincoln's curious behavior with women. It may be that he had self-doubts because he feared that he had acquired syphilis some-time in 1835 or 1836. The story comes directly from Herndon, who wrote in 1887 that Lincoln "went to Beardstown and dur-ing a devilish passion had Connection with a girl and Caught the disease."[42] It should be noted this story comes from before Hern-don's direct contact with Lincoln and is not attributed to him (i.e., Herndon does not preface the story with the telling phrase, "Lincoln told me once about the Beardstown girls," etc.), nor does Herndon say from whom he heard the story. Such criteria have always been the basis for determining the accuracy of Hern-don himself as a source. Furthermore, Herndon directly asked many of his New Salem informants whom he thought might know whether Lincoln had ever been with "bad women" and, as Wilson notes, the answer was "universally negative."[43] For all these reasons, it seems highly unlikely that Lincoln had a devil-ish passion for some Beardstown girl, and even less likely that he ever had syphilis. Milton Shutes, a medical expert writing in 1957, carefully sifted all the evidence for syphilis and concluded that it is virtually certain that Lincoln never contracted the disease.[44] What Shutes guessed—assuming the unlikely possibility that Herndon's story is true—is that Lincoln developed syphilophobia, which is not a matter of contagious sexual disease but a psycho-logical problem of sexual conflict centered on a man's fear of a contaminating injury to his penis. In an age haunted by the wide-spread existence of syphilis, a lack of treatment for it, and the fear of its spread through incidental contact, together with nineteenth-century cultural obsessions with the evils of masturbation, there are any number of possible psychosomatic reasons why a sexually naive man in his twenties might develop syphilophobia.

And so we return to psychological matters. Intimacy involves a merging of selves—both physical and emotional—in a union that can permit each partner to rise above his or her existential loneliness. In the formulation of the psychoanalyst Erik Erikson, intimacy is "the capacity to commit [oneself] to concrete affiliations and partnerships and to develop the ethical strength to abide by such commitments, even though they may call for significant sacrifices and compromises." Avoiding situations that have the potential of close affiliation and sexual union "may lead to a deep sense of isolation and consequent self-absorption."[45] This general characterization fits well with what we know about Lincoln. He could not go beyond himself because he had not fully consolidated the bases of his sexual or work identity. He lacked an inner coherence or identity that would permit him to transcend himself and reach out to another. Loss of self for such young men offers only the potential of psychic disintegration and frightening regression.

The theoretical connection between a lack of identity and a fear of intimacy is therefore far more than an accidental occurrence. Lincoln, in the 1830s, sought a unity among the several roles he was juggling: store owner, surveyor, rail splitter, lawyer, politician. By 1841 the lawyer-politician in him seemed dominant; but it was a recent and tentative consolidation that was neither immutable nor at the time the basis of anything more apparent than moderate professional success. His sense of self was fragile at best. For many less sensitive, it is all too easy to choose an identity from the available roles defined and outlined by parents, teachers, and social mores and expectations. But with Lincoln this was impossible, and its impossibility suggests an insight into a crucial aspect of greatness: the proud and obstinate refusal to wear the mask painted by others. He also sought a heterosexual union that kept eluding him. For a young man as confused as Lincoln, intimacy and love are bound to be approached ambivalently. Thus fear of intimacy and of the binding nature of sexual love contributed to Lincoln's identity confusion.

*Joshua Fry Speed, the most intimate friend
Lincoln ever had. Speed's courtship of Fanny
Henning helped Lincoln resolve his
confusion over his sexual identity. Courtesy of
Illinois State Historical Library.*

A full understanding of Lincoln's struggles with intimacy cannot be grasped by examining only his courtship of Mary Todd.
Of even greater significance was his relationship with Joshua Fry
Speed, whose patient friendship during these crucial years at first
aggravated Lincoln's conflicts, then served as the vehicle for their
resolution. The drama of Lincoln's courtship with Mary Todd has
obscured for most scholars the emotional centrality of his same-
sex friendship with Speed in the years before and just after the
winter of 1840–1841. This or that document seen in isolation
may provide some basis for a skewing of the story. But the only
way to make sense of *all* the evidence—especially the authentic

Lincoln letters—is to see the period from 1837 to 1842 as one piece. In that larger context, it hardly matters whether the engagement with Mary Todd was actually broken off in November 1840 (as Wilson argues), or even whether Edwin Webb may have been in Mary's sights for a brief period (as Baker argues). What does matter a great deal is the tortured feelings about love and sex that Lincoln experienced as he sought clarity of self in his late twenties and early thirties. It was already late in his life cycle for the resolution of such issues, to be sure, which probably accounts for the intensity of his struggles. But then creativity works in the margins of cultural norms that others so readily adopt.

Joshua Speed was an engaging young merchant who moved from Kentucky to Springfield in 1835. Lincoln's relationship with Speed began on his own arrival in Springfield in 1837. Lincoln, only recently admitted to the bar, had neither relatives nor friends on hand to see him through or help him pay his debts. He was probably already acquainted with Joshua Speed and certainly familiar with Speed's store.[46] He went directly there and asked how much it would cost to buy the material for a bed. Speed made the calculation and told Lincoln it would cost a total of seventeen dollars. As Speed later reported to Herndon, Lincoln asked for the money on credit until Christmas but in such a sad tone as to elicit Speed's sympathy.

> The tone of his voice was so melancholy that I felt for him. I looked up at him, and I thought then as I think now, that I never saw so gloomy, and melancholy a face. I said to him: "The contraction of so small a debt, seems to affect you so deeply, I think I can suggest a plan by which you will be able to attain your end, without incurring any debt. I have a very large room, and a very large double bed in it; which you are perfectly welcome to share with me if you choose." "Where is your room?" asked he. "Upstairs" said I, pointing

to the stairs leading from the store to my room. Without saying a word, he took his saddle-bags on his arm, went up stairs, set them down on the floor, came down again, and with a face beaming with pleasure and smiles exclaimed "Well Speed I'm moved."[47]

In 1838 Speed and Lincoln were joined in their room above the store by William Herndon, who later reported: "Lincoln, Speed, and I slept together for two or three years, i.e., slept in the same home, I being Speed's clerk; and Lincoln sleeping with Speed."[48] For a time Charles R. Hurst joined the dormitory, sleeping in a separate bed. Life in the store centered on open and congenial discussion and was pervaded by a rough maleness that sharply distinguished it from the sophisticated and slightly effete atmosphere of the coterie that met in the Edwards's home. According to Speed, discussion in the store revolved around Lincoln: "Mr. Lincoln was a social man, though he did not seek company; it sought him. After he made his home with me, on every winter's night at my store, by a big wood fire, no matter how inclement the weather, eight or ten choice spirits assembled, without distinction of party. It was a sort of social club without organization. They came there because they were sure to find Lincoln."[49]

Joshua Speed was the most intimate friend Lincoln ever had.[50] Ward Hill Lamon, in his 1872 biography, was the first to make this point.[51] Lincoln was good friends with his colleagues on the Eighth Judicial Circuit, especially David Davis, Ward Hill Lamon, and Henry C. Whitney, but never close in the way he was with Speed.[52] The only quarrel with the idea that Speed was at the center of Lincoln's emotional life later came from a jealous Herndon.[53] In fact the difference was complete. Lincoln liked Herndon but treated him condescendingly: He always called him "Billy" while Herndon called him "Mr. Lincoln." To Speed, Lincoln wrote: "You know my desire to befriend you is everlasting—that

I will never cease, while I know how to do any thing."[54] Even Herndon had to admit that Lincoln and Speed were unusually close.[55] Speed was an attractive young man, affable, kind, and easygoing. Ruth Painter Randall mentions his Byronic eyes and characterizes him as a rake, though the sources do not bear this out.[56] On the contrary, Speed seems to have been as innocent of sex as Lincoln, and when he began seriously courting Fanny Henning, whom he later married, Speed reported: "strange to say something of the same feeling which I regarded as so foolish in him took possession of me and kept me very unhappy from the time of my engagement until I was married."[57]

It would appear, therefore, that Lincoln and Speed's close relationship centered on their similar and reinforcing conflicts. Their sleeping in the same bed for three and one-half years, it would seem, intensified their closeness and aggravated their conflicts. It is probable that such close male contact during the years of Lincoln's greatest heterosexual tension heightened the difficulty he found in securing intimacy with a woman. Desire became complicated, though one can only guess from a distance in what specific ways. But it is telling that the period during which Lincoln slept with Speed began and ended with unconsummated female relationships, first with Mary Owens and then with Mary Todd. Speed provided an alternative relationship that neither threatened nor provoked Lincoln. Each of the two men found solace in discussing their forebodings about sexuality. Their intimate maleness substituted for the tantalizing but frightening closeness of women.

Such close male relationships were characteristic of early-nineteenth-century America and were quite common in an urban frontier town like Springfield, where there was a distinct shortage of eligible women.[58] In that pre-Freudian age, society legitimated such close male friendships, and it was not at all strange for men to sleep together in the same bed. This kind of sleeping arrangement grew out of economic necessity, and neither Speed nor Herndon found anything unusual in it. Inns at that time, with few rooms, simply separated the men from the women. Everyone crowded into all available space—for warmth as much as anything else.[59] Both before and after Lincoln met Speed it was a common experience for him to share a bed with other males. William Greene of New Salem days told Herndon that he had worked with Lincoln in Offutt's store and had "slept in the same cott & when one turned over the other had to do likewise." Later, on the judicial circuit that Lincoln and other lawyers rode for many months of every year, they regularly piled into crowded beds.[60] Spacious homes with individual chambers were extremely rare; the typical log cabin had only one room and one large bed, and only when that room began to burst with children was a loft put in.

Social custom and individual experience, however, are not always congruent. Just because many men slept together casually in inns and elsewhere during this period by no means proves that it was unimportant that Lincoln lay down in a crowded bed night after night for well over three years with his best male friend, whom he trusted above all with his deepest feelings. The question is, what does it mean? Lincoln was sensitive to issues of male closeness in a way that distinguished him from his peers. Mrs. Elizabeth Crawford, whom Herndon talked with in early 1866, remembered much about Lincoln from his adolescent days in Indiana. She shared with Herndon the "Chronicles of Reuben," a long satire that Lincoln had composed and read aloud to his friends. It told of the marriage of two brothers, Reuben and Charles, with two girls and also of the homosexual marriage of a third brother, Billy, with Natty:

> The girls he had tried on every side
> But none could he get to agree;

All was in vain, he went home again
And since that, he is married to Natty.

So Billy and Natty agreed very well;
And mamma's well pleased at the match.
The egg it is laid but Natty's afraid,
The shell is so soft that it never will hatch.
But Betsey, she said: "you cursed baldhead,
My suitor you never can be;
Besides, your low crotch proclaims you a botch
And that never can answer for me."[61]

The broken engagement with Mary Todd seems to be a less important psychological event for Lincoln than his separation from Speed. Certainly, the timing overlapped. Sometime in December 1840, and probably well before that, Speed decided to sell his store and return to Kentucky to attend to family matters (his father had died). He must have talked with Lincoln about the sale, for it required both men to find separate living quarters and of course leave their common bed, even though Speed did not leave Springfield until May of 1841.[62] The announcement of the sale of Speed's store in the local paper even appeared on January 1, 1841, the same day that Lincoln broke his engagement with Mary, though the precise day he and Speed went their separate ways is impossible to determine.[63] What the sequence suggests is that the impending separation from Speed threw Lincoln into a panic that shook his fragile sexual identity. In this state his fear of intimacy with a woman was revived, and he broke his engagement with Mary. One point is worth stressing: Lincoln's conflicts and fears operated at an unconscious level. It is highly unlikely, it seems to me (though it cannot be decisively excluded as a possibility), that Lincoln had a sexual relationship with Joshua Speed. Had Lincoln been homosexual, his relationship with Speed would have been less complicated—and he would not have become the

Lincoln we know in history. On the contrary, it was the unconscious level at which his feelings played out that made them for a time so confused and the struggles so intense but the larger meanings so interesting.

Abandoned by Speed and abandoning Mary, Lincoln gradually fell into a severe depression.[64] He was of course subject to depression throughout his life, but his most severe bout occurred in January 1841. On January 20 he wrote his friend John T. Stuart: "I have, within the last few days, been making a most discreditable exhibition of myself in the way of hypochondriaism." Three days later, also to Stuart, Lincoln noted in a tone of negative grandiosity: "I am now the most miserable man living. If what I feel were equally distributed to the whole human family, there would not be one cheerful face on the earth."[65] He came to refer to January 1, 1841, as the "fatal first," the memory of which was painful for him to recall. Speed and other friends worried over Lincoln's condition. "We have been very much distressed, on Mr. Lincoln's account; hearing that he had two Cat fits and a Duck fit since we left," Martin McKee wrote to John J. Hardin on January 27. Herndon wrote in retrospect: "Did you know that Mr. Lincoln was 'as crazy as a loon' in this city in 1841; that he did not sit, did not attend to the Legislature, but in part, if any (special session of 1841); that he was then deranged? Did you know that he was forcibly arrested by his special friends here at that time; that they had to remove all razors, knives, pistols, etc. from his room and presence, that he might not commit suicide?" He was confined to his bed for a week and only gradually resumed his legislative duties. During his depression he was tended by a kindly doctor, Anson G. Henry, who later wrote that Lincoln told him things he never said to anyone else. Afterward Lincoln was always eager to help Henry, and during his presidency Lincoln encouraged Henry to make long visits to the White House.[66]

Lincoln slowly recovered, though as late as June, Mary Todd noted that she had not met him in the "gay world for months." Speed, who remained in town until May, probably helped meliorate Lincoln's mood. Then Speed left for Kentucky to settle his family estate. Lincoln, emotionally unfit to be alone, went on a long visit to Speed's home, where he was welcomed warmly as a member of the family. In September Speed accompanied him back to Springfield and remained there until the end of 1841, although he was anxious to return to Louisville, where he had recently begun to court the lovely Fanny Henning.[67]

Speed was full of self-doubts about marriage, just as Lincoln had been. Lincoln seemed almost to welcome the appearance of his friend's dilemma, so similar to his own. After Speed's departure, Lincoln wrote to him frequently to offer advice: "I know what the painful point with you is, at all times when you are unhappy. It is an apprehension that you do not love her as you should."[68] Speed's letters in reply have been lost, but a month later

Fanny Henning, whose beautiful black eyes first attracted Joshua Fry Speed. Courtesy of Meserve-Kunhardt Collection.

Lincoln wrote: "I am now fully convinced, that you love her as ardently as you are capable of loving. Your ever being happy in her presence, and your intense anxiety about her health, if there were nothing else, would place this beyond all dispute in my mind. I incline to think it probably, that your nerves will fail you occasionally for a while; but once you get them fairly graded now, that trouble is over forever."[69]

Lincoln projected his own attitudes and conflicted feelings onto Speed, through whom he vicariously re-experienced the drama he had twice enacted in the previous decade. Lincoln related to Speed's difficulties in courtship with an intensity and involvement that suggests he saw Speed as a mirror of his own inner experience. "I now have no doubt," Lincoln told Speed, "that it is the peculiar misfortune of both you and me, to dream dreams of Elysium far exceeding all that any thing earthly can realize." Both also felt the same anxieties. Lincoln encouraged Speed to ease his "nervous temperament" and simply let himself love Fanny: "Say candidly, were not those heavenly *black eyes,* the whole basis of all your early reasoning on the subject?" Lincoln told him that Speed's deep fears for Fanny's health should at least reassure him of the "truth" of his "affection for her." He even suggested: "The Almighty has sent your present affliction expressly for that object." He concluded: "Why Speed, if you did not love her, although you might not wish her death, you would most calmly be resigned to it."[70] This juxtaposition of love and death suggests a morbid fascination with the destructive potentiality of sex.

The great event soon arrived. Speed was married on February 15, 1842, and all but tumbled out of his wedding bed to report the news of a successful consummation to his friend in Springfield. Lincoln wrote on February 25: "I received yours of the 12th. written the day you went down to William's place, some days since; but delayed answering it, till I should received the promised one,

Joshua and Fanny Speed after their marriage.
Courtesy of Lloyd Ostendorf.

of the 16th. which came last night. I opened the latter, with intense anxiety and trepidation—so much that although it turned out better than I expected, I have hardly yet, at the distance of ten hours, become calm." With clear relief Lincoln continued: "I tell you, Speed, our *forebodings,* for which you and I are rather peculiar, are all the worst sort of nonsense." Throughout this drama, Lincoln kept up his conspiratorial relationship with Speed that secured their intimacy, as he added tellingly: "I write another letter enclosing this, which you can show her [Fanny Henning], because, she would think strangely perhaps should you tell her that you receive no letters from me; or, telling her you do, should refuse to let her see them."[71]

This letter of February 25, which turned out to be the turning point in Lincoln's emotional life, suggests that at thirty-three Lincoln was a virgin and terrified of sexual intimacy. There is, however, evidence to the contrary. Lincoln himself told Speed on February 13 in a footnote to a letter: "I have been quite a man ever since you left."[72] This statement could refer to a sexual encounter. It could also express his good feelings at not being depressed, despite Speed's absence. Other evidence on this issue is clouded in fantasy and conjecture. John Hanks referred cryptically to the pretty women who "took Abe's eyes," and Herndon talked of Lincoln's "terrible passion for women." The best source, however, is Sarah Lincoln, who testified that Lincoln was not very fond of girls as far as she could tell.[73] Herndon also reported to Weik on January 5, 1889, a story reported to Herndon by Speed concerning Lincoln's visit to a prostitute. It is a preposterous story, however, that has Lincoln undressed and in bed with the woman before he asks how much she charges. On learning the fee is five dollars and aware that he has only three dollars, Lincoln gets up and dresses but offers her the three dollars for her trouble. "Mr. Lincoln," she replies, "you are the most conscientious man I ever saw."[74] Somehow, one senses a Lincoln joke that got lost in translation.

The letter of February 25 suggests that when Speed at last consummated his relationship with Fanny—and the sky did not fall in—Lincoln was liberated from his fear of marriage. Speed experienced what Lincoln could only fantasize about; he served as a kind of emotional proxy for his conflicted friend. Speed thus proved therapeutic. Within months, Lincoln began secretly to meet with Mary Todd again, and on November 4, 1842, the two were wed. A month before their marriage, there was one last expression of Lincoln's old inner conflict. On October 5, 1842, Lincoln wrote Speed: "But I want to ask a closer question—'Are you now, in *feeling* as well as *judgment,* glad you are married as you are?' From any body but me, this would be an impudent question not to be tolerated, but I know you will pardon it in me. Please answer it quickly as I feel impatient to know."[75] Lincoln apparently was satisfied with Speed's answer.

As this personal drama unfolded, Lincoln was well aware of the significance for him of his relationship with Speed. He had reported to Speed the "sleepless vigilance" with which he followed Speed's courting of Fanny. When Speed thanked him for his help, Lincoln responded that he was not sure he deserved gratitude for his role, since he had been "drawn to it as by fate." He explained: "I always was superstitious; and as part of my superstition, I believe God made me one of the instruments of bringing your Fanny and you together, which union, I have no doubt He had fore-ordained."[76]

For the rest of his life Lincoln retained affectionate feelings for Speed. He considered naming his first son Joshua, but in the end he and Mary chose Robert. He wrote Speed of problems with his children, something he never mentioned to anyone else. In a letter written in 1855, he unburdened himself to Speed on the complexities of his feelings about the political turmoil in the country. As president, he appointed Speed's brother, James, to his cabinet. Occasionally the Lincolns and Speeds visited each other, though Mary apparently had little enthusiasm for such visits. In the White House Lincoln once warmly welcomed Speed and talked of old times.[77]

After February 25, 1842, however, Speed had begun to lose emotional significance for Lincoln. Lincoln's letters became fewer and more formal. When Lincoln took care of the legal aspects of the sale of Speed's Springfield store, the letters the two exchanged contained little except matters of business. Though, in 1843, Lincoln had considered naming his first son Joshua, in 1846 he waited seven months to inform Speed of the birth of his second son, Edward. In 1848 the two even became angry with each other over a lost note that affected a case.[78] In the 1855 letter, in which Lincoln unburdened himself on politics, he sharply challenged Speed's ideas about slavery. After Speed's marriage, the intimacy drained from their relationship. Lincoln stumbled through his own crisis of courtship with only the vicarious assistance of Joshua Speed, but once it was over, Speed had little to offer. The friendship faded away.

The man pictured is believed to be
Thomas Lincoln, Abraham's father.
Courtesy of Meserve-Kunhardt Collection.

I happen temporarily to occupy this big White House. I am a living witness that any one of your children may look to come here as my father's child has.

A. Lincoln, August 22, 1864

3

FATHERS

———◆———

The issues of the self unite a host of complex themes from the past. Joshua Speed—and, later, Mary Todd—helped in Lincoln's search for sexual identity. The human animal, however, especially one as fiercely political as Lincoln, is more than a bundle of sexual drives. In a simplified (and therefore distorted) sense, Lincoln's young-adult struggles with intimacy reflected the confusions of his childhood relationship to his mother. But for a political man in nineteenth-century America, the vital issues of the public self clustered around Lincoln's relationship with his father. As Erik Erikson has noted in another context, to make sexuality available for mastery, "a man must confront his childhood and, above all, give an account of his conflicts with his father."[1]

In the spring of 1831, while Lincoln was helping take a flatboat of cargo to New Orleans with Denton Offutt, Thomas Lincoln moved to Charleston, Illinois. Over the years Thomas made a number of unfortunate land purchases, and he lived in poverty and disappointment until his death in 1851. In these two decades Lincoln occasionally visited his father and stepmother, though the record here is notably unreliable. Sarah said Lincoln used to visit her "every year or two," but it is unclear whether she meant for the entire period after 1831 or, more likely, for the years following Thomas's death in 1851. Usher F. Linder, a law associate, testified later that he first met Lincoln in Charleston when Lincoln was visiting his father's house. A few other such visits are acceptably documented. For example, in 1841 Lincoln traveled to Charleston to close a land transaction with his father. Occasionally he practiced law there, even though Charleston was not on the eighth circuit. The question is how often Lincoln took the trouble to travel the additional seven miles to Goosenest Prairie, where his father lived. Charles H. Coleman, who from fact and fiction put together an entire book on Lincoln in Coles

Lincoln as a father himself with his favorite son, Willie, inside fence, in the summer of 1860. Courtesy of Lloyd Ostendorf.

County, assumed that whenever Lincoln was in Charleston he went to see his father. It seems safer to assume the opposite: Lincoln generally avoided him.[2]

But no matter how often, or how seldom, Lincoln visited his father near Charleston, the record shows that his father never visited him in Springfield. Thomas and Sarah Lincoln did not attend Abraham and Mary's wedding, and none of Lincoln's four children ever met their paternal grandfather. Apparently, in all her life even Mary never laid eyes on Thomas. It seems therefore that on his rare visits to his father Lincoln went grudgingly and without his wife or children. Undoubtedly, Mary's social snobbery reinforced Lincoln's emotional distance from his father. She probably would have welcomed such a backwoodsman in her elegant house at Eighth and Jackson no more readily than she did the drunken, obstreperous Herndon. Herndon once told Weik: "You wish to know if Mrs. Lincoln and the Todd aristocratic family did not scorn and detest the Hanks and the Lincoln family and in answer to which I yell—yes." If Thomas and Sarah Lincoln had ever appeared at her door, Herndon said, "I doubt whether Mrs. Lincoln would have admitted them."[3] Still, Mary did not create the hostility between Lincoln and his father. Furthermore, Lincoln clearly separated the antagonism he felt toward his father from his abiding affection for his stepmother. It is therefore reasonable to suppose that Lincoln traveled to his parents' home near Charleston in the 1830s and 1840s to see Sarah and that he merely put up with the presence of his father.

As Thomas aged he became less and less capable of supporting himself and his wife. Lincoln gradually assumed responsibility for his parents' financial security, but he did so with marked irritation and resentment. The forty acres Lincoln purchased for Thomas in October 1841 was in fact a gift, for it allowed Thomas and Sarah full use of the property during their lifetime. Certainly

Lincoln himself had no intention of farming it. "*I* have no farm, nor ever expect to have," he told Speed in 1842.[4] Over the years Lincoln also periodically assigned legal fees to Thomas and gave him the power to collect on some notes (Lincoln regularly loaned money to friends and associates).[5]

But Thomas's needs exceeded Lincoln's generosity. On December 7, 1848, John D. Johnston, Lincoln's stepbrother, wrote to Lincoln on behalf of the illiterate Thomas to request a loan of twenty dollars to avoid the loss of his land. Johnston's letter, a curious document, reveals as much about Johnston as about Thomas. It begins with Thomas reporting: "I and the old woman is in best of health" and "soe is all of the relations at present." Then it notes with regret that Lincoln has failed to visit Goosenest on his way to Washington as Congressman-elect (though Lincoln and his family did manage a visit to the Todds in Kentucky). Thomas complains: "as you faild to come a past, I am compeled to make a request by Letter to you for the loan of, Twenty Dollars, which sum I am compeled to razes, or my Land will be sold." Thomas finds it embarrassing to have to borrow such a small amount to avoid so great a calamity as the loss of his land. "I doe expect you will think strang at this request, for that much money & it was eaquely as strange, to me & John." Thomas tries to explain that he forgot an old judgment against him and thinks he paid it, but lost the receipt "if we ever had one." The "we" here seems to be Thomas and Johnston, whose affairs were intermingled. Possibly the debt was Johnston's, and Thomas was covering up for his wayward stepson. In any event, Thomas appears to anticipate Lincoln's anger at the request, for he immediately adds: "I now you cant apreciate the reluctance that I have made this request of you for money but I am compeled to do so."[6]

To his father's abject plea, Lincoln replied with sarcasm and condescension. "My dear father: Your letter of the 7th was received night before last. I very cheerfully send you the twenty dollars, which sum you say is necessary to save your land from sale. It is singular that you should have forgotten a judgment against you; and it is more singular that the plaintiff should have let you forget it so long, particularly as I suppose you have always had property enough to satisfy a judgment of that amount."[7]

Just over two years later Thomas lay on his deathbed, and through John D. Johnston and a more distant relative, Harriet Hanks Chapman, he urged Lincoln to come and see him. Though the letters of Johnston and Chapman have not survived, it is apparent from Lincoln's reply on January 13, 1851, that Thomas knew he was dying and probably hoped for a final reconciliation with his estranged son. "Dear Brother," Lincoln responded to Johnston: "On the day before yesterday I received a letter from Harriet written at Greenup. She says she has just returned from your house; and that Father is very low, and will hardly recover. She also says you have written me two letters; and that although you do not expect me to come now, you wonder that I do not write. I received both your letters and although I have not answered them, it is not because I have forgotten them, or been uninterested about them—but because it appeared to me I could write nothing which could do any good." Lincoln's advice was to "procure a doctor, or any thing else for Father in his present sickness." He also gave two excuses for not coming: He was very busy, and Mary was "sick-abed."[8]

With the Illinois Supreme Court in session, this was indeed a busy season for Springfield lawyers. Still, Lincoln's presence was not required between January 13, the day of his letter, and January 17, the day of Thomas's death. In three cases, he was associated with other attorneys (in one case, Stephen T. Logan; in the others, William Herndon), who could have made the necessary court appearances or arguments. The only case that presented genuine difficulty, a case in which Lincoln alone represented the clients, came before the court on January 14. But it was common practice for lawyers to substitute for one another in times of overwork or emergency. There was also the possibility of an extension or postponement of the case.[9] And, though there was as yet no railroad line between Springfield and Charleston, the ninety-mile trip easily could be made in a day by horse or buggy.

Lincoln's reference to his wife's illness is somewhat more difficult to assess. Almost a year earlier their second son, Edward, had died, and Mary had collapsed in shock and for weeks remained in her room, weeping. Soon she was pregnant again, and their third son, William Wallace, was born on December 21, 1850, more than three weeks before Lincoln wrote Johnston that he could not visit his father. Though Mary was still recovering from childbirth, there were no complications, and Lincoln told Johnston he supposed her condition was "not dangerous." He was accustomed to her desperate pleas for closeness and attention, and he could spend months away campaigning or riding the circuit when it suited his needs. What she faced in mid-January 1851 was apparently one of her periodic bouts of depression, one associated this time with a minor physical illness. His use of this illness as an excuse for remaining in Springfield while his father was dying in Charleston appears, therefore, specious. He was trying desperately to justify his own inability to encounter a dying Thomas, despite his father's explicit plea.

Lincoln's letter to Johnston supports this interpretation. After explaining why he could not visit his father, Lincoln asks Johnston to "tell him [Thomas] to remember to call upon, and confide in, our great, and good, and merciful Maker; who will not turn away from him in any extremity." "He notes the fall of a sparrow," Lincoln says, referring to Matthew 10: 29–30 and *Hamlet* 5.2.231, "and numbers the hairs of our heads; and He will not forget the dying man, who puts his trust in Him." Then Lincoln adds a phrase that dramatically expressed his own deepest feelings: "Say to him that if we could meet now, it is doubtful whether it would not be more painful than pleasant." Possibly Lincoln was accurately predicting his father's reaction, but, more likely, the pain would have been Lincoln's, not his father's. Feelings have a way of finding expression, however confused, distorted, or disguised. In this letter Lincoln tried to convince himself that factors beyond his control—his busy schedule and his wife's illness—determined his behavior. But he realized the hollowness of these excuses, and so he turned to the absolving power of God. He simply could not bear the thought of meeting with his father on his deathbed.

If Lincoln had trouble dealing with his dying father, he was equally unable to handle the simplest of rituals our culture expects for the deceased. Lincoln did not attend his father's funeral, and he spent the rest of his life intermittently resolving to mark his father's grave in some appropriate way. Though he never got around to it, when his fourth son was born two years later, on April 4, 1853, Lincoln named him Thomas, after his father. There are many reasons for the naming of children, but in this case the timing suggests a kind of expiation or atonement for the guilt that Lincoln felt for the neglect of his father. During his final visit with his stepmother before leaving for Washington, in late January 1861, Lincoln visited his father's grave, which was "unmarked and utterly neglected," and at least thought of ordering a stone marker for the site. On December 19, 1867, Mary wrote to his stepmother: "My husband a few weeks before his death mentioned to me, that he intended *that* summer [i.e., 1865], paying proper respect to *his* father's grave, by a head and foot stone, with his name & age & I propose very soon carrying out his intentions." Mary, in her state of emotional disarray after the assassination, was even less capable than Lincoln of doing anything about the marker. The task was left to some local residents of Coles County, who finally erected a twelve-foot monument at the grave in 1880 —twenty-nine years after Thomas's death.[10]

★★★

This story of Lincoln's pained struggle to break free from and make sense of what he appeared to experience as the degraded, shameful image of his father was to have important political meanings. In his fertile imagination, Lincoln remade himself in relation to idealized others, most especially the nation's founders. As surrogate fathers in a psychological sense, the founders came to represent the integrity and authenticity so lacking in Lincoln's own sense of his biological father. The "fathers," on the other hand, those revered but distant others who created the nation and wrote stirring documents of freedom, filled the void of idealization in Lincoln's self.[11] And Lincoln's emotional and intellectual investment in these fathers was to prove a creative, healing force in a time of national breakdown.

Lincoln, of course, was not alone in idealizing the founders. In fact, he went along with one of the most powerful trends in American culture. The "post-heroic generation," as the historian George B. Forgie has called it, defined itself collectively in the shadow of these figures. Parson Weems's *Life of Washington,* for example, a book Lincoln absorbed as a child, painted a quite mythical picture of Washington and powerfully influenced Americans' reverence for Washington and other founders. When the Whig leader Henry Clay sought authority for federal expenditures on internal improvements, he found it in the Constitution and in the policies of Washington. Politicians North and South, from Daniel Webster to John C. Calhoun, talked of their special relationship to a mighty past.[12]

As with all such idealizations, however, the post-heroic generation remained ambivalent toward the fathers. Were the new generation merely to be quiescent and passive, protectors of the tradition, not actors within it? The founders were great; but to some, and perhaps to all at some level, the memory of the fathers was stifling. In the case of Lincoln, he engaged the founders with a passion that exceeded even what was common in the culture. They mattered. And yet Lincoln brimmed with ambivalence that carried over from the personal to the political.

These contradictions in Lincoln's thought burst forth in a speech he gave in 1838 before the Young Men's Lyceum in Springfield.[13] The panic of 1837 had created widespread social unrest and had intensified the growing discord over slavery. A spirit of mob violence prevailed in many areas of the country, as when, in the fall of 1837, a mob attacked the abolitionist press of Elijah P. Lovejoy in Alton, Illinois, and killed him when he attempted to defend it. In his speech, "The Perpetuation of Our Political Institutions," Lincoln dealt in a general way with the issues he felt the Alton lynching raised.[14]

The speech begins, as is so customary with Lincoln's rhetorical style, by placing us in the context of a continuous historical narrative that has a clear beginning: "In the great journal of things happening under the sun," he says, "we, the American People, find our account running, under date of the nineteenth century of the Christian era." The birth of Christ in this passage begins a historical sequence for Lincoln in a way that parallels the evocation, in another speech, of the signing of the Declaration of Independence: "Four score and seven years ago our fathers brought forth, upon this continent, a new nation, conceived in Liberty."

Lincoln then moves to a lofty description of the riches and abundance of America. This "fairest portion of the earth," he says, possesses the world's best land, soil, and climate; but the country's most important assets are its political institutions, which provide more civil and religious liberty than any other in history. But several potential dangers threaten this national experiment. He dismisses invasion by an outside force from Europe: Shall we expect some "transatlantic military giant," he asks, to "step the Ocean" and "crush us at a blow?" No, never!, Lincoln exclaims. The combined forces of Europe, Asia, and Africa with a Bonaparte at their head could not "take a drink from the Ohio, or make a track on the Blue Ridge, in a trial of a thousand years." The real danger, on the contrary, is from divisions within the country itself, most of all "the increasing disregard for the law," and what Lincoln calls "the growing disposition to substitute the wild and furious passions" for the "sober judgment of the Courts."

The spirit of mob violence often surfaced in Jacksonian America, but what Lincoln here calls the "mobocratic spirit" had been exacerbated by the economic panic of 1837. The event on everyone's mind—which Lincoln refers to in a phrase about shooting editors—was the death of Lovejoy. But there were other events as well. Lincoln finds that the mobocratic spirit prevails throughout the land: "Accounts of outrages committed by mobs, form the every-day news of the times," Lincoln says, from New England to Louisiana, "neither peculiar to the eternal snows of the former, nor the burning suns of the latter," and thus present in both slaveholding and non-slaveholding areas. The problem is basic, pernicious, and national: "Whatever, then, their cause may be, it is common to the whole country."

The danger the mobocratic spirit poses is surprisingly specific in its political outcome, according to Lincoln. Mob violence weakens the attachment of the people to the laws and makes it impossible for the people to govern themselves, that is, for democracy to operate effectively. "Whenever this effect [of weakening the attachment of people for the law] shall be produced among us; whenever the vicious portion of population shall be permitted to gather in bands of hundreds and thousands, and burn churches, ravage and rob provision stores, throw printing presses into rivers, shoot editors, and hang and burn obnoxious persons at pleasure, with impunity; depend on it, this Government cannot last." All laws, Lincoln says, must be obeyed, even bad ones. "There is no grievance," he states categorically, "that is a fit object of redress by the mob law." In an environment of weakened laws, wild and furious passions, and mobocratic rule, then, "new reapers will arise" and "seek a field," men of "ambition and talent" who will seek the gratification of their "ruling passion." These men—who suddenly become anthropomorphized as *a* man in the course of a paragraph—will emerge to overthrow the government and govern by authoritarian rule.

Lincoln imagines this new ruler as a man of "towering genius" who "disdains a beaten path." "Many great and good men," Lincoln says, have aspired to a seat in Congress, or a gubernatorial or even presidential chair. But such accomplishments would be too mundane for this new ruler, for such *"belong not to the family of the lion, or the tribe of the eagle."* Alexander, Caesar, or Napoleon would never have been satisfied with such circumscribed titles. On the contrary, this figure Lincoln evokes will add "story to story, upon the monuments of fame"; will deny there is glory in serving anyone else; will scorn to tread in the footsteps of *"any* predecessor, however illustrious"; and will be someone who "thirsts and burns" for distinction, even to the point of emancipating slaves or enslaving free men. Lincoln asks: "Is it unreasonable then to expect, that some man possessed of the loftiest genius, coupled with ambition sufficient to push it to its utmost stretch, will at some time, spring up among us?"

Lincoln concludes his speech with some considerations on

preventing the appearance of such a destructive genius in our midst. The answer he offers lies basically in reaffirming the work of the founders, those wise and learned men who created the republic and left us their priceless documents, the Declaration and the Constitution. (Lincoln, unlike many of his generation, especially Southerners, always considered the two as inseparable founding documents.) Our fathers who established this country, he says, "were the pillars of the temple of liberty; and now, that they have crumbled away, that temple must fall, unless we, their descendants, supply their places with other pillars, hewn from the solid quarry of sober reason." And he says with exuberance: "Passion has helped us; but can do so no more. It will in future be our enemy. Reason, cold, calculating, unimpassioned reason, must furnish all the materials for our future support and defence."

If that, then, is the argument of the speech, presented in some detail to suggest the richness of young Lincoln's impassioned rhetoric—there is no question his style improved with the years—it is open to many interpretations and has in fact occasioned more lively debate than any other single Lincoln document. One scholar, John Y. Simon, is worried about all the psychohistorical attention that has been lavished on the speech, since we lack a manuscript of it and have had to rely entirely on the version that appeared in the *Sangamo Journal* on February 3, 1838.[15] That version, of course, could have been altered between delivery and publication, perhaps incorporating suggestions of those who heard the speech, or, more disturbingly, could have been simply a second-hand account by a journalist who may or may not have accurately captured Lincoln's actual words. Simon fails to note, however, that appended to the text of the speech is a footnote to the effect that Lincoln had delivered to the *Journal* a copy of his speech. As a text, the Lyceum speech that has come down to us is therefore *more* reliable than a large number of Lincoln's other speeches, which are only available in newspaper versions without such an accompanying note.

Another issue has been raised by George Fredrickson, who argues that at the Lyceum young Lincoln was helping to define a conservative intellectual style in American politics that adamantly opposed the "trend toward general anarchy or majority tyranny." The Jacksonian spirit of unrestrained, romantic democracy strongly supported the expression of spontaneous popular feeling, as Fredrickson points out, and some Jacksonian theorists even defended in principle the rights of the mob. Other Americans, with a more traditional notion of order and community, "mounted a substantial counter-attack against the ideas and practices associated with the radical democratic impulse." Fredrickson sees Lincoln's Lyceum speech as a classic expression of this conservative response to the "mobocratic spirit" and as a statement of faith "in regular and established ways of making decisions and resolving disputes." The speech, Fredrickson says, is not open to psychological interpretation, because "it was not at all unusual for a lawyer to deprecate genius or defend calculating reason against exalted passion. It was, as we have seen, an integral part of the juridical defense of a procedural community."[16]

Psychological interpretation, however, is not separate from but congruent with other approaches. No doubt Lincoln's call for "cold, calculating, unimpassioned reason" was intended as an antidote to the "mobocratic spirit" that he saw in evidence throughout the land. That in no way, however, means that his call for reason and order lacked psychological meaning. Lincoln sought control in a number of areas. His passionate interest in order and reason, in fact, ran like a thread throughout his life, influencing not only his conception of the political process, but also his choice of career and his style of domesticity.

These issues were particularly keen for young Lincoln. In this regard, the Lyceum speech indirectly reflects Lincoln's anxiety over the emotional tumult of his courtships, broken engagements, and the forebodings he shared with Joshua Speed during the period that extended from the mid-1830s to the early 1840s. What Lincoln called forth from himself with a note of urgency was an imperfectly realized need for control, always the plaint of the troubled. As he put it in his contemporaneous temperance address: "Happy day, when, all appetites controlled, all passions subdued, all matters subjected, *mind,* all conquering *mind,* shall live and move the monarch of the world. Glorious consummation! Hail fall of Fury! Reign of Reason, all hail!"[17]

But to return to the Lyceum, it is not unlikely that Lincoln's immediate model for the towering genius who disdains a beaten path was Andrew Jackson, as Fredrickson suggests. It is also likely that if Lincoln was thinking of anyone in particular (which is not necessarily the case, given the way he anthropomorphizes the danger for rhetorical purposes), he had in mind Napoleon Bonaparte, whom he mentions twice by name in the speech. Maybe the danger is even more abstract. The sequence, after all, of mobocracy undermining democracy, which then gives way to autocracy or dictatorship, is precisely the model in Plato's *Republic.* Lincoln could have encountered some version of Plato's work in the early grammar books he used in school, which were quite advanced, or in newspaper articles or other kinds of popular stories.

Whatever the model, the towering genius of the Lyceum is an intriguing figure, one that has elicited a range of interpretations. Edmund Wilson was the first to say that the genius in fact reflects Lincoln's own projected image of his oedipal wishes for greatness. In this influential interpretation, Wilson argued that it was actually Lincoln himself who unconsciously desired to be a great world-historical figure who would rise above the emasculated fathers at any cost. Having created this image of the tyrant in the speech, however, Lincoln shrank from it with a shiver of unacknowledged recognition, which is the thematic sequence of the speech. The most important part of Wilson's interpretation, one often not fully appreciated, is that Lincoln's dark ambitions remained to motivate him later. The Lyceum, for Wilson, reveals the hidden truth of Lincoln as a purposeful tyrant who emerges full-blown during the war.[18]

Historians have all been touched, for better or worse, by Wilson. George B. Forgie, as noted, interprets Lincoln's image of the tyrant and his ambivalent attitude toward the founders as a cultural metaphor. Somewhat later, Dwight Anderson argued that the speech shows that Lincoln desired to slay the founders and take their place, that such feelings profoundly influenced his making of the Civil War, and that Lincoln found his immortality by becoming himself the Lyceum tyrant by the end of the war.[19] From Wilson to Anderson, such neo-revisionist interpretations read backward form a decidedly negative view of Lincoln's wartime leadership, a view that few share. I can find no justification for this theory in an offbeat psychological interpretation of an early speech, and it is not surprising that several leading Lincoln scholars have come down hard on such views, Don E. Fehrenbacher with Olympian disdain, and Richard N. Current with marked irritation.[20] It does seem imaginable, however, to be both careful and psychological. At least such is the goal.

Certainly, there is what one can loosely call "oedipal imagery" in the speech, especially in the contrasting images of the tyrant and the idealized founders whose work is trampled underfoot. The evil genius—a kind of Jacksonian Darth Vader—is thus vibrant, powerful, unfettered, and above and beyond history itself, while the founders and their work rot, subject to the abuse of nature: "They [the founders]," says Lincoln, "were a forest of giant oaks; but the all-resistless hurricane has swept over them, and left only, here and there, a lonely trunk, despoiled of its verdure, shorn of its foliage; unshading and unshaded; to murmur in a few more gentle breezes, and to combat with its mutilated limbs, a few more ruder storms, then to sink, and be no more." The metaphor suggests emasculation and castration at the hands of the aspiring son.

But such a Freudian view of the central themes in the speech, tangled as it has become with a derogatory view of Lincoln himself, obscures a number of other issues of the self in young Lincoln. Take, for example, what Edmund Wilson first introduced to us as the projective image of the tyrant in Lincoln's evocative phrases. A more nuanced view would note that Lincoln in his speech gives voice to a powerful and largely unacknowledged grandiosity that is grounded in a specific life crisis. Read psychologically, his brittle grandiosity is in fact the most striking and important aspect of the speech. Most other psychological commentators have assumed there is something evil in such self-imaginings, and that if Lincoln could at some level see himself as the towering genius at the Lyceum, that image must still be lurking in the shadows when he was president a quarter of a century later.

To a degree, of course, nothing in the self completely disappears, just as, in general, the more things change the more they are the same. But grandiosity works in complex ways. One expects, even welcomes, powerful ambition in a young man of greatness. Young Lincoln had to imagine himself as more capable than his accomplishment made visible at the time. He was not, to say the least, an ordinary small-town lawyer. Lincoln was a young man of driving ambition, a man who read Shakespeare and surely fantasized himself as one of the poet's troubled kings. This was a man who really did lift himself out of the backwoods, educate himself against great odds, marry up, and endure several political defeats to get elected twice as President of the United States. His terrible dilemma at the Lyceum was the discrepancy between fantasy and reality, ambition and fulfillment. Lincoln had done little to justify his own sense of self-worth that ranked him in his mind, unconsciously or not, with Alexander, Caesar, and Napoleon, let alone with his heroes, Washington and Jefferson. His soaring ambitions, thus frustrated, turned inward into some murky images in the speech. In time, Lincoln learned to bridle these feelings while simultaneously pushing forward vigorously to actualize his ambitions in the real world of politics. The United States is a free nation in no small measure because of these psychological changes within Lincoln.

The Lyceum was only the first articulated expression of what would be a host of speeches throughout his life that reveal Lincoln's enormously complex engagement with his own internalized image of the founders. In speech after speech in the 1850s, Lincoln invoked the spirit of the "fathers" as the basis for the salvation and rejuvenation of the country. No one more than Abraham Lincoln, it is fair to say, preserved the thought of the founders more keenly and intelligently as the nation hurtled toward civil war. During his debates with Stephen A. Douglas in 1858, Lincoln invoked with almost monotonous regularity the wisdom of the fathers and the power of their documents to solve current political problems. On February 27, 1860, at the Cooper Institute in New York City, Lincoln delivered one of his most important speeches before his presidency. In it he sought to understand "the frame of Government under which we live" and how slavery fitted into it. He carefully examined the attitudes of the thirty-nine signers, "who were our fathers," to see what they expected to become of slavery. He also addressed the vital issue of federal versus local authority in the territories. He concluded: *"As those fathers marked it [slavery], so let it be again marked, as an evil not to be extended, but ιο be tolerated and protected only because of and so far as its actual presence among us makes that toleration and protection a necessity."*[21]

After Lincoln was elected President, his view of his relationship to the founding fathers changed in subtle but crucial ways. Even during the interregnum and before the inauguration, all the states of the deep South had seceded and formed a new nation. Lincoln could no longer rely on the redeeming work of the founders to stave off the disaster of disunion. His election radically altered in his own mind his understanding of history. The change was apparent even as Lincoln left Springfield on his twelve-day journey to Washington. In an emotional farewell from the back of the train, Lincoln said goodbye to his friends and neighbors who stood in a drizzling rain at the depot on February 11, 1861: "I now leave, not knowing when, or whether ever, I may return, with a task before me greater than that which rested upon Washington." The Springfield *Journal* editor, who had "heard him speak upon a hundred different occasions," had "never seen him so profoundly affected."[22] With dramatic suddenness Lincoln assumed a position alongside the founders of the republic.

At Gettysburg, November 19, 1863, Lincoln subtly indicated his further reflections on his changed relationship to the founders.[23] He invoked the familiar respect for the fathers who had "brought forth, upon this continent, a new nation, conceived in Liberty, and dedicated to the proposition that all men are created equal." Then he stated a momentous issue for himself and the nation: whether the Civil War, symbolized by the battlefield where he spoke, would put an end to this great experiment. He concluded that the deaths were not in vain, that the nation—under his leadership, in a war for which he personally assumed responsibility—would have "a new birth of freedom," and that "government of the people, by the people, for the people" would not "perish from the earth."

The continuing war and its terrible carnage created for Lincoln something of a psychological and moral crisis. There seemed no explanation for the suffering, death, and destruction. In the past Lincoln had always related the great political issues of the day to the thought of the founders. But the war tore loose the nation's moorings in the past as well as his own. He began to find new meanings in the Father.

Never religious in a conventional sense and certainly not churched, Lincoln nevertheless seemed to believe in a deity. He had, of course, a firm grounding in the Bible. It seems he was genuinely cheered to know that others prayed for him. During his forty-nine months in office he issued nine separate calls to public penitence, fasting, prayer, and thanksgiving. Until the war, he had appeared to find ample basis for his evolving political positions in his own abundant common sense and in the documents of the founders. Then he began to look elsewhere. "Through this dreadful national crisis," Harriett Beecher Stowe noted in 1864, "he has been forced by the very anguish of the struggle to look upward." And up there was God, august, mysterious, majestic.[24]

In his Second Inaugural Address, March 4, 1865, a little more than a month before his death and with Union victory certain if not final, Lincoln dramatically illustrated the transformation of his thought. At the outset he established the South's responsibility for the war: "Both parties [North and South] deprecated war; but one of them would make war rather than let the nation survive; and the other would accept war rather than let it perish. And the war came." Lincoln then turned to the issue of slavery: "One eighth of the whole population were colored slaves, not distributed generally over the Union, but localized in the Southern part of it. . . . All knew that this interest was, somehow, the cause of the war." No one anticipated the magnitude or duration of the war that came, Lincoln continued. "Both [North and South] read the same Bible, and pray to the same God; and each invokes His aid against the other." The prayers of both could not be answered, and "neither has been answered fully."

The Almighty has His own purposes, Lincoln continued:

"Woe unto the world because of offences! for it must needs be that offences come; but woe to that man by whom the offence cometh!" If we shall suppose that American Slavery is one of those offences which, in the providence of God, must needs come, but which, having continued through His appointed time, He now wills to remove, and that He gives to both North and South, this terrible war, as the woe due to those by whom the offence came, shall we discern therein any departure from those divine attributes which the believers in a Living God always ascribe to him? Fondly do we hope—fervently do we pray—that this mighty scourge of war may speedily pass away. Yet, if God wills that it continue, until all the wealth piled by the bond-man's two hundred and fifty years of unrequited toil shall be sunk, and until every drop of blood drawn with the lash, shall be paid by another drawn with the sword, as was said three thousand years ago, so still it must be said "the judgments of the Lord, are true and righteous altogether."[25]

Here was a divine aim in the war. Here was a framework, an explanation, for what seemed as senseless as it was interminable. Here, too, was a feeling far different from the "cold, calculating, unimpassioned reason" of the Lyceum speech some twenty-six years earlier. Lincoln had warned strongly against the emergence of a tyrant who would take advantage of social chaos, but in the process only thinly disguised his own identification with that towering genius. Later, as the country moved toward war over slavery, Lincoln became a passionate spokesman for a return to the wisdom of the fathers and their successors such as Henry Clay. These men emerged in Lincoln's thought as our only source of wisdom and guidance in perilous times. Then came the war, and with it Lincoln assumed a place in history which he quickly realized put him on a par with the founders. Suddenly, those revered, distant, idealized figures lost their psychological significance. Lincoln had been lifted by history to look directly into the eyes of his heroes. It was a startling experience. And his gaze drifted upward. Finally only God, and no man, could supply the meaning of human existence.

Mary Todd Lincoln. Courtesy of Illinois State Historical Library.

What changes time *brings to us all—I sometimes feel as if I had lived a century.* My life *is not dated by years.*

Mary Todd Lincoln, December 5, 1869

4

MARY

Her earliest photograph dates from 1846. It shows an attractive young woman in her mid-twenties gazing expectantly at the camera. Full cheeks, though suggesting a tendency toward plumpness, only accentuate the softness and femininity. Light brown hair is pulled back from a high forehead. The eyes and nose are regular, even pleasant. The mouth pulls together tightly above a rounded chin. A long graceful neck plunges into folds of obscuring Victorian fabric. Short arms rest uneasily, one of them propped against a chair, as the subject waits rigidly through a long exposure. The hands seem large for the body, and the fingers long.

Other sources add lifelike details to this stark black-and-white daguerreotype. "Her features were not regularly beautiful," recalled Mary's childhood friend, Mrs. Elizabeth L. Norris, "but she was certainly very pretty with her clear blue eyes, lovely complexion, and soft brown hair." She had a bright and intelligent face, and "no Old Master ever modeled a more perfect arm and hand."[1]

Mary took great pride in her soft complexion, graceful arms, and full buxom figure. In her early years the fashion forbade much décolleté, but by the 1860s plunging necklines and bare shoulders were in style. Mary, then a matronly forty, eagerly adopted the new mode. She was short (five feet, two inches) and seemed shorter beside a husband who was extraordinarily tall for the time (six feet, four inches). Yet she carried herself well and "was graceful in her movements," a fine and experienced dancer, familiar with the best technique and able to move easily across the floor.[2]

This attractive woman had a complex personality. Vivacious, infectiously enthusiastic, delightfully witty, she could make a bishop forget his prayers, as her brother-in-law once said.[3] Her letters bustle with energy, haste, and excitement. Of an 1840 trip to Missouri, she wrote that she "remained a week, attended four parties, during the time, once [sic] was *particularly* distinguished for its brilliancy and *city like* doings, the house was very commodious, four rooms & two halls, thrown open for the reception of the guests, in two, dancing was carried on with *untiring vigor,* kept up until 3 o'clock."[4] She described the Virginia reel as "poetry of motion," yet confessed she was nearly exhausted at the "*desperate exertions*" of the dance. Then she referred to "*some letters*" (perhaps from Lincoln) that "were entirely *unlooked for.*"

Mary's letters of this period seem to burst from the page. The sentences run on with few paragraph breaks but with occasional dashes. Indiscriminate underlining gives a feeling of exaggerated drama. The diversity of topics testifies to the range of Mary's interests and the extent of her involvement in the world around her. She describes an incredibly busy schedule, with "scarce a leisure moment" to call her own. She delights in gossip: "I know you would be pleased with Matilda Edwards, a lovelier girl I never saw. *Mr. Speed's* ever changing heart I suspect is about offering *its young* affection at her shrine." The mention of Speed reminds her of "*Mr. Webb*, a widower of modest merit" and of her sister's "most agreeable party," with over a hundred guests. She refers to two married friends, then asks: "Why is it that married folks always become so serious?" She expresses ironic pleasure that another friend is about to commit the "*crime of matrimony*." (These references are the only suggestions of her engagement to Lincoln, which is to be prematurely ended in two weeks.) Without a breath she moves abruptly into politics, noting her elation at the 1840 election of William Henry Harrison as President. Apparently she worked for Harrison during the campaign: "This fall I became quite a *politician,* rather an unladylike profession, yet at such a *crisis,* whose heart could remain untouched while the energies of all were called in question?"[5] Politics, love, marriage, friends, relatives, parties, and the weather all dance across the page.

At that time Mary had a capacity for self-reflection and ironic humor that gave depth to her somewhat superficial concerns with the swirl of social life around her. Would her real nature be satisfied with the excitement of continued parties? She doubts it. "I would such were not my nature, for mine I fancy is to be a quiet lot, and happy indeed will I be, if it is, only cast near those, I so *dearly love,* my feelings & hopes are all so sanguine that in this dull world of reality tis best to dispel our delusive day dreams so soon as possible."[6] She laughs at her own frailties and at her plumpness. She describes herself as the "same ruddy *pineknot*" but without quite the same "exuberance of flesh," though with "quite a sufficiency."[7] There is a certain reflective detachment in her descriptions of the most trivial occurrences. She provides concrete information (for example, how many guests were at the ball), describes the courtships of others as an outside observer might, and easily separates her own fantasies and dreams from the lives of those around her.

There was gaiety and brightness in young Mary Todd. She "was one of the brightest of all the circle in Springfield at that time [ca. 1840]," as her friend, Mrs. John T. Stuart, later commented. "She could entertain a roomful with her ready wit."[8] Her overly protective biographer Ruth Painter Randall says she had a "natural cheerfulness," which makes her gaiety sound almost genetic.[9] Mary cut quite a figure in Springfield. Once, when she and her friend Mercy Levering were cooped up at home by heavy rains, she finally could stand it no longer and decided to set out for town. With some wooden shingles she thought she could lay a movable track and thus advance over the mud. The two young women made it to town reasonably well but then had to confront the dismaying prospect of a return by the same tedious method. Instead of trying it, Mary enlisted a dray to haul her home, though Mercy declined to accompany her. Mary's ride created a sensation. Here was Springfield's leading belle plopped unceremoniously in the rear of a lowly wagon. A socially conscious young Dr. E. H. Merryman took note of the event in a humorous poem, which begins:

> Up flew windows, out popped heads
> To see this lady gay
> In silken cloak and feathers white
> A riding on a dray.

The poem concludes with a rather cruel reference to Mary's plumpness:

> At length arrived at Edwards' gate
> Hart backed the usual way
> And taking out the iron pin
> He rolled her off the dray.[10]

There was a proud, stubborn streak in young Mary. She knew what it meant to ride in a dray, just as she knew it infuriated her family for her to fall in love with the lowborn and apparently hapless Abraham Lincoln. She pursued her unflagging interest in politics, even though she was aware it was "unladylike." In love, too, she stubbornly clung to the memory of Lincoln for a year and a half, even though he had broken their engagement. She wrote Mercy Levering in June 1841 that she had been "much alone of late" and had been left to the solitude of her own thoughts and "some *lingering regrets* over the past, which time can alone overshadow with its healing balm." If only Lincoln would return to her company, "much, much happiness" would it afford her.[11] She remained quietly faithful all that summer, fall, and the following winter, waiting patiently for him to wrestle his own inner demons to the ground. There is no indication he asked her to wait; on the contrary, he seemed unable to communicate anything to her until the spring of 1842. Perhaps she sensed time would heal the wounds. So she waited.

There is an old Todd family tale that when Lincoln first met Mary at a ball he said he would like to dance with her in the worst way, and she reportedly commented later how accurate that was. Lincoln obviously could handle such repartee, but most of the other young men in Mary's life suffered severely from her occasional biting sarcasm. "Without designing to wound," Elizabeth Norris later recalled of Mary in Kentucky, "she now & then indulged in sarcastic, witty remarks that cut like a Damascus blade —but there was no malice in it—She was impulsive & made no attempt to conceal her feelings."[12] In the summer of 1842 Mary was apparently the prime mover, along with Julia Jayne and Lincoln, in writing the "Rebecca Letters," which ridiculed James Shields and nearly resulted in a duel between him and Lincoln.[13]

Sarcasm, of course, is the less gentle side of humor. It tells more about the insecurities and foibles of the joker than about the person who is the butt of the jokes. In the case of young Mary her sarcasm was associated with a ferocious temper. Her rages were legion, though they were worse in the matron, Mrs. Lincoln, than in the young Mary Todd. Young Mary was impulsive, quixotic, nervous, and frenetic, a coiled bundle of energy under relatively good control but ready at any point to burst forth. At this point in her life her capacity for genuine warmth and sympathy for others, her self-reflection, and the effusive enthusiasm of ripe youth partially hid the potential meanings of her rage. But several observers close to Mary later commented on the contrast between her happy, warm self and the rage beneath. "She was very highly strung," wrote her sister Emilie Todd Helm, "nervous, impulsive, excitable, having an emotional temperament much like an April day, sunning all over with laughter one moment, the next crying as if her heart would break." Her face was an index to every passing emotion.[14]

★★★

Lincoln's cousin, Dennis Hanks, noted that Mary came from "blue blood, blue grass Kentucky stock." She was indeed the scion of a distinguished Kentucky clan. Her father, Robert Smith Todd, was the owner of a fine house and a number of slaves and was a leader in Whig politics. Their house in Lexington was a center of informed political debate with guests that included Henry Clay. At thirteen, so the story goes, Mary rode out to Ashland, Clay's home just outside Lexington, to show him her new white pony. And reportedly she was once romping through the house when her elderly grandmother cautioned, "Sit down Mary. Do be quiet. What on earth do you suppose will become of you if you go on this way?" "Oh, I will be the wife of a President some day," carelessly answered the petted child.[15]

Her father was born in 1791, the seventh of eleven children of the distinguished Levi Todd. Robert Todd entered Transylvania University at fourteen years of age, then clerked in an office, studied law under the tutelage of George M. Bibb, and was admitted to the bar in 1811. He soon excelled in business, politics, and Lexington public life. After opening a fancy retail store in 1817, he expanded into other retail enterprises and into the cotton manufacturing business, with a large packaging plant and a wholesale outlet. In 1835 he became the first president of the new Branch Bank of Kentucky. He also wielded political clout. He served repeatedly as the clerk of the Kentucky House of Representatives and in 1831, when Lexington was incorporated, he was elected to its first board of council. Though high-strung and impetuous, he was highly successful and widely admired for his wealth, power, and family background.[16]

In 1811 Robert married his second cousin, Eliza Parker. Her family was just as distinguished as his; she had relatives who had been friends of George Washington.[17] Settling down to a comfortable life, Robert and Eliza began to produce children with regularity: Elizabeth (1813), Frances (1815), Levi (1817), Mary (December 13, 1818), Robert (1820), Ann Maria (1824), and George (1825). Eliza died from complications following George's birth, and her death left an unhealed wound in seven-year-old Mary. She remained permanently vulnerable to separation and loss, and later, as her own children one by one died, she lost her psychological moorings in reality.

The death of her mother left Mary alone, unwanted, and something of a bother to her father, to the unmarried aunt who moved in, and to the overworked household slaves: Jane Saunders, the housekeeper; Chaney, the cook; Nelson, the body servant, coachman, and jack-of-all-trades; and the two who cared for the children, "Mammy Sally" and Judy, the nurse.[18] "Mammy Sally" perhaps filled some of the void in Mary's life, but nothing Mary did could bring her father more closely into her orbit. Within a year he seemingly rejected her when he took a second wife, Elizabeth Humphreys, who began dutifully to produce new babies for him, eight of them in thirteen years. Robert Todd probably felt that by remarrying he was providing a better home for all his children. But Mary's need for his attention and love precluded a sharing of affection with her second mother and those hateful new babies. Mary's resentment of her stepmother—and of her father—may have received some outside reinforcement, for Grandmother Parker, who lived next door, detested the second Mrs. Todd. Mary's situation intensified her willfulness and tendency to tantrums. In confused expressions of undirected rage she seemingly cried out for support, love, and nurturing from her father, her missing mother, and anyone else who might help her. Her calls went largely unheeded. As an adult, she attached herself to Lincoln with all the intensity resulting from these unfulfilled childhood longings. She adored him for his calm, fatherly presence, and nothing made her happier than when he called her his child-wife.

Mary's stepmother, "Betsy" Humphreys Todd, seems to have been incapable of responding to Mary's needs. Her unfeeling way is suggested by an incident that occurred in 1848, when Mary was staying in her father's house with her two sons, five-year-old Robert and two-year-old Eddie, while Lincoln served as a congressman in Washington. As Mary told her husband in a long, rambling letter, Robert had brought home a cat, to the immense delight of Eddie. "Ma came in, she you know dislikes the whole cat race." In a "very unfeeling way" the old woman ordered the nearest servant to throw the cat out. Eddie began screaming violently, but "she never appeared to mind his screams." Mary concluded: "Tis unusual for her *now a days,* to do any thing quite so striking, she is very obliging and accommodating, but if she thought any of us, were on her hands again I believe she would be *worse* than ever."[19]

Mary was writing Lincoln from her father's home late on a Saturday night. The children were finally asleep and she was alone, longing for her husband and writing him how "very sad" she felt at their separation. Such a setting was calculated to revive childhood wishes and memories. In her "dreamy" state Mary transferred to Lincoln her childhood longings for her father. The cat incident marked Betsy as an intruder and solidified Mary's relationship with her father-husband. It confirmed the wickedness of the stepmother and reinforced Mary's unconscious desire for her husband-father to make her his child-wife.

Mary adjusted in a complex way to what were for her the confused and unempathic family relationships that followed her mother's death. She grew up "without learning the essential lesson of self-restraint," as Ruth Painter Randall quaintly puts it.[20] Such a view makes the tantrum a problem of discipline and fails to appreciate the desperate search for inner cohesion and meaningful attention that is the psychological message of an incoherently screaming child. A relevant anecdote is one that Elizabeth Norris, Mary's friend and roommate in the Todd home for several years, recalled of Mary as an early adolescent. Mary and Elizabeth wanted hoopskirts so as to look grown-up for church. Mary conceived a plan to make the hoops out of dried willows, but these spread the skirts awkwardly and unevenly. Still, Mary was determined to wear the hoops, and she sneaked out of the house to avoid her stepmother's censure. Betsy, catching sight of her from a window, insisted that she come back and take off the ridiculous outfit. In her room Mary burst into furious and futile tears.[21]

The hoops, it seems, symbolized maturity for Mary. The stepmother's harsh response failed to grant Mary independent initiative or to recognize her awkward but genuine expression of individuality. The scene reveals the sexual tension between Mary and Betsy. Mary had gone to great effort to make herself pretty, only to have Betsy tell her how ugly and stupid she looked. In this struggle Betsy emerged victorious, but in the process she only made it more difficult for Mary to develop her sexual identity.

The story of the willow hoops reflects Mary's resourcefulness and creativity. When Elizabeth Norris first met her, at the age of ten, Mary was "bright and talkative & warm hearted." She seemed "far advanced, over girls of her age, in education." Her school was the center of her psychological existence. The principal, Mr. Ward, was a harsh taskmaster, but Mary never came under his censure. Instead, she seemed to find solace in the rigorous schedule, "pouring [*sic*] over her books" by the light of a candle and often getting up before breakfast to complete her lessons. Cold though the winter days often were, Mary never complained. "I never saw any display of temper on her part," Norris recalled, "or heard her reprimanded."[22]

At fourteen, Mary progressed to Mme. Victorie Charlotte Leclere Mentelle's select school, just outside Lexington, to board there Mondays through Fridays for the next four years. The school emphasized the fine graces required of a lady—Mary became a superb dancer, for example—but it also provided an intellectually stimulating environment for a smart young girl. Mme. Mentelle required her charges to speak French while at school, and dancing lessons alternated with courses on the classics. Here Mary received a remarkable and quite atypical education for an antebellum southern belle. She became witty, articulate, and outspoken with both peers and adults. She learned to enjoy the finest French authors and could astound visiting Frenchmen with her Parisian accent.

 finishing school

At nineteen, Mary had not yet completed her education. After spending the summer of 1837 in Springfield with her sister, Elizabeth Edwards, she returned to Lexington and spent the next two years studying under Dr. Ward, her earlier principal. Her work with him amounted to a kind of graduate study, and the results were impressive. She now was "forever reciting" poetry, to the delight and amusement of her friends. "Page after page of classic poetry she could recite and liked nothing better." When she went back to Springfield in 1839 to live with her sister, the twenty-one-year-old Mary was an accomplished woman, fully prepared to assume a leading position in the Springfield coterie. Even her worst enemy of later years, William Herndon, could not help giving a favorable description of the young Mary. According to him, she was pleasant, polite, civil, graceful, intelligent, witty (though sometimes bitter), polished, well educated, a good linguist, a clever conversationalist, a little proud and sometimes haughty but a very shrewd young woman.[23]

★★★

Lincoln called her "Molly" before the birth of their first son, Robert, in 1843. After that, she was "Mother" or occasionally "little-woman" or "Puss" or "child-wife." She found security in his fatherly presence and remembered later that "he was never himself" when she was not perfectly well. Lincoln enjoyed Mary's enthusiasm for fine clothes and seemed proud of her good looks. She in turn delighted in making herself pretty for him. Her total love for him magnified his public and private virtues and minimized those of his political opponents. "Mr. Douglas," she once commented, "is a very little, little giant by the side of my tall Kentuckian, and intellectually my husband towers above Douglas just as he does physically." When in 1855 Lyman Trumbull defeated Lincoln for the Senate, there was a hint of double-dealing on Trumbull's part, but Lincoln soon accepted the inevitable and patched up fences with his former friend. Mary, however, refused ever again to speak with Lyman Trumbull or with his wife, Julia, who had been one of her best friends. Even the amicable Dr. Anson G. Henry could not mediate between Mary and Julia. "Mary and

Julia have both made me their confidant telling me their grievances, and both think the other *all* to blame," Henry wrote his wife in February 1861. "I am trying to make peace between them."[24]

Mary's first years of marriage were troubled by problems of financial insecurity, continuing tension with her Todd relatives, and the lack of a home she could call her own. She and her husband moved at first to the Globe Tavern, where they rented a room for four dollars a week. For Mary, raised in genteel comfort, it was an awful experience to begin married life in a single rented room. She was aggressively materialistic, and at the Globe she had to endure the constraints of possessing neither money to buy things nor space to display them. She soon came to hate boarding houses. She only lasted briefly at Mrs. Sprigg's in Washington in 1847. And after 1865 she continually lamented her cramped hotel quarters and the shame of not owning a house appropriate for a President's widow. Her post-1865 attempts to buy a house seem to have repeated her earlier experience when she and Lincoln carefully husbanded their resources to escape the confining atmosphere of the Globe.

Mary's father, Robert Todd, visited the Lincolns shortly after their marriage. Though impressed with his son-in-law (in a way the Edwardses had never been[25]), he apparently thought Mary lacked the comforts she required, for he began to give her $120 a year and continued to do so until his death in 1849. The money was more than enough to pay the wages of a maid. Mary's sister, Elizabeth Edwards, and Elizabeth's husband always objected to Lincoln, whom they thought never quite met Todd standards. Mary, ever loyal to Lincoln, held her own in this struggle. Nine months after her marriage she gave birth to Robert at the Globe Tavern rather than in the comfort of the Edwards home. Years later she recalled her "darling husband" bending over her with love and tenderness at the birth.[26]

Mary felt it impossible to remain at the Globe Tavern new baby. So while hoping to buy a house of their own, the Lincolns moved in 1843 to a rented one. Finally, in 1844, they bought their home at Eighth and Jackson for $1,500, paying $1,200 in cash and a transferred title to a lot valued at $300.[27] In this house Mary defined her own style of domesticity, one that was distinct but reflected the middle-class taste of the period. Her entire upbringing, as well as her personal needs, influenced her decision to devote body and soul to husband, children, home.

In their life together, as Randall describes it, Lincoln and Mary "knew drudgery, monotony, illnesses, clashes of nerves and viewpoints, scoldings, 'blues,' fears, disappointments, small disasters—all the elements that go into the daily exasperation of the average household." To this home, as to others, "the husband returned after the day's work to tell his wife all that had happened to him that day," and the wife told of babies learning to talk in "such a dear, funny combination of sounds" that both of the parents laughed. "There was love in the house on Eighth Street, there was fun and playfulness, there was the joy of children."[28] This rosy picture, though true as far as it goes, misses the significance, for Mary, of Lincoln's reserve. "You are aware," she wrote Josiah G. Holland in 1865, "that with all the President's deep feelings, he was *not* a demonstrative man, when he felt most deeply, he expressed the least."[29] In this statement she accurately identified an important aspect of Lincoln's personality. She also revealed an underlying note of resentment—that is, she believed in his love but needed much more attention and care than he seemed constitutionally able to give. He was absent physically for much of the time and, when home, was not always there in an emotional sense. Once, for example, he was reading before the fire and was so absorbed in his book that he let the fire get low. Mary asked him three times to build it up, but he did not hear

Just before leaving Springfield in 1861, Mary posed with Willie (left) and Tad. Eddy, born in 1846, died in 1850 without a picture having been taken of him. Courtesy of Meserve-Kunhardt Collection.

her. Finally, in a rage, she picked up a piece of firewood and went at him.[30]

Herndon interprets this fireplace incident, which he picked up from a servant in the Lincoln home, as evidence of his hero's "domestic hell." Actually, it suggests Mary's frustration with Lincoln's emotional distance, and it shows her inability to contain her anger. To some extent, her anger was justified. She probably felt hurt by the implicit snub in Lincoln's lack of response to her requests, though his absorption in his book by no means indicated a lack of love for her. She could be horribly frustrated with his refusal to become a total part of her. Desperately in need of Lincoln, Mary often summoned him home from the office to help handle household emergencies, especially those relating to the children. For much of her life, however, she had to cope without him, as he rode the circuit or went off campaigning for months at a time. Her response to his absences was decidedly ambivalent. She wanted the income that the lucrative practice on the circuit brought, and she longed for the fame of political success, yet his absences could devastate her. In 1859 she sent a note to ask Ozias M. Hatch, who was planning to leave for Chicago, to contact Lincoln there and tell him *"dear little Taddie"* was ill. "The Dr. thinks it may prove a *slight* attack of *lung* fever. I am feeling troubled & it would be a comfort to have him, *at home.* He passed a bad night. I do not like his symptoms, and will be glad, if he hurries home." But Lincoln stayed in Chicago to make a speech and did not start home for several days.[31]

A Springfield neighbor, James Gourley, once stated: "I don't think that Mrs. Lincoln was as bad a woman as she is represented; she was a good friend of mine. She always said that if her husband had stayed home as he ought to that she could love him better; she is no prostitute, a good woman. She dared me once or twice to kiss her, as I thought, refused, wouldn't now." Gourley also reported that once in terror Mary had wakened him and pleaded hysterically with him to come spend the night in her house. Lincoln was away, and apparently the maid was letting men slip in the back door to visit her. Mary frantically appealed to Gourley: "Come—do come & stay with me all night—you can sleep in the bed with Bob & I. I don't want boys: they go to sleep too soon & won't & can't watch. Come do—Sleep with Robt & myself."[32]

★★★

The relative abundance of information obscures rather than clarifies the Lincolns' complicated relationship. Herndon does little to help. For him, Lincoln's "domestic hell" was a central fact of the hero's life. "Poor Lincoln," Herndon thought, "was woman-whipped." Mary berated her husband for answering the doorbell himself rather than sending a servant; for using his own knife in the butter; and for lying on the floor to read a newspaper or a book. It might seem odd that Herndon could view Mary so favorably as a young woman and yet see her as such a shrew after marriage, when "she became soured, got gross, became material, avaricious, insolent." He explained the change by reference to Ann Rutledge: "Mrs. Lincoln's knowledge that Lincoln did not love her and did love another caused much trouble between them. I say, Lincoln told her *he did not love her.* The world does not know her, Mrs. Lincoln's sufferings, her trials, and the cause of things." In Herndon's view, what had been admirable pride and genteel breeding in Mary became aristocratic, haughty, and imperious manners. "She was cold as a chunk of ice," he believed.[33]

Relations between Mary and Herndon were bad from the start. As a young man, he once asked her to dance at a ball. Intending to compliment her, he told her she danced like a serpent. This she took as a distinctly ungracious comment, and soon a kind of silent war developed between them.[34] She never relented. When Herndon traveled to Washington in 1863 to try to get a job for a friend, he ran out of money and had to borrow twenty-five dollars from Lincoln. Mary snubbed him. Privately, he complained of her wickedness and felt sorry for her poor husband.[35]

In the triangular relationship of Lincoln, Mary, and Herndon, a curious set of exclusive intimacies developed. From her point of view, her love and needs excluded anyone else from a closeness to Lincoln. He had to envelop her, comfort her, love her as a husband *and* as a father. The lover expects fidelity, but the child demands absorbing attention; in Mary the lover and the child merged. Herndon also sought an impossible closeness with Lincoln.

All he wrote about Lincoln implies wonderment and awe. Lincoln seems to have recognized the idealizing needs of his junior partner and skillfully played on them. Though Herndon was only nine years younger, Lincoln liked to lecture him as a father would a boy. When Herndon was arrested for drunkenness he turned to Lincoln to bail him out and help him save face. And after Lincoln died, Herndon lived only to produce what he hoped would be the definitive biography of the great man.

Lincoln thus aroused the love of one man and one woman who, like children in a situation of intense sibling rivalry, detested each other. When open warfare broke out between Herndon and Mary in 1865, it only brought to the surface the suppressed tensions that dated from the early 1840s. There was a sexual basis for this rivalry. It is most explicit in Herndon's insistent and even obsessional interest in Lincoln's sex life, which he believed had been richly varied before Lincoln's marriage. He leaves to the imagination the question of whether Lincoln consummated his relationship with Ann Rutledge, but he leaves no doubt that Lincoln enjoyed the pleasures of farmers' daughters, prostitutes, and others.[36] Lincoln's closeness to Speed upset Herndon; he could not understand it but wished for something like it for himself. Then Lincoln married and, in Herndon's eyes, became oddly devoted to his nasty little wife. "Lincoln had terribly strong passions for women," Herndon once declared, "could scarcely keep his hands off them, and yet he had honor and strong will, and these enabled him to put out the fires of his terrible passion."[37] The fires of terrible passion probably were Herndon's own, and so were the frustrations, the ungratified longings. Raw, elemental jealousy prompted the virulent hatred between Herndon and Mary as each sought possession of the elusive Lincoln.

On the issue between Herndon and Mary, most authors have taken one side or the other. Edmund Wilson, agreeing with Herndon, has referred to the "tantrums and aspirations of his [Lincoln's] rather vulgar wife."[38] On the other hand, Ruth Painter Randall, Irving Stone *(Love is Eternal),* and, most recently, Jean Baker have leapt to Mary's defense. But such simple-minded scholarly quarreling is tiresome and merely replays old arguments without advancing our understanding. Mary is a complex figure who elicits mixed responses. She was a blend of willful, stubborn, outspoken manners and a quiet, passive femininity. She defined her life in Lincoln's shadow and then refused to stay there. She could be warm and genuine one moment and manipulative, petty, and imperious the next. At times she was in a rage, at other times collapsing with a migraine headache. "And you are entirely free from head-ache?" Lincoln wrote her on April 16, 1848. "That is good—good—considering it is the first spring you have been free from it since we were acquainted."[39] In addition to her short-term vacillations, Mary underwent a long-term change. The bubbly, vivacious, engaging young woman almost seems a different person from the dour, self-pitying widow.

Herndon's material tends to support the view of Mary's contrariness. For example, Herndon relates an incident with a Mr. Tiger, which he picked up third-hand. Tiger's niece, Sarah, had worked for Mary as a maid sometime in 1850. All went well until Mary got into one of her "insane mad spells" and insulted and slapped the girl, who ran home to her uncle. Tiger went to see Mary. He found her standing in the yard, which was strewn with Sarah's trunk and clothes. He attempted to learn Mary's side of the story, but rational discussion seemed impossible. "Mrs. Lincoln got madder and madder," Herndon comments, "boiled over with her insane rages, and at last struck Tiger with a broom two or three times." Tiger, now angry himself, sought out Lincoln for an apology and reportedly found him telling jokes at the Edwards store. He called him outside and demanded that he punish Mary and apologize to him. Lincoln sadly appealed to him: "Friend Tiger, can't you endure this one wrong done you by a madwoman without much complaint for old friendship's sake while I have had to bear it without complaint and without a murmur for, lo, these last fifteen years?"[40]

It matters little whether Lincoln was in the Edwards store, or when the episode occurred (Lincoln had not known Mary for fifteen years by 1850), or whether he said exactly what he is quoted as having said. It does matter whether something like this incident occurred at some time during the Lincolns' Springfield years. And that seems likely. Furthermore, the point of the anecdote— Mary's erupting, irrational anger—finds adequate documentation in a variety of sources. Neighbor Gourley noted that Lincoln and Mary got along fine "unless Mrs. Lincoln got the devil in her"; Lincoln would then pick up one of his children and walk off, paying no heed to her "wild furious condition." Mrs. George C. Real reported that she and her mother once went to call on the Lincolns. As they approached the house the back door flew open and Lincoln came rushing out. Mary was fast on his heels throwing potatoes at him. Another of Herndon's informants told of Mary chasing Lincoln with a butcher knife. Lincoln, apparently realizing that people were watching, stopped short and wheeled around, caught Mary by the back of her neck and seat of her pants, and carried her inside the door, saying, "There, now, stay in the house and don't be a damned fool before the people." Herndon also recalled from his personal experience Lincoln's frequent gloom at the office when chased from home. And so it goes. After 1860, visitors, friends, neighbors, relatives, journalists, the devoted and the spiteful, all commented on Mary's ferocious and unpredictable temper. The little girl who stomped her feet —because she could not secure a disoriented world and capture the attention of her busy and remote father—gave way to a housewife who startled those around her with periodic outbursts of furious, irrational rage.[41]

★★★

The Lincolns generally stayed at home in the evenings. An Irish servant, Mrs. Mary Gaughan, recalled that they were "very domestic in their tastes although they were great entertainers and had numerous guests. They very seldom went out visiting, preferring the pleasures of their own home." Mary would work around the house or sew; Lincoln would read. Their home was a private sphere that both of them protected. A young friend of Robert's from Phillips Exeter Academy, Frank Fuller, who visited the Lincolns in July 1860, noted how warmly Mary had received him and how interestingly she had talked of poetry with him. Lincoln impressed him even more favorably. To some, the Lincoln privacy seemed unnaturally exclusive. Ward Hill Lamon thought the home "forbade the entering guest," and Herndon believed that Lincoln dared not invite his friends home. This view implies that Lincoln needed to protect himself against Mary, but, in fact, the Lincolns' private style reflected her character and needs, not his.[42]

Mary's life centered on giving birth, on making the household "work," and on adjusting to Lincoln's irregular presence. Robert was born in 1843, Eddie in 1846, Willie in 1850, and Tad in 1853. Eddie died at the age of four, but as late as 1856 Mary still had three lively boys, aged thirteen, six, and three. They absorbed her attention. As she commented later, if she erred in her child-rearing, it was because she was too indulgent. She took pride in the boys' appearance and fussed over their clothing. In 1853 she asked a friend, Elizabeth Dale Beck, who was traveling to St. Louis, to buy a white fur hat for the baby Tad. "I should like white trimmings & white feather," she wrote, "if you find any to your taste, of the prettiest quality." Some years later Mary, giving a party for Willie on his ninth birthday, sent hand-lettered invitations to over fifty of his young friends.[43]

Mary was always deeply involved in the children. For "any big man or woman" who visited the Lincoln home, Herndon said, Mary would dress up the boys, trot them out, "and get them to monkey around, talk, dance, speak, quote poetry, etc., etc." The boys' performance would inspire her to excessive praise, which would annoy the visitor and embarrass Lincoln. "After Mrs. Lincoln had exhausted the English language and broken herself down in her rhapsodies on her children, Lincoln would smooth things over by saying: 'These children may be something sometime, if they are not merely rare-ripes, rotten types, hothouse plants. I have always noticed that a rare-ripe child quickly matures, but rots as quickly.'"[44]

This account suggests Mary's conflicted identification with the boys' natural exhibitionism. She seemed unable to set limits for herself or them. Lincoln would put her down, gently but firmly, and thus show her, his "child-wife," when to stop. Similarly, on June 2, 1848, he responded to her wish to come visit him in Washington (she was in Lexington): "Will you be a *good girl* in all things, if I consent? Then come along and that as *soon* as possible." Earlier that year he had told her to stop putting the "honorable" on her letters to him. "I like the letters very much, but I would rather they should not have that upon them. It is not necessary, as I suppose you have thought, to have them come free."[45]

Mary, who needed Lincoln's fatherly help and support, found that problems with the children proved to be an effective basis for manipulating him into a more central place in the household. Some problems, of course, were real. Children can hurt themselves, run away and get lost, eat poison left for rats, fall into rivers. Mary, however, seemed full of fears even when all was well. When she sensed a hint of danger she panicked, and when disaster actually

Robert Todd Lincoln as an adolescent,
looking cross-eyed and a bit glum.
Courtesy of Louis A. Warren
Lincoln Library & Museum, Fort Wayne, Indiana.

struck she collapsed. In the middle of a letter to Speed in 1846 Lincoln noted that a messenger had come to his office to tell him that Bob, then three, was lost. Lincoln rushed home, only to discover that the boy had already been found and whipped. By the time he returned to his letter, Lincoln jokingly guessed that Robert had run away again. But Lincoln was not always there to help Mary; indeed, he was seldom there when she most needed him. A neighbor, Elizabeth A. Capps, recalled how hysterical Mary became if a child was lost and how, when Robert ate some lime, she started screaming in helpless terror, "Bobbie will die, Bobbie will die" (Capps's father came to the rescue and washed the boy's

Willie Lincoln in Washington, D.C., 1861, age ten years. His death the next year cast a long shadow over the lives of both his parents. Photograph by Matthew Brady. Courtesy of Louis A. Warren Lincoln Library & Museum, Fort Wayne, Indiana.

mouth out). The child in her spilled over anxiously to the children she tended.[46]

Mary's psychological vulnerabilities made her unusually suscep-tible to the devastating effect of death. Everyone, of course, must face the loss of loved ones, but few experience the relentless pro-cession of deaths that Mary did. On July 16, 1849, her father died; in January 1850, her grandmother; and on February 1, 1850, her little Eddie, who had never even had his picture taken. At the loss of her son, Mary went into deep mourning, cried bitterly, even stopped eating. Lincoln once bent over her and pleaded with her, "Eat, Mary, for we must live." "God gives us our loved ones," she wrote much later, "we make them our idols, they are removed from us, & we have patiently to await the time, when, He reunites us to them. And the *waiting* is so long!"[47]

The Lincolns responded to the wrenching loss of Eddie by deciding to have another child; within a month Mary was pregnant. The hope of renewed life, Lincoln's devoted support, and the new meaning of religion in her life gradually brought Mary out of her despair. By spring she was well enough to travel with Lin-coln and Robert to Lexington to visit her family. Mary had always had trouble with separations, and after 1850 she developed a morbid fear of loss, especially when Robert left for Exeter in 1859 (and then for Harvard in 1860). On August 28, 1859, she wrote her friend Hannah Shearer that she felt "quite lonely" now that Bob was gone. It seemed "as if light & mirth, had departed with him." She wrote long letters to him, and she traveled a good deal, but the inner emptiness remained. She confided to Hannah Shearer, on October 2, 1859: "Since I last wrote you, I have been wandering. Mr. L & myself visited Columbus & some beautiful portions of Ohio, & made a charming visit to Cincinnati. I am again at home and Mr. L. is in Wisconsin. I miss Bob, so much that I do not feel settled down, as much as I used to & find myself going on trips quite frequently." The following summer Mary reported to Adeline Judd that her boy Robert had been gone a year and she felt "*wild* to see him."[48]

Mary's capacity for denial was profound. As a sad widow after 1875 (when she was briefly institutionalized on Robert's initiative), she came to feel quite differently about the separation from her son in 1859. By 1877 Robert seemed to her a "bad son" and a "wretched young man, but old in sin" with a "mean nature," a person who must yet render account to his Maker: "And God, does not allow, sin, to go unpunished." Mary continued: "In our household, he was always trying to obtain the mastery, on all occasions—never daring of course to be insolent, to my amiable devoted children or myself, when my beloved husband, was near, it was a great relief to us all, when he was sent to school, *then* we had a most loving peace." One thing Mary was certain of: "*Distance or time does not weaken remembrance.*"[49] This letter was written to Edward Louis Baker, who was the grandson of her sister, Elizabeth Edwards. All of her intense hatred for Robert she poured out in this letter to Baker, a letter that served to eliminate Robert and put Baker in his place. Her unconscious substitution of her devoted young friend Baker for Robert helped her to mourn the "loss" of her hated son.

In her marriage Mary devised a variety of strategies for handling her extreme sensitivities. She manipulated Lincoln, bringing him home to handle minor crises with the children; she fleetingly identified with her boys in an effort to find escape; and she tried to center attention on herself and her problems with periodic rages. She also sought—in clothes, money, furniture, and other objects—substitutes for the confused and uncontrollable world of people. She always accumulated her possessions aggressively, taking particular pride in her clothes. When she was a child, her homemade hoop became a symbol of her call for recognition and love from her father and for distance from her stepmother. Later, she pushed hard to escape from the Globe Tavern and then furnished and enlarged her own house, despite some tension with Lincoln over the costs. She saw that both she and her children always kept up with the fashions. Henry Villard noted her "splendid toilette" at the February 1861 farewell party for Springfield friends. But clothes and things proved inadequate substitutes, and she manipulated them with the same ambivalence as she did people. As early as 1848 Lincoln wrote her from Washington: "Last Wednesday, P. H. Hood & Co., dunned me for a little bill of $5.38 cents, and Walter Harper & Co., another for $8.50 cents, for goods which they say you bought. I hesitated to pay them because my recollection is that you told me when you went away, there was nothing left unpaid. Mention in your letter whether they are right." Herndon, in thinking Mary became materialistic and avaricious after her marriage, accurately but ungenerously captured her desperate need to acquire.[50]

The losses Mary experienced from 1848 to 1850 marked the end of one phase of her life: her relatively gay, open, vivacious youth that had merged into her early years of marriage. After 1850 she was very definitely a mature woman, a matron really, with the lines beginning to harden around her mouth, her body growing plump and soft, and her hands hardening with toil. After the birth of Tad in 1853 she developed serious gynecological problems. "My disease is of a womanly nature, which you will understand has been greatly accelerated by the last three years of mental suffering." So she wrote her friend Rhoda White on May 2, 1868. "Since the birth of my youngest son, for about twelve years I have been more or less a sufferer."[51] Mary's disease may have played a major role in shaping her life after 1853. It probably ended sexual intercourse between the Lincolns, who had previously spaced the birth of their children quite regularly, but who had no more children after that year.[52] And if abstinence proved necessary because of Mary's condition, it was further reinforced by the separate bedrooms that were built into the remodeled and enlarged house in 1856.[53] Mary was only thirty-five in 1853, probably still far from menopause and the end of her childbearing years. There were then no effective contraceptives, and abortion would have been out of the question for the Lincolns. Four children were perhaps enough anyway. But the apparent end of a sexual relationship seemingly contributed to the charting of a new course in the marriage. Mary turned increasingly outward and away from her complete absorption in home, husband, and children, though without direction or unifying purpose. After 1853 her domestic style clearly began to alter. Social obligations, frequent parties, politics, and her husband's career assumed more and more attention. Mary never abandoned her original commitment to her home and her children, and so she hovered uncertainly between her self-conception as a passively devoted wife and her emerging identity as a semi-public figure.

On November 23, 1856, and again on February 16, 1857, Mary wrote a long letter to her sister, Emilie Todd Helm, and these letters reflect her recently consolidated position between the private and semipublic spheres. The letters deal with politics, parties, family, friends, church, and marriages, and they are among the best examples of Mary's discursive style. Lydia Matteson is about to marry; the Bakers are still with the Edwardses. Louisa Lies has recently married. Robert Scott is courting Julia Ridgely, whose brother Charley is to marry Jennie Barrett this winter. O. B. Ficklin came to tea; he is as "rough & uncultivated as ever altho some years since married an accomplished Georgia belle," who apparently should have changed things. Dr. Smith, their minister, plans to resign because he cannot live on the limited salary he is given. The winter has been quiet, partly because of the scarlet fever among children. Still, there has been a round of parties: "Within the last 3 weeks, there has been a party, almost every night & some two or three grand fetes, are coming off this week." Mary herself is still recovering from a party she has just given for three hundred people. Three days ago Governor Bissell gave a large party. Miss Dunlop is spending the winter in town and looking very pretty, but "the beaux do not appear so numerous as the winter you passed here." Dr. and Mrs. Brown are on hand; he has charge of the First Presbyterian Church now.[54]

And so it went. Mary reported to her friend Hannah Shearer that there had been "a continued round of *strawberry* parties" and that during the past week she had spent five evenings out. She also reported giving a "strawberry company for 70 people." Isaac Arnold described her as "busy, animated, and gay" at these gatherings. According to this former Springfield friend, she was the chief attraction of fancy parties with her genial manners and "wit and humor, anecdote and unrivalled conversation." The journalist Henry Villard filed a story on the party the Lincolns gave as a farewell to their Springfield friends just before their departure for Washington. He noted that hundreds attended. "Mrs. Lincoln's splendid toilette gave satisfactory evidence of extensive purchases during her late visit to New York."[55]

Mary's lifelong fascination with politics found ready expression after 1854, as Lincoln's renewed interest in public issues converged with her tentatively expanding concerns. The young woman who had acted so "unladylike" in 1840 on behalf of Harrison continued to follow political events after 1842, and in the mid-1850s her interest became a passion. She strongly supported Lincoln's ambition, even though his speeches, the meetings, and the relentless campaigning took him away from home. She liked to attend the functions where he spoke, and she thrilled to his oratory. Mary was more than the little woman at home; she supported

Lincoln's drive upward and provided a stable center of gravity for his reach out into the chaos of politics in the 1850s. She seemed totally identified with his successes and failures. Gustave Koerner recalled seeing him in a hotel lobby in Alton before his debate there with Douglas in 1858. Lincoln, an old friend and political ally of Koerner, asked him to come upstairs and see Mary, then told him: "Now, tell Mary what you think of our chances! She is rather dispirited." Two years later Mary wrote her friend Hannah Shearer: "I scarcely know, how I would bear up, under defeat. I trust that we will not have the trial." Lincoln recognized the extent of Mary's investment in his career and could respond sensitively to her fears. On election night in 1860 he waited quietly in the telegraph office as the returns came in. When he had won New York—and the election—he turned to Lyman Trumbull and said: "I guess I'll go down and tell Mary about it."[56]

★★★

Mary's involvement in Lincoln's career and her strong support for his ambition has led to the mistaken idea that she played a major role in shaping his political ideas.[57] Her influence never extended that far. On November 23, 1856, she tried to explain his position on slavery to her sister, Emilie Todd Helm. She said he had supported Fremont for the Presidency, but was not an abolitionist. "All he desires is, that slavery, shall not be extended, let it remain where it is." She herself had preferred Millard Fillmore in the same election: "My weak woman's heart was too Southern in feeling, to sympathize with any but Fillmore." What really appealed to her about him was his nativism: "If some of you Kentuckians, had, to deal with the wild Irish, as we housekeepers are sometimes called upon to do, the southerners would certainly elect Mr. Fillmore next time." Lincoln had only disdain for the base prejudice that fueled the nativist movement. On

*Mary at the first inaugural ball. Note her hair
decked with flowers and pulled tightly into a bun.
Courtesy of Meserve-Kunhardt Collection.*

August 24, 1855, in a long letter to his old friend Joshua Speed, he attempted to explain where he stood in the muddled political world. "I am not a Know-Nothing. That is certain. How could I be? How can any one who abhors the oppression of negroes, be in favor of degrading classes of white people?" It is bad enough, he continued, to exclude Negroes from a position of equality guaranteed in the Declaration of Independence; the Know-Nothings would exclude Negroes and Catholics and foreigners alike. "When it comes to this I should prefer emigrating to some country where they make no pretence of loving liberty—to Russia, for instance, where despotism can be taken pure, and without the base alloy of hypocrasy."[58] Mary had come a long way politically from her slave-owning past to endorse Lincoln's opposition to the spread of slavery, but she remained stubbornly unsympathetic with his egalitarian beliefs.

★★★

Mary Lincoln was hardly a popular first lady. "The Hell-cat," Lincoln's secretary John Hay observed on April 9, 1862, "is getting more Hell-cattical day by day." Again he wrote: "The devil is abroad, having great wrath. His daughter, the Hell-cat, sent Stackpole in to blackguard me about the feed of her horses. She thinks there is cheating round the board and with that candor so charming in the young does not hesitate to say so." Hay had long since learned to manipulate Mary and he always seemed to dislike her. He even lacked empathy for her difficult period of grief following the death of her third son, Willie, in February 1862. In Randall's view, Hay failed to understand that "mental illness was involved," though in fact he seemed quite convinced she was crazy. The press relentlessly criticized her. Newspapers then were generally intensely partisan, and partisan feeling ran high during the war. Noah Brooks, who was to replace John Hay, only obliquely praised Mary in a dispatch for his California paper: "It is not a gracious task to refute these things [the criticisms of Mary], but the tales that are told of Mrs. Lincoln's vanity, pride, vulgarity and meanness ought to put any decent man or woman to the blush. . . . Mrs. Lincoln, I am glad to be able to say from personal knowledge, is a true American woman."[59]

All the complexities of Mary's character contributed to her public image in the White House. Her new position underlined her real or apparent faults but obscured her virtues. Her contemporaries never knew how often she visited hospitals and prisons in Washington, for she did not gather reporters around her during the visits. She never seemed to lose completely her empathic touch, but her compassion was evident only in quiet and private ways. After her friend Hannah Shearer lost a son late in 1864, Mary wrote her: "Since we were so heavily visited by affliction, almost three years since the loss of our darling idolized Willie, with the sensitiveness of a heavy sorrow, I have shrank, from all communication, with those, who would most forcibly recall my sorrow to my mind. Now, in this, the hours of *your* deep grief, with all my *own wounds* bleeding afresh, I find myself, writing to you, to express, my deepest sympathy, *well knowing* how unavailing, words, are, when we are broken hearted."[60]

Mrs. President Lincoln was not a simple midwestern housewife thrust suddenly onto center stage where she found the attention—and criticism—impossible to handle. For much of her life she had dreamed of and even prepared for the position she occupied as first lady. In some ways she proved ready for the demands of her position. She turned out to be a competent and gracious hostess, with her "levee" on Friday evening, reception on Saturday afternoon, and balls and dinners on special occasions. The French nobleman de Chambrun seemed quite impressed with the social style of her White House.

At first many of the leading ladies in Washington snubbed her as a parvenue. She responded bitterly and used her position when she could to undermine her tormenters. She faced an inherently difficult situation: Her position required that she regularly entertain political friends and opponents, travelers from near and far, and diplomats; yet the war occupied the entire period of her stewardship over the White House. Many critics were bound to see any entertaining as frivolous at best and, at worst, a criminal waste of public money when soldiers without blankets were dying in defense of the country.[61]

Mary's southern background also generated harsh criticism. After all, she had come from a slave-owning family that remained decidedly southern in its loyalties after 1861. Seven of her immediate male relatives fought for the Confederacy: one brother, three half-brothers, and three brothers-in-law. However, she seemed to feel no attachment to these members of the Todd clan. She told Reverend N. W. Miner, a Springfield neighbor who visited the White House during the horrendous battle of Shiloh in April 1862, that she had two brothers then fighting for the South in that very battle. "I hope they are either dead or taken prisoner," she commented vigorously. Miner was taken aback, but Mary explained: "They would kill my husband if they could, and destroy our Government—the dearest of all things to us; and I repeat it —I hope they are either dead or taken prisoner." Mary expressed the same sentiment to her seamstress, Elizabeth Keckley, on the death of her brother, Captain Alexander Todd. "He made his choice long ago. He decided against my husband, and through him against me. He has been fighting against us; and since he chose to be our deadly enemy, I see no special reason why I should bitterly mourn his death." In her public role, however, Mary never seemed able to convince everyone that she was loyal. In the minds of many, she bore the stigma of a traitor.[62]

Refusing to leave politics entirely to Lincoln, Mary meddled in small matters of influence and large matters of policy. Even before the inauguration she had let the excitement of her new position go to her head. In a confidential letter of January 17, 1861, she urged David Davis to use his influence with Lincoln to keep the offensive Norman Judd out of the cabinet. She knew that a word from Davis would "have much effect." The absurdity of seeking to have Davis influence her own husband is striking. When she traveled east to buy clothes, she dispensed gratuitous political advice all along the way. Writing to Lincoln from New York, November 2, 1862, she hinted that "all the distinguished in the land" were concerned that he replace McClellan, and she asked that an army promotion be given to Alexander T. Stewart, who owned a prestigious New York store to which she was apparently in debt. By then, she had accumulated a host of shady figures and sycophants who attended dutifully to her vanity and their own greed. Among them were Henry Wikoff, a great talker, flatterer, cheat, and liar; his flamboyant and disreputable friend, Dan Sickles; and Oliver S. Halsted, a munitions lobbyist in search of big deals. All three received the devoted attention of a needy Mrs. Lincoln, who prided herself on her intuition that told her what people were really like.[63]

Elizabeth Keckley, a mulatto seamstress and a former slave who had worked for the wife of Jefferson Davis, began service with Mary soon after she moved into the White House. In time Elizabeth became a confidante to whom Mary entrusted secrets that apparently she told no one else. This relationship has contributed to the questionable notion that Mary played an important role in shaping Lincoln's attitudes toward blacks and his policies on emancipation. Mary herself encouraged this idea, as when she wrote Elizabeth on October 9, 1867, that she had never failed to urge her husband to be an extreme Republican. Actually, she had exerted little influence on Lincoln in regard to this or any other political subject. As early as January 1861, she had felt forced to turn to David Davis to influence Lincoln; she had lost a voice in the new government before it even began. In late November 1864, she dashed off notes in which she asked Oliver S. Halsted and Charles Sumner to prevent the appointment of Nathaniel Banks to the cabinet. It never seemed to occur to her simply to talk with her husband about the matter.[64]

The presidency and the war created a vast chasm between the Lincolns. Mary tried reaching out but without much success. On November 3, 1862, she wrote from New York: "I have waited in vain to hear from you, yet as you are not *given* to letter writing, will be charitable enough to impute your silence, to the right cause." She begged: "One line, to say, that we are occasionally remembered will be gratefully received by your very truly, M. L." A year later Mary, again in New York, wired Lincoln: "Reached here last evening. Very tired and severe headache. Hope to hear you are doing well. Expect a telegraph to-day." He responded: "All going well. A. Lincoln." Mary's inability to bridge the gulf between herself and Lincoln intensified her well-established physical and emotional problems. Anson G. Henry, who visited the White House in February 1864, found that she was in bed, "not being very well."[65]

The mounting tension climaxed in March 1865. Lincoln had ridden out to City Point to review some troops, and Mary followed in a carriage with Colonel Horace Porter. She either began the day with a migraine headache or acquired one in the carriage when it hit a bump and she severely knocked her head. She arrived somewhat late, and the review had already begun. Lincoln ended the review with a beautiful young woman, Mrs. Ord, riding beside him in front of the troops. Mary went berserk with jealousy. The officers in her carriage had to restrain her physically from jumping out. When Mrs. Grant tried to calm her, Mary angrily accused her of complicity in the affair. And when Lincoln and Mrs. Ord came up, Mary lashed out at Mrs. Ord and reduced her to tears. Then she turned on Lincoln in furious anger as the generals, their aides, their wives, and the Army of the Potomac watched. Lincoln put his arm around her and turned her aside, calling her "Mother" and speaking softly. Gradually he quieted her.[66]

Had it not been for the demands of war, Lincoln might have been more reassuring to Mary all along. In his heart he seemed to remain devoted to her. At one White House reception he turned to a woman at his side and called her attention to the beautifully dressed Mary. "My wife is as handsome as when she was a girl, and I, a poor nobody then, fell in love with her; and what is more, I have never fallen out." When he was killed in Ford's Theater, he was holding her hand. But most of the time his preoccupations were too great for him to be close to Mary and involved in her world in anything except a peripheral way. Besides, he tired of her impetuosity and her unforgiving hatreds. On April 9, 1865, returning from Richmond on a boat, Mary spied Washington from a distance and commented with a shudder that the city was full of enemies. Lincoln responded with an impatient gesture. "Enemies," he said, "never again must we repeat that word."[67]

The wartime Lincolns were apart physically and emotionally. Mary, lacking the resiliency of her youth, had a heavy public task to perform as manager of the White House. Lincoln, of course, was under almost inhuman pressure from the time of his election until his death. There were few fleeting moments when Mary could share an intimate word with her husband. Guests or relatives usually accompanied the two on carriage rides.[68] Lincoln ate little if any breakfast, began work early, and stayed late. He and Mary tried to keep together as a family for the midday and the evening meals, but the demands of the war and the office frequently interfered. As they long since had decided to sleep apart, no loving embrace ended the difficult day.

In the early part of the presidency, Mary tried to define for herself a politically important position in a kind of kitchen cabinet —without success. She also energetically played her role as hostess, but ran into relentless criticism. By the end of the first year in Washington, things had soured for her. She was ridiculed in the press and in Washington society both as a hostess and as a person. Many doubted her loyalty to the Union. Lincoln was caught up in the war, which was going badly. Her only source of comfort was her children, who were always there, dependent and needy, and from whom she could get a measure of strength and renewal. Willie's death on February 20, 1862, removed what was perhaps the last prop to Mary's tenuous hold on reality. She adhered to the ritualized Victorian forms of mourning but in her devastating grief carried everything to excess. She went to bed for months and cried uncontrollably. She discontinued entertaining for the rest of the year, and, as she had done after Eddie's death, she even stopped eating for a time. She wrote Julia Ann Sprigg on May 29, 1862, "We have met with so overwhelming an affliction in death of our beloved Willie a being too precious for earth, that I am so completely unnerved, that I can scarcely command myself to write." Mary begged Julia to visit her and ease her "crushing bereavement."[69]

Mary's anger at her loss expressed itself even against God. "How often I feel rebellious," she wrote on July 26, 1862, "and almost believe that our Heavenly Father, has forsaken us, in removing, so lovely a child from us!" Later she repressed this anger toward God and turned it on herself. In 1864 she wrote her old friend Hannah Shearer that with Willie's death she had passed through a "fiery furnace of affliction" (a metaphor she borrowed from Lincoln). She went on to say that Willie's death had been a kind of divine punishment for getting too wrapped up in "our own political advancement."[70] Mary's partly conscious reasoning apparently was that God willed her to care for her children but that she had abandoned them in the search for political advancement, so He took Willie away.

A fascinating series of letters from Elizabeth Edwards, who came from Springfield to stay with her sister through the worst period of mourning, to her daughter, Julia, provide a unique opportunity to follow the course of Mary's reaction to Willie's death —and the strains it put on those close to her. At first Elizabeth felt only sympathy for Mary. She wrote Julia on March 1, just a week after Willie's death: "Your Aunt Mary still confines herself to her room, feeling very sad and at times, gives way to violent grief. She is so constituted, and the surrounding circumstances will prevent, a long indulgence of such gloom." The next day Elizabeth told Julia how glad she was to be with Mary and comfort her, for Mary had been "utterly unable to control her feelings. Mary has confined herself to her room, and bed, until this morning, when I persuaded her to put on the *black dress*." Later that month, on March 12, Elizabeth reiterated her sympathy for Mary and expressed a touch of self-satisfaction at her efforts. "I feel very much for her, and am satisfied that my presence is more soothing than anything else at present."[71]

Already beginning to tire of Mary's relentless suffering, Elizabeth noted how depressing it was to be absorbed in Mary's sorrow. She also expressed the hope that her niece, Mary Wallace, would substitute for her in a month or two. By April she had come to feel that Mary was indulging her grief. Elizabeth's request to be replaced became insistent. "Your Aunt Mary wonders if Mary Wallace will not feel like coming on, when I am ready to leave —Mention it to her—and I would advise it by all means." Elizabeth was quite aware of Mary's antagonism toward most members of the Springfield Todd clan and seemed to fear those old hatreds would keep Mary Wallace from replacing her. Elizabeth therefore went to some length to convey to Julia that Mary's desperate state would override such feelings. "Without a doubt," Elizabeth wrote Julia on April 9, "she [Mary Wallace] will be treated with the greatest kindness, for a companion is absolutely necessary for her Aunt, who is at times very gloomy."

Elizabeth began to feel trapped in Mary's clawing needs. On April 19 she wrote Julia that "The daily routine here is especially irksome to me." By April 26 Elizabeth was past sympathy for Mary and concerned only with her own escape. She told Julia that Mary was so "nervous and dependent upon the companionship of some one" that she would definitely be friendly to any visitor, even one from the family. And she noted, "The truth is I am not very happy." Elizabeth left soon on the pretext of an urgent summons from home. Mary Wallace never came.[72]

Mary's seamstress, Elizabeth Keckley, later described another aspect of Mary's unhinged state after Willie's death. For months Mary was unable to mention Willie's name or look at his picture. She never again entered the guest room where he had died or the Green Room where he was embalmed. "There was something supernatural in her dread of these things," Mrs. Keckley reported, "and something that she could not explain." Mrs. Keckley also reported the scene when Lincoln threatened to institutionalize Mary if she failed to recover. He led her to a window and said, "Mother, do you see that large white building on the hill yonder. Try and control your grief or it will drive you mad and we may have to send you there." Jean Baker, Mary's most recent (and highly protective) biographer, raises doubts about the story, and therefore about the Keckley testimony in general, on the grounds that one could not see the Hospital for the Insane from the White House. She is mistaken, however; it is only later buildings that obscure the view.[73]

In her despair Mary turned to spiritualism to recapture contact with Willie. A séance was held at the Soldier's Home in the summer of 1862, and there is some indication that the séances continued long after that. Lincoln, suspecting fraud, successfully had at least one of Mary's spiritualists exposed. Mary eventually repudiated the more extreme claims of the spiritualists—for example, that during a séance one actually converses with the dead —and retreated to a more religiously legitimated, though still rather mystical, idea that she described in a letter of November 20, 1869: "I am not EITHER a spiritualist—but I sincerely believe

—our loved ones, who have only, 'gone before' are permitted to watch over those who are dearer to them than life."[74]

A large part of Mary's sanity died with Willie. Emilie Todd Helm, who visited late in 1863, noted in her diary how Mary visited her one night in a "deep pit of gloom and despair" and reported that Willie came to her every night and stood at the foot of her bed "with the same, sweet, adorable smile he has always had." Sometimes he came with Eddie and twice with her brother, Alec. Emilie was frightened by her sister's unnatural behavior, but she went on to make the psychologically astute observation that Mary's hold on the dead in part reflected her fears about Robert's going into the army. This was an important issue with the Lincolns. Robert was an able-bodied, adult male throughout the war. Lincoln felt it was unfair for him to send hundreds of thousands of young men to their deaths in the war while Robert remained safely ensconced at Harvard. But the desperation of Mary's opposition persuaded him to wait until Robert's graduation in 1864. Even then he delayed until the first part of the following year, when he sent Robert as a personal aide to Grant, and thus safely removed him from battle.[75]

There had always been a sense in which Mary's response to the unloving and uncontrollable world of people was to seek substitute gratification in money, clothes, furniture, and various possessions. Things at least stood still, could be admired and fondled, and never died. Yet her ambivalence toward people spilled over to their inanimate surrogates. As she lost her own center of gravity during the war, Mary turned with alarming vigor to her clothes and household furnishings for fulfillment. One of the first letters she wrote after Willie's death was to Ruth Harris to order some mourning clothes. The bonnet she requested was to be elegantly plain and genteel; she ordered the crepe to be the finest jet black English variety and the trimming to be small and delicate. In everything, Mary commanded, Harris was to use only the very best material. Any gift that arrived at the White House she felt was hers personally—grapes from Ohio and cider from New York, an elaborate tablecloth from Constantinople, yards of lace and China silk, fabrics embroidered in France, books, jewelry, anything at all. She also bought vast quantities of everything. At the start of her stewardship of the White House, Congress authorized $20,000 for her to fix up what all agreed had become a rather dilapidated old house. Mary briefly had a marvelous, if manic, spree purchasing only the best furnishings for the White House. There was quickly an uproar over her extravagant purchases. But, even worse, she had forgotten to keep track of her expenses and substantially overran her appropriation. When Lincoln found out, he was furious and determined to pay for Mary's purchases of "*flub dubs*," as he reportedly called them. In the end, however, Congress paid.[76]

Mary spent her own money with equal indiscretion. In 1866, when she was desperately trying to sell some of her White House possessions, Mary listed her *unused* jewelry, hoping for close to a full refund from the New York store where it was purchased. The items included earrings, a gold card case, a diamond ring, a pearl bracelet, an onyx breastpin and matching earrings, a pair of enameled sleeve buttons, and on and on. Mary also could be intermittently tight with money; when she interviewed Elizabeth Keckley in 1861, she stressed her poverty and hoped Keckley's terms would be reasonable. But Mary's caution hardly prevailed.

By the summer of 1864 her debts were enormous and she lived in constant anxiety that Lincoln would discover the truth, though it is difficult to believe Lincoln was not aware of the situation. It is more likely that out of empathy for her he simply avoided confronting her. She often wrote telegrams to creditors, telling them their payment was coming soon. Once she made a revealing slip: She wired George A. Hearn of New York, "Will you send your check today?" As the pressure mounted Mary feared most of all that Lincoln would not be reelected and her secret debts would be revealed. She poured out her heart to Mrs. Keckley and became obsessed with her fears of Lincoln's political fate. By September she saw her problems as partly the result of her husband's honesty. "Poor Mr. Lincoln," she wrote on September 23, 1864, "who is almost a monomaniac on the subject of honesty." When at last the victory came, Mary drew a deep sigh of relief. But her happiness proved short-lived.[77]

★★★

Mary's final chapter is a tale of unrelieved sadness. She had collapsed after the earlier deaths, but the loss of Lincoln on April 14, 1865, affected her traumatically. She went to bed, numb, lost, confused, utterly helpless. For five weeks she lay there, unable to supervise packing or make preparations for the future. She later repressed all memory of the first few days following the assassination. She was unable to attend the funeral service in Washington on April 20. De Chambrun stopped by that afternoon to leave his card and noted Mary was still "completely insane."

Except for her youngest son, Tad, her only extended human contact in this desolate period was with the kindly doctor, Anson G. Henry, who had long ago attended Lincoln in his worst depression, in January 1841. Henry wrote his wife in May 1865, that Mary refused to be comforted. Still he spent several hours a day with her, talking largely about religious matters and the hovering spirits of the dead, and these discussions seemed to relieve Mary somewhat. Henry also helped Mary in her struggles with the city of Springfield to bury Lincoln where she intended, in Oak Ridge Cemetery, just north of town. Several enterprising Springfield citizens, wishing to honor Lincoln (and perhaps with an eye on the commercial merit of the idea), proposed a downtown burial site with an appropriate monument. The body was halfway across the country, wending its slow way home, when Mary discovered what was afoot. She asked Henry to write the letter. "I have been requested by Mrs. Lincoln to say," wrote Henry on May 1, "that if her wishes and directions in regard to her husband's remains are not complied with she will remove them to Chicago next June."[78]

Mary had always been ambivalent about Springfield, and the fight over Lincoln's remains hardly endeared her to its citizens or made a return there desirable for her. She also could not face living so close to the grave. After a brief visit to Oak Ridge Cemetery in December 1865, Mary wrote a friend that "The further removed I am, the better, it will be, for *my reason,* from *that* spot." Mary felt this keenly, for her constrained financial situation made it increasingly difficult to survive anywhere except Springfield, where, of course, she owned a home. Lincoln left an estate of liquid assets valued at $83,000. The administrator of the estate until it was settled in 1868 was David Davis. He performed well, for during these three years he regularly paid interest of about $1,500 to Mary and each of the boys and increased the capital to $110,000, which was divided three ways in 1868. In December 1865, Congress voted Mary a one-time sum of $25,000. Mary always felt unfairly treated because Congress at first refused and then only reluctantly voted her a pension in 1869. But she always had assets and an adequate income, except for her debts from her personal spending sprees in the White House. These debts drove her to abstraction.[79]

Mary chose to live in Chicago. There she stayed in some dreary rooms in a Hyde Park hotel, secluded, alone, bitter, broken with grief, racked by migraines, pouring out her heart in letters to almost every correspondent. On May 9, 1865: "I go hence, broken hearted, with every hope almost in life—crushed." On May 14: "In my crushing sorrow, I have found myself almost doubting the goodness of the Almighty." May 29: "To rejoin my Husband, who loved me so devotedly & whom I idolized, would be bliss indeed. I am scarcely able to sit up & fear it will be some time, ere I can summon strength of mind or body either, to receive friends." July 11: "I have almost become blind with weeping." And another letter on the same day: "I am realizing, day by day, hour by hour, how insupportable life is, without the presence of the *One,* who loved me & my sons so dearly & in return, was idolized. Tell me, how *can,* I live, without my Husband, any longer?" July 17: "If it was not for dear little Taddie, I would pray to die, I am so miserable." July 26: "The world looks darker to me than ever & my heart aches, for my bereaved Sons." August 17: "My heart is indeed broken, and without my beloved husband, I do not wish to live. Life, is indeed a heavy burden, & I do not care how soon, I am called hence." November 29: "I have been so wild in my despair over the loss, of my idolized husband." December 8: "Only those, who suffered & lost . . . can fully understand the return of anniversaries." December 11: "My overwhelming sorrow, removes me, from the world." And finally, December 24: "I pour my sad tale, into your sympathizing ear."[80]

Over the years Mary returned often to the theme of her grief. This sampling of her 1865 letters suggests the extent of her pervasive sense of gloom. She never really resolved these feelings of loss, anger, and helplessness, which in turn accentuated the more unlovely characteristics of her personality. She was intensely envious when Ulysses S. Grant received several houses and a large pension after the war, while the family of the martyred President had to struggle. "Alas, alas my burden of sorrow is too heavy for me to bear," she moaned in self-pity to Elizabeth Blair Lee on August 25, 1865. A few months later her tone was almost a parody of self-pity. "Yet I cannot express to you, how painful to me, it is, to have *no* quiet home, where I can freely indulge my sorrows —*this is* yet another of the crosses, appointed unto me." Her brooding envy of Grant consumed much of her energy. "Life is certainly, *couleur de rose* to *him*—," she wrote Sally Orne on December 30, 1865, "if it is, all *darkness & gloom* to the unhappy family, of the fallen chief."[81]

Mary's self-absorption had always made her relatively insensitive to the feelings of others; after 1865 her despair blinded her to the ways she manipulated people. In August 1865, for example, Mary wrote Sally Orne a long, self-pitying letter that began with an attempt to evoke pity in Mrs. Orne: "Bowed down & heart broken, in my terrible bereavement." Mary dwelt on her afflictions at the loss of her devoted and loving husband and declared she would welcome death, which would give her a chance to rejoin Lincoln. Mary's real purpose, however, was to get Sally Orne to sell the dress Mary had worn at the second inaugural ball. Mary bleakly painted her financial picture: She said her pension was $1,500 per year, which was a little misleading. She and Tad together received $3,000, which would have been adequate except for her wartime debts. She then described the dress and asked Mrs. Orne to sell it in New York. Apparently, the idea of selling something excited Mary, for she went on to mention to Mrs. Orne some magnificent material she would like to sell. Nothing came of these feelers to Sally Orne, so Mary turned hopefully to Elizabeth Keckley; that in turn led to a scandal in 1867.

Mary's idea had been to sell all her old dresses in New York, and Mrs. Keckley agreed to help. The two met furtively and tried to peddle the clothes through a pair of disreputable brokers. With Mary's support, the brokers first tried bribing politicians to promote purchase of the clothes with public funds, then they gathered the support of well-known figures for an auction, and, finally, took all the dresses on tour. From the beginning Mary manipulated Mrs. Keckley in a variety of conscious and unconscious ways. Mrs. Keckley genuinely wanted to help and endured a great deal herself as events unfolded. But it seems Mrs. Keckley also resented the way she had been handled through it all, and in 1868 she published her book (an "as told to" volume), *Behind The Scenes,* which revealed all the unhappy details of the clothes scandal as well as the impulsive purchases Mary had made while in the White House that had originally created her indebtedness. The book even included twenty-four of Mary's most personal letters.[82]

Mary's real and imagined financial problems, her grief, and her loneliness were all endlessly complicated by her physical problems. Whatever was wrong gynecologically seemed to worsen after the assassination, and her headaches were a continuous torment. The five weeks following the assassination and the train trip to Chicago were one great headache. After that her life revolved around her headaches. In December 1865, Mary told Mary Jane Welles that she was incapacitated for three days of every week with severe headaches. The following May, Mary again mentioned that for three days a week her headaches were so severe she could barely sit up. Sometimes she overcame her worst agonies to write letters to friends, but only when urgent financial pressures forced her out of bed. At her insanity hearing in Chicago in 1875, a doctor testified she had told him that during one of her headaches "an Indian was removing the bones of her face and pulling wires out of her eyes." This was used as evidence that she was hallucinating, though it may simply have been a graphic attempt to describe her pain.[83]

Mary was sad and suffered greatly, but she kept her spunk. She may have humiliated herself in badly planned attempts to raise money, but she never repudiated her debts. She lived alone and went hungry rather than move in with relatives (at least until after her institutionalization in 1875). She never accepted defeat.

She dragged herself from bed to write spiteful, angry letters and then returned to lie awake hating. And she never lost her interest in politics. She regularly absorbed the contents of seven papers: *The Chicago Tribune, Times,* and *Evening Journal; The Illinois State Journal,* for news of friends and enemies in Springfield; *The New York Times* and the *Tribune;* and *The Washington World.* She hated the way journalists dealt with her and the world, calling them vampires, but she could not stop reading.[84]

★★★

The fight in Mary, however, should not obscure the desperation of her state. Physically and emotionally, she was a wreck. She was helpless, in debt, and constantly making bad decisions about her life. Her personality was increasingly brittle. Her warmth, intense loyalty, and empathy could no longer stem the tide of envy, greed, suspiciousness, and sensitivity to slight that spurred feelings of revenge, stubbornness, and self-absorption. Not surprisingly, in psychological terms, what emerged finally as the trait that was to bring about her institutionalization was her paranoia. She wrote Dr. Henry on July 17, 1865, of her overwhelming sorrow at all the enemies she had to contend with. She came to feel betrayed by her political friends—David Davis, James Harlan, Edward Stanton, and Joshua Speed's brother, James—on the pension issue. "All, they desire is to be inquisitive and they are *not* friends & will *never* assist us—Therefore, let this, be an end, to *them.*" In time these fears and pervasive feelings of danger gave way to actual paranoia. The turning point seemed to be the death of Tad in 1871. Smoke from a neighboring chimney suggested to her that the city was about to burn. When she entered a public dining room, she whispered, "I am afraid; I am afraid." In March 1875, she and her son, Robert, stayed in a Chicago hotel in separate rooms. She was terribly restless and once left her room improperly dressed. Robert tried to calm her by putting his arm around her and leading her back. Mary turned away violently, screaming, "You are going to murder me."[85]

There was a real basis to some of her fears. Robert was having her followed by a Pinkerton detective in early 1875, and her insanity hearing that May was a carefully staged setup. The day before it was to begin Robert called together several physicians and an old friend of his father, Leonard Swett. Robert got the doctors to agree that he had a case for the committal of Mary. He then asked Swett to be the one to pick her up at the hotel at one P.M. and take her to the two P.M. trial. Mary knew nothing of these arrangements. She was astounded when Swett arrived the next day, but went along without physical resistance. She refused to take Swett's arm, however, and suggested to him that he should attend to his own crazy wife when he finished with her. At the trial Robert and Swett at first had some trouble with their prearranged defense counsel, Isaac Arnold. It seems he expressed some misgivings about carrying out his task because he was personally convinced of Mary's insanity. Swett persevered, however, and pointed out that Arnold had to defend Mary or she would get some "mischievous lawyer" who would "make us trouble."[86]

The trial brought forward depressing evidence of Mary's state as various witnesses testified to her paranoia. John Fitzhenry, a hotel waiter, said he was called to her room where he found her "carelessly dressed" and complaining of vague fears. Charles Dodge, another hotel employee, reported that she complained to him of a stranger in her room who was about to molest her. Other witnesses reported her hallucinations. A certain Maggie Gavin testified that Mary heard voices through the wall. Robert himself made that more specific: She had met a "wandering Jew" in Florida who had taken her pocketbook and now talked to her through the walls. There was also plenty of evidence presented of her superfluous buying and the risks of her walking around with $57,000 in securities sewn into her petticoats. It was an embarrassing trial for all concerned. People like Swett felt guilty, and Robert himself never really got over it.[87]

Mary sat through it all quietly, but on the evening of the trial's completion she tried to commit suicide. She slipped past the guards at her hotel room and went to buy some laudanum from a local druggist. However, he recognized her. After that, Mary spent three months in Bellevue Hospital, well cared for by Dr. R. L. Patterson. In the fall Mary's sister, Elizabeth Edwards, took her home to Springfield.

Mary's behavior continued to worry Robert. He wrote Elizabeth Edwards on January 17, 1876: "I am very much afraid that things are going on from bad to worse as they did last spring—and that if they get worse it will be necessary to place my mother again under Dr. Patterson's care." Robert backed off, however, and Mary stayed in Springfield.[88]

Her life ended sadly. On June 15, 1876, a second trial judged her sane and restored her rights. After that she traveled frequently but kept the Edwardses as her base. She wrote voluminously, mulling over the past with friends and fretting over her finances with her Springfield banker, Jacob Bunn. In her last years she seemed numb with hurt. Her old friend and neighbor, N. W. Miner, who had since moved to New Jersey, saw her once in New York in 1881. Mary had traveled there for medical treatment. Miner was aghast when he met her: Her hair was prematurely gray, her eyes half-closed with excessive weeping, and she was staying alone in an old and dingy hotel.[89] She died in her sister's home in Springfield on July 15, 1882, at the age of sixty-three. She spent the last few months sleeping on one side of the bed. The other space she kept for Lincoln.

The first known photograph of Lincoln, 1846. He was thirty-seven years old, hopeful, reflective, and uncertain. Courtesy of Library of Congress.

In this troublesome world we are never quite satisfied.
                    Abraham to Mary Lincoln, April 16, 1848

5

A LITTLE WORLD MADE CUNNINGLY

By the 1840s Lincoln had "made it" in the cherished American sense. He was far beyond his rural roots and rapidly emerging among Illinois Whigs as a sought-after lawyer and political leader. He owned a nice home in Springfield, had married well, and children were entering his life in regular intervals of three to four years. The first photograph of Lincoln, taken in 1846, nicely captures the contentment of a successful man with a promising future. He would often joke of his "poor, lean, lank, face," but in this picture at least there is a hint of bourgeois self-satisfaction in the slight tilt of the head and jaunty thrust of the chin.[1] He seems to be a young man who expected to be taken seriously.

And yet there is a tension in the eyes that has an almost haunting quality. They are surprisingly round and deep, set off in the photograph by shadows that only enhance their mysteriousness. Nor can the mystery of Lincoln's eyes be dismissed as an artifact of early photographic technique, which required the subject to sit motionless for several minutes while the plate was exposed. "My old, withered, dry eyes," Lincoln said on hearing a moving speech by Alexander H. Stephens in 1848, "are full of tears yet." He was thirty-eight years old. A decade later, in a fragment on the struggle against slavery, Lincoln referred to his "own poor eyes" that might not last to see the final victory. The eyes, it seems, captured Lincoln's early sense of life's mournful tasks, which in turn aged him prematurely. Before his fortieth birthday Lincoln contrasted himself with the young men of Illinois politics. In his private life he was "Father" to Mary's "Mother." He joked at times of his need for spectacles and his poor eyesight, but there is something curiously sad and moving when a healthy, vigorous middle-aged man refers to himself as old.[2] His eyes suggest a kind of premature insight that carried its burdens and took its toll.

★★★

Two points are quite well documented in Lincoln's relationship with Mary. The first is that from the outset Lincoln developed a powerful attachment to his vivacious young wife. A week after their wedding of November 4, 1842, he ended a business letter with the cryptic note, "Nothing new here, except my marrying, which to me, is a matter of profound wonder." Later the following spring James C. Conkling met Lincoln in Bloomington and reported that he had "found Lincoln desperately homesick and turning his head frequently towards the south." After the stress of their tumultuous courtship, Lincoln seemed to embrace Mary fervently, to find deep needs for love and devotion satisfied in her. Separation came as a painful experience.[3]

It is equally clear that by the 1860s Lincoln believed Mary bordered on insanity and required a patient, humane tolerance. He watched her collapse after Willie's death in 1862. When her sister's help proved futile, he exerted a measure of control and told her she must restrain herself or he would have her committed. He carefully and discreetly exposed the fraudulent psychic medium to whom Mary turned in the spring and summer of 1862. "The caprices of Mrs. Lincoln, I am satisfied, are the result of partial insanity," he said once to a visiting reporter, and asked whether her malady was "beyond medical remedy to check before it becomes fully developed?"[4]

These two ends of the spectrum frame the essential issues in Lincoln's complicated relationship with Mary. From the beginning she met some important needs in Lincoln, but her own problems gradually diminished her central emotional position in his life. These problems were sufficiently severe to cause Lincoln to see her as nearly insane. The psychological movement along this emotional spectrum occurred erratically and is difficult to place in chronological sequence. Nevertheless, there is a marked change in all facets of Lincoln's life with Mary around 1854. The coincidence of this dating with larger political events is hardly accidental. It suggests that a multitude of private and public concerns prompted an emotional reordering of Lincoln's self-organization at this time.

Life at Eighth and Jackson subtly combined themes of intimacy and distance. In this tight house, which until 1856 consisted of only one floor, the Lincolns defined their family style. Four rooms and a kitchen separated the functions of daily life. On either side of the entrance two parlors—one formal, the other informal—clearly expressed the family's genteel aspirations. The bedroom for both the Lincolns and their children was at the back of the formal parlor, behind a partition that has since been removed. These close sleeping quarters joined intimate relations with child-rearing. It is striking how the arrangement of the house spatially allocated the back corner and smallest room to private family activities. The most conspicuous space is reserved for the parlors. In other words, the home de-emphasized intimacy in favor of more formal encounters—sitting around the fire, talking, playing with the children. Next to the bedroom was the dining room laid out with respectable dignity: a table with four chairs, a serving table, and a sideboard. Behind the dining room, and quite separate from the four central living rooms, was the kitchen. It was ample and well equipped but apart, no longer the central motif so characteristic of room arrangements in earlier periods.

The architecture of the house confirmed and reinforced the domestic aspirations of the Lincolns. It looked inward, away from the world, turning closely around a central axis. The world was deliberately excluded, a private enjoyment of family domesticity deliberately pursued. In this, of course, the Lincolns typified a style of family life that was increasingly important and prevalent after 1820, especially among white, urban, middle-class families. The Lincolns, however, perhaps even more vigorously than most, sealed off the family unit from outside contagion. Few friends "dropped by," and the neighbors kept an amicable but respectable distance: Few of the reminiscences of neighbors describe scenes occurring within the house. Herndon groused about the way Mary excluded him, David Davis, and other friends from the Lincoln home.[5] Lincoln was willing to tolerate Mary's idiosyncratic exclusion of people like Herndon from the home because it reflected his own protective conception of the hearth. In a sense, a tightly cohesive nineteenth-century family like the Lincolns survived only so long as it could effectively maintain the sharp line between itself and the community.

The Lincolns also kept apart from their troublesome relatives. Lincoln frequently visited his country kin near Charleston, but they never visited his home in Springfield. The one exception was a daughter of Dennis Hanks who showed up as a domestic in the Lincoln home in 1844. The relationship between her and Mary, however, was a disaster and the poor girl was driven away.

The relationship with the Todds was somewhat more complex. The Lincolns married without the Todd family's approval, but Mary's father was quickly won over. He even gave Mary money. It is speculation, but it is difficult to believe a man as proud as Lincoln relished such gifts that tied his wife to her father. But it is not speculation that the relationship between Lincoln and the other Todds was highly strained. Matters even reached the point of a lawsuit in 1853, when Mary's tempestuous brother, Levi, accused Lincoln of embezzling funds collected for Robert Todd on an earlier suit in Illinois. Lincoln was enraged. He wrote his lawyer in Louisville that he found it difficult to suppress his indignation at the charge. When the lawyer delayed in settling the case, Lincoln's frustration mounted and he let him know that the matter upset him a great deal. The case left a bad taste in Lincoln's mouth. Perhaps it helped him deal with the Todds' southern loyalties during the war.[6]

The Lincoln family's need for exclusivity also provides perspective on Mary's difficulty in keeping servants. Anyone from the outside was an intruder, and Mary wanted her maids to be "submissive." She wrote in 1859 to her friend, Hannah Shearer: "My seamstresses bear such different testimony to my honesty & justice, that it is a matter of unimportance & therefore, we will forever drop the subject." Lincoln, it seems, tried to handle the situation by paying some servants extra to endure his wife. But in a larger sense both Mary's refusal to deal with the issue and Lincoln's slipping money to servants to buy peace reflect a vital, unspoken agreement in the family to keep the world at bay, to solidify or attempt to solidify a cohesive domestic unit.[7]

The sources do not allow a complete reconstruction of the rhythm of daily life for the Lincolns. One can only gain glimpses of this little world cunningly turned in on itself. The formality of the dining room and the parlor suggests a rigorous scheduling of domestic behaviors. Dinner was probably normally served at the same time each night, and an evening pattern of talking, reading, and then sleeping kept to. There is a sense that Lincoln deviated somewhat from the script. To Mary's dismay he lounged on the floor at times, answered the door with his tie loose, and allowed himself to slip into distant worlds of thought and perhaps periodic depression.

As for the family's expenses, Lincoln, who from the mid-1840s on earned a very respectable $1,200 to $1,800 a year, bought his own rather expensive suits and ties and handled such matters as the purchase of a new carriage, but he left the responsibility for food, children, and household in Mary's hands.[8] He certainly paid the bills and probably gave Mary adequate pocket money to run the house. He also allowed her to use various charge accounts in town. In the 1840s these expenditures seemed within reasonable bounds. There is no reason to suspect tension over money, though Mary's delight in material possessions may have helped her endure Lincoln's active and lucrative work on the circuit.

Lincoln's absences from his home are a crucial and highly controversial issue in grasping the rhythm of his life with Mary. No discussion of Lincoln and Mary, their home and children, or indeed the deeper meanings of Lincoln's thought can ignore his pattern of distancing and separation in his mature years. The facts are fairly clear; their meaning ambiguous. Two interests, law and politics, pulled him away. The pull of politics was erratic and obviously regulated by outside factors. Lincoln was a loyal Whig throughout the years before 1854 and, during election years, regularly met requests to talk on the issues and in support of local candidates. In 1844 he worked vigorously and unsuccessfully to garner support for his candidacy to the United States House of Representatives. Then, in 1846, he defeated Peter Cartwright after a busy two months of campaigning. From the fall of 1847

Lincoln was in Washington and apart from his family except for the few months of the stay when Mary and the children were there (December 1847 to March 1848). The pace of Lincoln's political work slacked off some between 1849 and 1854 but remained an important ingredient in his life. After 1854, however, politics increasingly consumed Lincoln. His success as a lawyer—with income like the notable fee of $5,000 charged to the Illinois Central Railroad in 1857—supported long periods of politicking.

The more constant pull on Lincoln was the circuit. Unlike other lawyers, Lincoln was unique in his practice of attending every court on the circuit and remaining until the end. Herndon embellished here a good deal. He has Lincoln growing sad as the other lawyers start home for the weekend to see their wives and babies, having learned not to encourage Lincoln to come with them. Herndon's account appeared in a letter he wrote to his

William Herndon in the 1850s, when he was Lincoln's law partner. Courtesy of Illinois Historical Society.

A Little World Made Cunningly

coauthor, Jesse Weik, in 1887. The final presentation of this matter in the 1889 biography called in the authority of David Davis, who was quoted as saying how odd it was to everyone that Lincoln never went home on Sunday from the circuit. "At first we wondered at it," Davis said, "but soon learned to account for his strange disinclination to go home. Lincoln himself never had much to say about home, and we never felt free to comment on it. Most of us had pleasant, inviting homes, and as we struck out for them I'm sure each one of us down in our hearts had a mingled feeling of pity and sympathy for him." The editor of the 1930 edition of Herndon's book, Paul Angle, could not contain himself on this point and added a gratuitous footnote that Lincoln worked hard on the circuit and must have been too tired to travel home on Sunday. But Judge David Davis also worked prodigiously on the circuit. He seldom missed traveling home on his day off, no matter how tired he might have been, and even found time while listening to dull cases to write passionate letters to his young wife. It was undoubtedly a bother to travel to Springfield on horseback along muddy roads from, for example, Taylorville. But it was not an impossible trip; the other lawyers regularly traveled that twenty-five miles and other routes on weekends.[9]

To get a sense of the pattern of Lincoln's absences from home, one need only consult the remarkably complete three-volume study, *Lincoln Day by Day,* which traces Lincoln's activities on a daily basis for his entire life.[10] In the spring of 1843, for example, Lincoln took two one-day excursions before leaving on the court circuit on April 12. He remained away until May 4. On his return he managed to remain pretty much at home through the summer, except for one-day trips on May 22, June 5, and July 15. Then on September 6 he left for the fall circuit and stayed away until September 25, when he returned for a weekend, and left again to return October 9. He was then home until October 16, when he left for another week of circuit work. He took a final two-day trip that year in early November. In the course of the year Lincoln had been gone a total of some ten weeks, including three weeks in the spring and more than five weeks in September and early October. Few trips occurred between mid-October and early April, and throughout the summer Lincoln traveled only erratically. One interesting point is that Lincoln broke up the fall term with two visits. At least sometimes he came home.

The pattern for 1843 holds for most of the following 1840s, except when Lincoln was in Washington. Lincoln seldom went away from home until the spring term of the circuit began in April, and then he usually broke up his trip into units of two or at most three weeks. In 1844, for example, Lincoln was away from April 3 to April 16, May 6 to May 10, May 27 to June 6, July 15 to July 21, September 5 to September 16, September 21 to October 7, and October 21 to November 11. He also took several one-day trips. That year he was gone some fourteen weeks. In 1846 he took his first really extended trip, when he was gone eight weeks between June and July 25 campaigning for the House seat.

After Lincoln returned from Washington in March 1849, he tried to minimize his travel. He was gone only one week in June and was out on the fall circuit from September 20 to September 25 and October 1 to October 13. In 1850, however, legal work took a heavy toll. He was gone for two weeks between April 3 and April 18, four weeks between May 1 and June 1, four weeks for a summer trial in Chicago, which ran from June 30 to July 26, a couple of one-day excursions in August, then six weeks on the circuit from September 18 to October 31. The last trip of that year was from November 14 to November 21.

A subtle shift had occurred in the pattern of Lincoln's absences between 1843 and 1850—they had lengthened. In the early days of his marriage he seldom stayed away more than two weeks and determinedly broke up longer trips into two- and three-week units. In 1850, however, he took five long trips that lasted two, four, four, six, and one weeks, in that order. The six-week trip on the fall circuit (September 18 to October 31), apparently without a visit home, is the most striking. The same pattern holds true for the next few years. In 1852, for example, Lincoln was gone for six extended trips: three weeks in April, four in May, one in June, five in September and October, two in November, and, unusually, two more in the first part of December. In 1854 Lincoln seemed so caught up in circuit life that he stayed out during the spring term for six and one-half weeks from April 5 to June 30.

After the mid-1850s Lincoln again altered the rhythm of his travels, quite dramatically increasing both the frequency and duration of his trips. Several factors contributed to the change. He was more noted and therefore in greater demand as a lawyer, and he was also more centrally engaged in political activities, which meant more short visits to speak throughout the state. It all crowded in. In the mid-1850s travel was made easier by the railroads, which by then had a fairly extensive set of routes throughout Illinois. The existence of the railroads, however, did not seem to bring Lincoln home more often; it just took him away more often. During 1856, for example, Lincoln was away from home a total of nearly twenty weeks. He remained out on the spring circuit for eight weeks (April 2 to May 29) and then took thirteen more trips that year. Six of these trips were one- to three-day excursions, but of the remaining seven, four were at least a week, two were two weeks and one—when he was out on the fall circuit —three and one-half weeks (October 3 to October 27).

This objective evidence of the pattern of Lincoln's absences from Mary and home can also be approached more subjectively. Herndon noted in a letter written August 4, 1857, that he had to start some court work because Lincoln was absent. There is nothing really remarkable about the reference in Herndon's letter except that it is made gratuitously. It suggests that Herndon felt Lincoln was usually absent. Lincoln himself often mentioned facts of his travels in letters, because so much of his mail reached him on the run. He also used his absences to ward off students who wished to apprentice themselves with him. For example, he told Isham Reavis in 1855 that he was "from home too much" for it to be advantageous for a young man to read law with him. Three years later he used essentially the same excuse with James T. Thornton: "I am absent altogether too much to be a suitable instructor for a law-student."[11]

All this evidence of Lincoln's absences from home suggests a number of important conclusions. Lincoln established the general pattern of persistent separation from home at the very beginning of his marriage. Obviously, real need for an income prompted frequent trips on the circuit. He was good at that kind of work, he found it afforded pleasure, and it yielded a good income. The pattern of separations was that few lasted over two weeks, and the most likely time of separation was in the spring and fall. Lincoln was always home between December and April and usually absent only for short trips in the summer. The most important exception in the first decade or so of the marriage was between spring 1848 and spring 1849, when Lincoln was in Washington (Mary was with him there briefly but soon left to stay with her family in Kentucky). After the early 1850s the pattern of that first decade accelerated markedly: The total number of weeks Lincoln was away increased from an average of twelve weeks a year to approximately twenty weeks a year, *and* the rhythm changed. In the first decade of marriage, Lincoln seldom left his home for more than two weeks; in the 1850s the same kinds of activities (riding the circuit, for example) took him away for as long as eight straight weeks.

It seems that during the first decade or so of his marriage, Lincoln wrestled with his conflicted intimacy with Mary and home. He needed to leave often, but took emotional sustenance from the episodic refueling he received at home. To push this idea somewhat further, it seems probable that Lincoln embraced the periodicity of his relationship with Mary, the closeness–separation–closeness that defined its contours. In the early years at least he was homesick while absent (as reported in Conkling's 1842 letter) but was sometimes preoccupied while with her (resulting in incidents with Mary like the one Herndon describes in front of the fireplace). This kind of complex tie to Mary carried with it a deep devotion and fidelity; the stories of Lincoln's sexual capers are ludicrously apocryphal. But conflict created a need for regulated distance from Mary. The background for such a pattern was perhaps Lincoln's childhood experience of the death of his mother: his resulting need to repeat that loss, and his desire for recovery in minute doses as an adult. To "lose" Mary when he departed for the circuit evoked significant feelings of dread and, probably more often, depression in Lincoln. He needed the circuit life, however, both to support his material aspirations and to free him temporarily from a transference figure of such potent significance. Once separated, however, Lincoln seemed desirous of returning and reestablishing ties with Mary. He came back often in these years and was apparently away no more than absolutely necessary.

The memories of Whitney, Herndon, and Davis are thus quite wrong and misleading if one collapses the entire eighteen years between 1842 and 1860. These old friends are, however, right on target for the period after the early 1850s. By then Lincoln was quite willing, even eager, to travel a great deal. He rode the circuit without returning home for as long as eight weeks. He never seemed reluctant to be away; on the contrary, his cohorts on the circuit remember him as a boon companion. He seldom wrote home.[12] And he kept adding new legal and political responsibilities to an already tight schedule. The creative tension that defined Lincoln's relationship with Mary in the 1840s and early 1850s loosened considerably after 1854.

For Mary, of course, Lincoln was an intensely idealized figure on whom she came increasingly to lean for life itself. Lincoln in turn welcomed and perhaps needed such idealization and adoration. What emerges in the few letters Lincoln wrote Mary during their long separation in 1848 is a wistful loneliness and an immersion in family life, colored by a fatherly remoteness that created distance as it united. The background of these letters was Mary's departure from Mrs. Sprigg's boardinghouse in Washington after a stay of several months. She was quite unhappy with the accommodations and probably disappointed that no one paid any attention to her as the wife of a junior congressman. Though the letters date from the early period of Mary's absence, this separation lasted a year. Whether other letters were written and lost is uncertain. For some reason a special dread descended on Lincoln in that spring of 1848. "In this troublesome world," he wrote on April 16, 1848, "we are never quite satisfied. When you were here, I thought you hindered me some in attending to business; but now, having nothing but business—no variety—it has grown exceedingly tasteless to me. I hate to sit down and direct documents, and I hate to stay in this old room by myself."[13]

Lincoln then proceeded to comment on mundane but clearly meaningful details of family life mentioned by Mary in her earlier letters. He commented on a robbery in Mary's grandmother's house and thought it was unwise for her to stay alone. He asked Mary to send his greetings to John Parker. Lincoln then told her he had tried to find the "little plaid stockings" for Eddie but was unsuccessful: McKnight was out of business now and Allen had none of that description. Lincoln commented that an old friend of Mary's from St. Louis would be leaving Washington soon and offered to drop off a package in Lexington. One can see clearly his fatherly, controlling tone in the way he handled certain items of business. For example, Lincoln expressed pleasure that Mary was enjoying herself but cautioned against hurting her father by getting too close to the family of one of Robert Todd's staunch personal and political enemies. It is remarkable that Mary should have needed such advice. Lincoln immediately followed up this passage by alluding obliquely to Mary's disruptive presence in Washington. "All the house—or rather, all with whom you were on decided good terms—send their love to you. The others say nothing." The comment appears to be a backhanded way of under-lining his caution not to offend her father needlessly by her wanton friendships.

Scolding in turn gave way to a gentle reprimand. As we have seen, Lincoln asked Mary to please leave the "Hon." off her letters to him. He granted that her motivation was probably to insure free posting, but he assured her it was unnecessary. Lincoln was uncomfortable with the pretentiousness of the modest title: He would rather be an honorable "Mr." than an unnoticed and ignoble "Hon." The gap between the false dignity of his real position in Washington and his soaring ambitions could not be covered by recourse to title. Mary, who so fiercely identified with Lincoln's ambitions, in this sense prodded him with the title. Lincoln with-drew from embracing such empty symbols and in the process established an important point with Mary.

The reprimand over the title put Mary in her place and per-mitted Lincoln in his secured position of authority to be tender and fatherly. He referred condescendingly to her frequent head-aches, noting that this was the first time since they had met that she did not suffer from them. He even allowed himself a hint of sexual play, though in a vein that underlined her hefty and aging body. "I am afraid you will get so well, and fat, and young be wanting to marry again. Tell Louisa I want her to watc a little for me. Get weighed, and write me how much you weigh." Lincoln was lonely and yearned for contact with Mary. And yet his expressions of love, modest but real, deliberately dwelt on Mary's excruciating migraines and her fat body. Lincoln took away something vital as he provided crucial sustenance, distanced as he expressed love, and in every way forcefully clarified his position of authority. It is no wonder Mary idealized him; that was the only emotional position he allowed her to assume.

Lincoln's next letter to Mary sharply defined her subordinate position to him as it playfully acceded to her wish to come visit him in Washington. He opened with excuses for not answering right away (essentially that he was tired and busy). Lincoln then addressed directly the matter of her visit and the unspoken problem it posed. "Will you be a *good girl* in all things, if I consent?"[14] The allusion here is clearly to problems Mary caused before at Mrs. Sprigg's, her tantrums, and her general discontent with Washington. Lincoln perhaps occupied a humble niche in Congress, but he was sufficiently self-conscious of his position to try to avoid any obvious embarrassments. If Lincoln put Mary down, however, he quickly recovered himself. For he added after this proviso: "Then come along, and that *as soon* as possible." In fact, as he thought about the visit (if free from turmoil) he became quite openly eager to see her: "Having got the idea [of a visit] in my head, I shall be impatient till I see you." And Lincoln concluded the letter after discussing some money matters: "Come as soon as you can. I want to see you, and our dear—*dear* boys very much. Every body here wants to see our dear Bobby."

Mary then delayed some before she left Lexington, causing Lincoln anxiety. Having "got the idea" in his head, he wanted a family reunion. He even ended his third letter (July 2, 1848) with

A Little World Made Cunningly

153

a note of impatience: "Father expected to see you all sooner; but let it pass; stay as long as you please, and come when you please. Kiss and love the dear rascals."[15] This last and final letter in the series was unusually full of family concerns. Lincoln told Mary to be sure to arrange matters with the mail. He also mentioned friends and relatives: "Give my kindest regards to your uncle John," Lincoln noted, "and all the family. Thinking of them reminds me that I saw your acquaintance, Newton, of Arkansas, at the Philadelphia Convention."

These letters suggest in concrete ways the assorted needs for which Lincoln turned to Mary for gratification. But by the mid-1850s, their relationship had subtly changed as Lincoln's outlook expanded. Their sense of private space radically altered; after 1856 they moved from the tight four-room house that looked in on itself to a genteel home that allocated space generously. This larger house gave the family members much greater privacy as it turned outward to the world: Lincoln's separate bedroom doubled as an office where he met many important political figures in the late 1850s.

Lincoln's shifting field of vision after 1854 had enormous consequences for the country; it also tended to leave Mary alone, abandoned to meet her mounting needs without emotional resources. Deep childhood wounds reopened in Mary as the distance between husband and wife increased. His perception of her insanity, which was undoubtedly partly true, also perhaps carried a measure of desire on his part. His essential human kindness kept him near her, and she could never have survived without it. But in another sense her insanity filled the emptiness Lincoln created as he enlarged his vision. The change around 1854 represented for Lincoln a complex transition from a conflicted private world of meanings that never worked themselves out to a public arena of political rhetoric that he domesticated. Lincoln's personal issues of loss and reunion proved remarkably continuous as he translated his private experience into an idiom that made sense of much larger concerns. After 1854 Lincoln turned outward and attempted, as Erik Erikson might say, to solve for all what he could not solve for himself alone.

★★★

Lincoln's relationship with Mary carried the essential weight of his conflicted ties to home and family. But the children also represented another crucial aspect of his domesticity. "My Friends," Lincoln said to those gathered at the depot on his departure for Washington in 1861, "No one, not in my situation, can appreciate my feeling of sadness at this parting. To this place, and the kindness of these people, I owe everything. Here I have lived a quarter of a century, and have passed from a young to an old man. Here my children have been born, and one is buried."[16]

Such direct public reference to his children was rare for Lincoln. On the question of his relationship to his children, myth and the projected fantasies of various authors cloud our vision even more than is usual in the Lincoln story. The most abundant source is Herndon, and, of course, he had an ax to grind whenever he mentioned Lincoln's domestic affairs. Mary hopelessly idealized Lincoln's relationship with the children, and Lincoln himself, as usual in personal matters, left few verifiable written clues. Furthermore, there is little information from the children themselves. Only Robert lived to maturity, and he was generally reticent about revealing concrete details of his childhood. Robert was caught up in his painful relationship with his mother and, subsequently, saw his role as protector of his father's story from meddlers like Herndon. We are left, therefore, with only bits and pieces of often questionable evidence from which to draw conclusions.

At the most superficial level Lincoln clearly seemed to love and enjoy his children, as well as children generally. According to his old friend, Ward Hill Lamon, Lincoln was extremely fond of his children and was patient, indulgent, and generous with them. He often walked in the country with them on Sunday afternoon, "giving himself up entirely to them," rambling in green fields and cool woods, "amusing and instructing them for a whole day at a time." The Lincolns' neighbor, Noyes W. Miner, later illustrated Lincoln's love for children with an evocative anecdote: Troops of children from the block would watch for Lincoln's return from his law office for meals; they would then "gambol by his side, and as many as could get hold of him, would swing from his hands. He had a kind word & a smile for all." Mrs. George C. Heal, the daughter of a Lincoln acquaintance, recalled much later her experiences visiting the home. Lincoln would give her "hossy" rides, holding her hands and putting her on his leg, chanting, "This is the way the lady rides—Nim—Nim—Nim!" Then he would speed up some. "This is the way the gentleman rides —Prim—Prim—Prim!" Then at full gallop: "This is the way the countryman rides—Giddy-up—Giddy-up—Giddy-up!"— which led to shrieks of delight. It seems Lincoln would play these games with the little girl while Mary and Mrs. Heal's mother were in the adjoining room "gossiping."[17]

This kind of post-assassination anecdotal material may simply reflect the need to see Lincoln as a Christ-like figure, suffering the little children to come unto him. Another group of anecdotes, which have a hint of vitality, are perhaps more authentic. Once a neighbor, Mrs. Bradford, saw Lincoln pushing a baby carriage down the street, a decidedly unmasculine thing to do in this period. When she upbraided him for doing Mary's work rather than being down in his law office, Lincoln looked at her (probably suppressing a comment about busybodies) and said, "I promised" and went on about his business. Another time Lincoln was seen carrying Tad, who always received special attention, to his office, even though the boy was already half-grown. Frances Wallace, Mary's sister, told Lincoln that the boy could easily walk and thus implicitly chided him for overindulgence. Lincoln replied, undoubtedly with tongue in cheek: "Oh, don't you think his little feet will get too tired?"[18]

This theme of Lincoln's gentleness with children and indulgence of them to a fault occurs repeatedly in the literature. From Mary's perspective it was admirable. "Mr. Lincoln," she told Herndon in 1866, "was the kindest man and most loving husband and father in the world." Furthermore, he gave everyone in the family "unbounded liberty" and was "exceedingly indulgent" with the children. What indulgence meant specifically for Mary is unclear, but it involved a loving recognition of the boys' achievements and an absence of restraint. Mary quoted Lincoln to Herndon: "It is my pleasure that my children are free, happy and unrestrained by parental tyranny. Love is the chain whereby to bind a child to its parents." For Herndon, such indulgence of the children was despicable. Herndon, it seems, came to hate the little Lincoln brats, and felt his partner was "so blinded to his children's faults" that if they "s[hit] in Lincoln's hat and rubbed it on his boots, he would have laughed and thought it smart." Lincoln often brought the boys to the law office on Sunday and let them play while he worked. They would pull the books from the shelf, bend the points of the pens, overturn inkstands, scatter law papers, throw pencils into the spittoon, and piss on the floor. Lincoln would work calmly through it all. Nothing disturbed his serene good nature.[19]

In order to put Herndon's account into perspective, it is worth noting that this picture of Lincoln's brats in the office was tied directly to Herndon's unflattering characterization of Mary: The reason Lincoln brought the children to the office at all was so Mary could go to Church "*to show her new bonnet.*" Furthermore,

Herndon saw the boys' behavior as somehow Mary's fault. Herndon himself was unable to handle the anger he felt toward the boys who, as extensions of Mary, drove a wedge between himself and Lincoln. He frankly confessed wanting to wring the boys' necks and pitch them out the window when Lincoln brought them to the office. He held back, however, out of respect for Lincoln, "and left for parts unknown."[20]

Lincoln's "indulgence" of his children thus carried contradictory meanings for different observers. For our purposes, however, it is worth stressing the points of agreement. Lincoln seemed eager to let the children grow without much parental restraint, to find their own way in a complex world. In modern terms, he was permissive. He was quite willing to flout social codes of behavior that defined his role as in the office and Mary's as with the children. The officious intrusions of friends and relatives had no effect on him. His large, doting spirit also seemed to spill over to other children, and he became the delight of the block. His tolerant, humane kindness, which so appealed to Mary and made him able to bear her odd behavior through many trials, blinded him to obvious faults of his children. He seemed to encourage their freedom and to let discipline go by the wayside.

Nevertheless, Lincoln's ties to his children were complex. Lincoln's frequent separations from Mary also meant he was away from the boys. Lincoln in large part was an absent father. Mary basically raised the children. It was her interaction with them that set the contours of their personality. The boys' wildness perhaps reflected Lincoln's tolerance, but surely it also grew out of Mary's trouble in dealing with the people in her life. One reason Lincoln could tolerate so much from his children may have been that he saw them so infrequently.

Lincoln wrote Mary on July 2, 1848, that "Father" expected to see her and the boys soon.[21] One can read this to show what

The Globe Tavern, where the Lincolns first lived after their marriage in 1842. Courtesy of Illinois State Historical Library.

a "good" father Lincoln was, but it is striking that Lincoln wrote the note because it had been a long time since he had seen his family. He also used the third person to refer to himself. This grammatical distancing tended to elevate Lincoln within the family, to split him off as a godlike figure apart from the rest. It also separated himself from his own experience. Only rarely—as in his autobiography, when matters also touched close—did Lincoln fall back on the third person to talk about himself. It was a sign of ambivalence. And in this letter to Mary the ambivalence seemed to center on fatherhood.

The birth of Lincoln's first son on August 1, 1843, had been a joyous event. It seemed to relieve Lincoln of a confused sense of potency and togetherness that had undermined much of his earlier relationship with Mary. It is interesting in this regard that in the months before the baby's birth, Lincoln felt a strong connection to Joshua Speed, to whom he wrote when Mary was five months pregnant, "About the prospect of your having a namesake at our house cant say, exactly yet." Lincoln followed this letter with several more to Speed inviting him to visit Springfield. On May 18 he assured him that a room could be prepared at the Globe Tavern. And on July 26 he urged Speed again to visit with Fanny, for "We are but two as yet." It is unclear when "Robert" replaced "Joshua" as the baby's name, but the source is clear: Robert was the name of Mary's father.[22]

The best and only extended account of Lincoln's feelings about any of his children came in a letter he wrote to Speed on October 10, 1846. The lead topic of the letter was to announce the birth of another boy, Eddie, on March 10, 1846. Lincoln, however, proceeded quickly to a discussion of Robert. The boy was "short and low," Lincoln reported, and probably always would be. He was talking all right and seemed "quite smart enough." But Lincoln was oddly uncomfortable with Robert's talents. "I some times fear he [Robert] is one of the little rare-ripe sort, that are smarter at about five than ever after." Robert was then just three. Lincoln, it seems, felt an ambivalent fondness for his first-born, a recognition of Robert's potential that carried with it an inability to tolerate the competitive thrust of Robert's intelligence.

Robert was also something of a troublemaker for Lincoln, full of "that sort of mischief, that is the offspring of much animal spirits." As Lincoln was writing his letter of October 10 to Speed from the office, a messenger came to fetch him home to find the lost Robert. By the time Lincoln returned home the child had been found and whipped, so he went back to his office to finish describing the scene to Speed. Lincoln concluded his letter ironically by speculating that Robert by then had probably run away again.[23] Lincoln thus unburdened himself about his son—in a way never again to be repeated—to his old friend, Speed, whom

Lincoln once again placed in the role of emotional intermediary. As Speed once helped Lincoln reach out to Mary, Lincoln now wanted him to help deal with his son. The situations, however, were entirely different. Speed could, of course, do little, and besides, Lincoln was well past the period of his greatest psychological openness to outside influence.

But Lincoln's disappointment with Robert and his antagonism toward him continued. Two years after his letter to Speed, Lincoln dreamed of something bad happening to Robert. It seemed to foreshadow the future. He wrote Mary: "I did not get rid of the impression of that foolish dream about dear Bobby till I got your letter written the same day."[24] There are several second-hand reports of prophetic dreams Lincoln had during the war, but they were only recorded later and their meaning is clouded by the passage of time. The reference in this letter, however, is quite specific. Lincoln had had some dream of young Robert that boded evil. He apparently felt it was sufficiently real to be prophetic and had to write Mary immediately to assure himself of Robert's safety. Having heard that all was well, Lincoln dismissed the dream as "foolish." Before that, however, it was clearly a serious matter. It is speculation no doubt, but Lincoln's dream of evil befalling his five-year-old son probably reflected his own ambivalence toward his firstborn. In some way Robert obstructed Lincoln's largely unconscious grandiosity, limiting by his presence the father's tendency to fill the male space within the family.

Robert carried a heavy burden of Lincoln's expectations. All of the father's educational deficiencies and social aspirations united in Robert. Thus the eldest boy was to have the kind of schooling that Lincoln never had; he was even to go to Harvard. There is some indication it was Lincoln's idea that Robert attend Harvard. Robert, however, remembered it as his own idea in his brief autobiographical statement for the Harvard Class Book of 1864.

In that statement, Robert described the inadequacy of his educational experience in the 1850s at Illinois State University, which was then in Springfield: "The government was very easy, and we did just what pleased us[,] study consuming only a very small portion of our time." Robert eventually came to question the value of such laxity: "I became aware," he continued, "that I could never get an education in that way and resolved to enter Harvard College." He imagined it would be easy to get into Harvard, but soon had the "honor to receive a fabulous number of failures." He resolved, however, "not to retire beaten" and took President Walker's advice to take a preparatory year at Exeter. The year at Exeter worked out well, though Robert had to give up his hope of entering Harvard as a sophomore. He was "obliged" to enter as a freshman in 1860.[25]

Robert seemed proud he had stuck by his goal of getting into Harvard. "After the commencement in 1860," he said, "I was able to inform my father that I had succeeded in entering College without a Condition—quite a change from the previous year." At Harvard, Robert managed with gentlemanly C's; he studied enough, he said, to satisfy himself without being overly earnest about it. If he excelled, it meant confronting his awesome father directly; if he failed totally, he equally risked losing a large measure of love. So he ambled along. He was active in a variety of enterprises in college and was proud to report his election as vice-president of the Hasty Pudding Club.[26]

Robert thus fulfilled Lincoln's contradictory feelings about education. Lincoln recognized the inadequacies of his erratic schooling. At the same time, as a self-made man, he took pride in the learning he acquired on his own. Some of the advice he gave young lawyers suggested, in fact, that they forget formal schooling altogether. Just read, he said, and keep on reading. Robert had all the best schooling and yet never quite made the mark.

Lovely

There was, however, a certain closeness between Linco.. Robert. Lincoln visited him at Exeter during that first winter away from home; in fact, a reason for accepting an invitation to speak at Cooper Union in New York in 1860 was to combine it with a trip to see Robert. Robert eagerly welcomed his father, who made quite an impression on his schoolmates. They spent some time together alone, though most of their few days together were crowded with speeches Lincoln had to make. Years later, Robert found a way to spend time with his father during the war. Lincoln often walked to the telegraph office in the War Department alone at night to check the progress of a battle. Robert recalled later that during the winter of 1865 he told his father he wished that he would not do that at night without letting him know, so that he could accompany him. Lincoln as a result woke Robert up on a "number of occasions" and the two walked together to the telegraph office.[27]

In many respects Robert was much like his father. For example, he was reported to have a good sense of humor. An English observer once commented that Robert "when once he had shaken himself free from his jokes, was vigorous enough."[28] In his autobiographical statement there is humor in his reference to his "fabulous failures" in the Harvard exams and how some "filthy lucre" got him out of a scrape at Exeter. He seemed to play on words as his father did, though less gently; sarcasm often infected Robert's jokes:

Not very long ago in trying a suit, Mr. Lincoln addressed the defendant, Mr. Windet,—a man who was hopelessly insolvent, but given to great schemes about which he did a great deal of talking. Mr. Lincoln pronounced the defendant's name with the accent on the first syllable. The gentleman corrected him saying, "Mr. Windet, if you please, sir, Mr. Windet" accenting the last syllable. Mr. Lincoln replied very quietly: "I beg your pardon, sir; but I think that I am to be

A Little World Made Cunningly

excused for not knowing whether to associate more of wind or debt with you."[29]

The letters he wrote seldom show any humor at all. At best he mustered a sense of irony. "Please accept my thanks for your kindness in sending me the bag of 'Lincoln' Coffee," he wrote John Hanna in 1884. "It is rather singular that this brand should be used in Costa Rica, and it gives me great pleasure to receive it on account of this peculiar circumstance."[30]

Robert was also ambitious, shrewd, capable. He was a successful lawyer in Chicago through the 1870s. Between 1879 and 1884 he then served competently as Secretary of War. After that he returned briefly to various legal and business interests in Chicago before accepting (somewhat reluctantly) appointment as Minister to Great Britain. He returned to Chicago in 1893 to begin a long and prestigious association with the Pullman Railroad Company. He became president of the company in 1901 and in the course of the next decade guided it through its greatest period of financial growth.[31] After 1911 he went into semi-retirement as chairman of the board. He spent as much time as possible in his beloved Vermont home, which he named Hildene. There he played golf, wrote letters, and dabbled in astronomy. He died in 1926, just short of his eighty-third birthday.

In a sense Robert lived out with a vengeance his father's upwardly mobile aspirations. He became a millionaire and the confidant of the powerful. He served on important boards and ran one of the nation's leading companies. He lived sumptuously and socialized only with the best people. He went to England in part because of the "social benefits" that came with the job. Robert also seemed to identify with Lincoln's alienation from Thomas, which in Robert became a generalized feeling of shame about his father's rural roots. He disdained the bad spelling of the frontier.

Thomas Lincoln, Robert said, "was poor and unable to give him [Lincoln] an education." He also suggested that Lincoln's parents, who lacked opportunity, were lazy: "It is well known that my father's parents were poor and unlearned, and without opportunity," he wrote in 1884, "if they had the inclination, of doing more than keep slight traditions of their relations, and I know little of what those were."[32]

Robert treasured his father's memory and saw himself as the caretaker of the Lincoln tradition. His ownership of the Lincoln papers gave meaning to his role as protector. He let no one see the papers, except his secretaries, John G. Nicolay and John Hay, for their approved biography. As a stubborn final gesture, Robert also imposed a twenty-one-year cloture on the papers after his death in 1926 to frustrate Albert Beveridge, whose work on Lincoln Robert disliked. During his lifetime Robert received hundreds of letters requesting relics, mementos, autographs, or information from the Lincoln papers. For many respondents Robert developed a form letter that his secretary, Charles S. Sweet, could send out. But Robert himself responded directly to a surprising number of these requests. He was particularly likely to write back when asked about photographs or paintings of Lincoln. In 1887, for example, he told Ewing Hill that "I do not know of any portrait of him [Lincoln] standing erect which is at all satisfactory. There is such a large painting in the President's house, but if I owned it I would burn it." He said he liked the Volk life mask because it showed Lincoln without a beard. He preferred that to the ones with a beard, which for Robert were less "familiar." Robert replied without irony or resentment to one extraordinary request for an original copy of the Gettysburg Address.[33]

Robert had strong views about what was acceptable and what should be discarded in the books on his father that came pouring out after 1865. He was "indignant" about Ward Hill Lamon and felt Herndon was entirely untrustworthy. In 1884 he tried to discourage a publisher from putting out a book by Jane Swisshelm. Her material, Robert felt, was a "miserable mess of misstatements," "trash," and "invention," and it would be a "wretched thing" to publish it.[34] He did, however, approve of Nicolay and Hay's work and felt Isaac Arnold's one-volume study the best short biography available. Robert wanted everything about Lincoln to be factually correct but he refused access to the material that would have made for accuracy. He provided information to selected respondents over half a century and seemed baffled as to why everyone kept getting the Lincoln story all wrong. He hoped silence would stifle the inquisitive, but instead it only spurred them on.

Scholars for nearly a century have been angry at Robert because he kept them away from the Lincoln papers. But what has not been appreciated is the vital meaning of the papers for Robert. The secrecy accomplished several psychological objectives. It kept Lincoln alive and close to Robert in a special way. Any human relic carries this meaning, but Robert built his self-conception around his unique connection to his father. In his letters, for example, Robert wrote somewhat tiresomely of which were the best and worst photographs or paintings of Lincoln, whose biography was awful, whose good, and he diligently recorded his own memories of selected events. This circumscribed focus on the past preserved Lincoln for his son. It also controlled Lincoln and kept him near, as Robert never could as a child. In the Lincoln legacy Robert retained a hold on his father that gratified enduring childhood longings.

Robert found painful any situation that publicly honored his father with him present. As a rule he religiously avoided such events, although he often felt obliged to provide lengthy, somewhat gratuitous explanations for his actions. For example, in January 1900, he turned down a request to speak at a birthday ceremony honoring Lincoln. "I do not know whether my reasons for this are sufficient," he wrote, "but they seem very good to me. While I am most sincerely gratified for the admiration of his character, which is the burden of so many speeches at meetings of this kind, I am more comfortable in reading them than I would be in a company listening to them; and if I were present, it would very commonly happen that I would be much embarrassed in trying to avoid speaking myself. This I am most unwilling to do."[35] Such scenes seemed to overwhelm him. He refused to attend the re-burial of his father's remains in 1902 and stayed away from the dedication in 1909 of the cabin in which Lincoln may have been born. He avoided any public encounter that risked comparing him to Lincoln; he never once gave a speech about his father.

As he aged, however, Robert came to accept the inevitable constraints on his control of his father's memory. His acceptance of these constraints came slowly and painfully. He was enraged at Herndon's 1866 lecture on Ann Rutledge and furious at Lamon's 1872 *Life*. By the turn of the century, however, Robert was able to brush aside much of the foolishness about his father. For example, he wrote to a friend in 1900 that a respectable business-man had reported proudly to him that his brother had served in Lincoln's bodyguard of a hundred men over six feet tall. "I did not think it necessary to say to him," Robert concluded, "that there never was such a bodyguard."[36]

Robert's adult encounters with the memory of his father were complicated by the troubles with his mother. In his autobio-graphical statement of 1864, Robert neglected to mention his mother's date of birth, and his hand jiggled and forced him to write over the "my" of "my mother" when he mentioned her. After the war, Robert tried living with Mary in Chicago as he began his law practice, but the strains were incredible. Mary de-scribed, for example, Robert's overwhelming sense of shame when the "old clothes scandal" broke in 1867. Later, as Mary's condition deteriorated, her paranoid fantasies about Robert confirmed his feeling that the "dreadful circumstances" surrounding his father's death had "deranged" his mother mentally. Her actions, he said, distressed him "beyond any power of description." The clothes scandal and her hundreds of letters to all and sundry begging for money were only a part of what he had to "grieve and be mortified about." There was also "any quantity of newspaper publicity about her actions and writings . . . it all nearly wore my life out."[37]

Robert remained confused about his mother throughout his life. He hardly ever talked about her in private and drew a public screen over the events surrounding her committal. He even tried to cover up the episode by searching out and destroying Mary's letters from the period. He gave up, however, because there were simply too many letters.[38] Robert took on with a grim, almost fatalistic determination what he saw as his responsibility to commit her. "I can only do my duty," he wrote on June 1, 1875, "as it is given me to see it."[39] The fatalism Robert expressed reflected perhaps his fantasy of acting out his father's wishes. The committal curiously linked him with his father's convictions about Mary's insanity and Lincoln's threat to commit her after Willie's death in 1862. Robert probably sensed what his father had told Mary. But even if he somehow missed the family secret, he could not avoid Elizabeth Keckley's 1868 book, which reported Lincoln's threats. The unspoken support for Robert's committal of his mother was thus his awareness, however dimly acknowledged, that he was acting as Lincoln's surrogate.

Robert lacked spontaneity and zest. His thousands of letters are characterized by a flatness of tone, a decided lack of affect. He seemed to block any mourning response to his mother's death; at least he failed to discuss her death in his correspondence. Occasionally, he got mad (at Herndon, for example) and he deeply grieved over the death of his son, Jack (Abraham Lincoln II) in 1890. But these were the exceptions. Herndon, as we might suspect, rather overstated his case against Robert: "He has the insane rage of his mother without the sense of his father. Robert Lincoln is a wretch of a man." He was also a "little wee bit of a man," "silly, cold and selfish, a Todd not a Lincoln," "little, proud, aristocratic and haughty," and "his mother's 'baby' all through." If we remove the venom from Herndon, it offers a measure of insight into the cold and haughty demeanor of Robert Lincoln.[40]

The other children were different, though none lived long enough to make possible anything but the most cursory comments about their personalities. Eddie lived only four years. Tad, born in 1853, was the oddity in the family, an appealing yet helpless and possibly somewhat retarded child. He was twelve or so before he could read. He lisped slightly. He was delightfully impish. Lincoln went to great lengths to entertain Tad; he played blind man's bluff with him, for example, and would trip over furniture to insure Tad would escape. During the war, Tad ran wild in the White House. He dressed up in uniforms, interrupted cabinet meetings, and drove Nicolay and Hay to distraction. But he never upset Lincoln, who responded easily to Tad's helplessness. Tad was like a puppy whose uncomplicated presence helped defuse some of the family tensions and conflicts.[41]

Finally, there was Willie, born in 1850, who was the favorite. He was lively, poetic, and smart. Willie, according to Mary's niece, Elizabeth Todd Grimsley, was a "noble, beautiful boy." He had "great mental activity," an unusual intelligence, a wonderful memory, and was frank and loving. The impression one gets is that Lincoln so obviously favored Willie it never had to be remarked upon. Willie's death in 1862 etched massive new lines of sorrow in Lincoln. "I never saw a man so bowed down with grief," wrote Elizabeth Keckley, describing Lincoln reacting to the boy's death, "murmuring 'My poor boy, he was too good for this earth. God has called him home. I know that he is much better off in heaven, but then we loved him so. It is hard, hard to have him die!' Great sobs choked his utterance. . . . I did not dream that his rugged nature could be so moved."[42]

It is interesting to compare Robert, born in 1843, with Willie, who was born in 1850. Robert was born into the family when Lincoln was most a part of it. He carried the full burden of Lincoln's conflicts over fatherhood and his contradictory expectations for his son. With seven years between the birth of these two sons, and with Lincoln's greater emotional distance from the family itself, Robert could relate warmly and easily to Willie. The conflicted intensity of the early years of marriage heavily burdened him. The freer sense of Lincoln family life in the 1850s allowed the talented Willie breathing space. He took advantage of it.[43]

He studied with nobody.

A. Lincoln (on himself), June 1860

6

LAW AND ORDER

———◆•◆———

No assessment of the mature Lincoln can proceed without some understanding of his activities as a lawyer. In practical terms it was his legal work that supported his lifestyle and defined his place within the larger community. Lincoln seemed to find or consolidate in the law a sense of order that perhaps served as an antidote to his domestic turbulence. One might even argue that Lincoln's search for order was the defining characteristic of his adult life, public and private, and that his failure to find effective order domestically prompted an analogous engagement with larger issues in the community. In this sense, law and Lincoln's self-conception as a lawyer helped bridge the gap from private to public.

It all began somewhat inauspiciously. Speed noted that Lincoln at first lacked confidence as a lawyer and embraced his new career with diffidence. He seemed intimidated by the high-powered lawyers with whom he came into contact.[1] Lincoln did write some legal documents for Bowling Green, the local justice of the *largest trial practice*

peace in New Salem, and was himself sued several times. But Lincoln completely lacked formal training in the law. He picked up Blackstone's *Commentaries* on John T. Stuart's urging and read intently and alone whenever he could. "If you are resolutely determined to make a lawyer of yourself," Lincoln later counseled an aspiring lawyer, "the thing is more than half done already." There is no need for formal schooling, he went on, just a determined crack at the books. "Get the books, and read and study them till, you understand them in their principal features; that is the main thing. . . . Always bear in mind that your own resolution to succeed, is more important than any other one thing." "The books and your capacity for understanding are just the same in all places," he once told someone else. "Begin with Blackstone's *Commentaries* first and after reading it through, say twice, take up Chitty's *Pleadings,* Greenleaf's *Evidence,* and Story's *Equity* in succession. Work, work, work is the main thing."

Lincoln even seemed to feel it was better not to have formal training in the law, partly, it appears, because solitary study gets the job done faster. All this was later to be romanticized greatly in the literature, but it is worth recalling that Lincoln had no other choice and was himself unusually talented. The limits of his legal knowledge were also quite apparent to his partner. It has been noted that Lincoln appears never to have read a law text after he was accepted into the bar; his knowledge came from attending carefully to each case. "Mr. Lincoln," David Davis said in 1866, "was not a general reader in any field of knowledge; he was purely a practical man, and when he wished to know a fact, he trailed it up and dug it up, root and branch . . . [and] used his information for practical ends."[2]

Lincoln was what lawyers call a litigation man. He worked the courts, where he was aggressive and tenacious. He was also busy: He had the largest trial practice of all his peers in central

Illinois. In 1853, Lincoln and Herndon were responsible for one-third of all cases that were heard at the Sangamon Circuit Court, at a time when forty lawyers practiced there. More than half Lincoln's cases involved real property and mortgages, simple contracts, or issues of procedure. The next largest category of cases concerned personal property. There were numerous divorce cases but few wills. As Lincoln matured and his skill became better known, his practice included substantial work in federal trial court. He was quite well known as an appellate lawyer, and he and his partners handled 411 cases before the state's highest court. Some two-thirds of his practice dealt with common law issues, while only six percent involved criminal law, despite his notoriety in a few cases such as his defense of Duff Armstrong, who had been accused of murder.[3]

Herndon noted that Lincoln was incredibly shrewd as a trial lawyer, able to sway juries by his honesty, humor, and lucidity. "Great in court anywhere," David Davis told Herndon, who jotted down notes of the conversation, "if he thought he was right. He inquired more into cases than into the Philosophy: was a good Circuit Court Lawyer." Lincoln was well prepared and seldom caught off guard by the testimony of the opposition. With a jury he was direct, simple, and clear. "Billy," Lincoln told Herndon, "don't shoot too high—aim lower and the common people will understand you. They are the ones you want to reach—at least they are the ones you ought to reach. The educated and refined people will understand you anyway. If you aim too high your ideas will go over the heads of the masses, and only hit those who need no hitting." Lincoln was also calm and used anecdotes effectively. All remarked on his skill. The same traits that worked with juries also made him a favorite of his peers. Henry C. Whitney remembered fondly Lincoln's reply to his question of whether in an attachment suit a service of the attachment writ on the defendant had the force of a summons. Lincoln pondered the matter, cast his eyes up to the ceiling for a long minute and finally replied roguishly: "Damnfino."[4]

He took the cases as they came: a farmer suing his neighbor for stealing his pig, a wife seeking divorce, a slave suing for freedom, a property dispute, anything and everything. Lincoln believed strongly in the ethics of his profession and seemed to feel even the devil deserved an advocate. Thus in 1847 he represented Robert Matson, who was suing to recover his runaway slaves. Matson had brought his Kentucky slaves into Illinois to work on his farm, and they had run away and later brought suit for their freedom. Lincoln and Usher Linder defended Matson. In his argument, Lincoln granted that the slaves would be free if they had been permanently brought into Illinois to work, but in this case were only in transit. Lincoln lost the case, and reportedly Matson never paid his fee. From later statements it is clear Lincoln detested the fugitive slave law, but here as elsewhere he buried his personal feelings in the interest of serving his client.[5]

Herndon noted that Lincoln often began a day in the office sad and gloomy but that the melancholy lifted as the day progressed. The work and the human contact it involved brought Lincoln out of himself as he listened to endless tales of anger, misdeeds, and woe. He searched people out, probing and questioning, trying to put them and himself at ease. Herndon recognized the subtlety of Lincoln's style but remained somewhat ambivalent about it. By the time Herndon wrote his book in the 1880s, most of his ambivalence had fallen away. A letter he wrote in 1857, however, captures better than any source what the office was like when Lincoln was there, as well as some of Herndon's deeper feelings about his partner: "I am now in my office writing this letter," Herndon told Wendell Philips, "with a good hickory fire in the stove and several good jolly fellows keeping it warm. Lincoln— the joker—the funny man—is cracking his jokes:—he beats Hale to death *in that line*. By the by—do you know Lincoln? as we say west he is a 'hoss' I am the runt of the firm and no 'hoss,' yet I suppose will pass among the crowd as a Liberty lover—a fool and a Reformer."[6]

Their practice became huge—eventually, Lincoln and his partners handled nearly five thousand cases during twenty-five years of work. Lincoln's professional standards are reflected in his advice to students:

> Never let your correspondence fall behind. Whatever piece of business you have in hand, before stopping, do all the labor pertaining to it which can then be done. When you bring a common-law suit, if you have the facts for doing so, write the declaration at once. If a law point be involved, examine the books, and note the authority you rely on upon the declaration itself, where you are sure to find it when wanted. The same of defenses and pleas.

Still, things could be a bit rough around the edges. A student clerking in the office later reported that seeds once actually sprouted in a dusty corner. At times Lincoln simply forgot things, large and small. "I am ashamed of not sooner answering your letter," he wrote Richard S. Thomas on June 27, 1850. "My only apologies are, first, that I have been very busy in the U.S. Court; and second, that when I received the letter I put it in my old hat, and buying a new one the next day, the old one was set aside, and so, the letter lost sight of for a time." He wrote Milton K. Alexander on June 13, 1854: "It pains me to say that I forgot to attend to your business when I was in Clinton, at court in May last. Your best way would be to address me a letter at Clinton, about the time I go there to court in the fall (Oct. 16th I think) and then it will be fresh, & I will not forget or neglect it."[7]

One careful student of Lincoln the lawyer has noted that such sloppiness was hardly out of place for the times. The fact is that everything was done on the run, and copying was for all intents and purposes nonexistent. There was no way all the relevant documents could be at hand, or even carefully protected in one place. If crucial arguments, precedents, and the nature of the law were not in your head, you were lost. Lincoln apologized for any obvious error or inconvenience he caused a client, and in general those who employed him were quite satisfied with his work. He was also supremely honest—he told students that if they could not be honest lawyers, "resolve to be honest without being a lawyer" —and gave two pieces of very sound advice:

> Discourage litigation. Persuade your neighbors to compromise whenever you can. Point out to them how the nominal winner is often a real loser—in fees, expenses, and waste of time. As a peacemaker the lawyer has a superior opportunity of being a good man. There will still be business enough.
>
> Never stir up litigation. A worse man can scarcely be found than one who does this. Who can be more nearly a fiend than he who habitually overhauls the register of deeds in search of defects in titles, whereon to stir up strife, and put money in his pocket? A moral tone ought to be infused into the profession which should drive such men out of it.[8]

Much of Lincoln's law practice appears erratic but should really be seen as fluid because it was often, if not usually, carried out on the circuit, in motion and under pressure, without time for adequate preparation. The circuit was a wonderfully premodern system devised to accommodate a changing but thinly populated state. When Lincoln first became a lawyer, there were seven state circuits, with judges elected by the legislature. This system dated from the Illinois constitution in 1818. The grouping of counties in each circuit, however, was constantly changing throughout the 1830s and 1840s, because new counties were being formed as the state's population increased and shifted north. For example, between 1837 and 1839 the legislature recognized twenty-one new counties. The eighth circuit itself was formed in 1839. It was huge and included seven counties (Sangamon, McLean, Livingston, Macon, Christian, Logan, and Menard). Over the next six years, nine more counties were added (Dewitt, Shelby, Champaign, Mason, Pitt, Woodford, Moultire, Edgar, and Vermillion). At its largest the eighth circuit covered a thousand square miles, two-thirds of the width and one-third the length of the state.

The entire court—judge, lawyers, and clerks—moved among county seats throughout the circuit. The court would be in session in each county seat for a few days to a week, depending on the volume of business, and then move on. The whole circuit was covered once in the spring and once in the fall. The court settings were usually quite humble, a log cabin adapted for the purpose or an unpretentious state building. The system had an impromptu quality that some observers at the time regarded as incompetence.[9] It was impossible to carry books along, so most cases were argued on the issue of right or wrong rather than on precedent.

There was often little time for a lawyer to prepare or even to learn the facts of a case. He might of course have made previous contact with a client and, through letters, worked out an argument based on precedent from research in Springfield. In such cases Lincoln and others worked with local "partners," through loose affiliations with lawyers in the county seats. Lincoln had some seventy-five such casual, ad hoc arrangements over the years.[10] More often, however, a lawyer was approached to handle a case as he arrived in town. An afternoon in the town square, talking and joking with the local residents the day before court opened, was the principal way to bring in business.

Conditions for the lawyers on the circuit were primitive. Much of their time was spent in arduous travel between county seats. In the years when Judge Treat presided over the eighth circuit (1843–1848), the caravan usually moved by horseback. Between 1848 and 1860, when David Davis was the judge, they moved at first by buggy over the improved roads and, by the mid-1850s, by train. In the court, which met every day except Sunday, the lawyers had to argue cases before juries that refused to recognize legal pretensions. Food and lodging varied but were never elegant. If the night had to be spent along the route between county seats, which was often, everyone might have to crowd into a log cabin, perhaps on the floor. Even in the towns, there was seldom enough space in the local hotel for everyone in the caravan, so lawyers usually slept two (or sometimes more) in a bed. The food was abundant but usually terrible. Most lawyers tried to return home on weekends but still faced long and frequent separations from wives and children. Circuit life could be frustrating, disruptive, hard, and lonely.[11]

But Lincoln loved it. He was as happy on the circuit as he ever was in his life. He never complained of the physical hardships and seemed to thrive on the quiet loneliness of the circuit. He would bounce along on his horse for hours, absorbed in his book, and he read Euclid in the peaceful time after others were asleep. He was known to slip away quietly by himself, once to spend an entire evening at a little magic lantern show intended for children. The rough male camaradarie of aspiring professionals in primitive conditions also appealed to Lincoln. It provided, especially, an ideal audience for his spontaneous, warm humor. David Davis used to hold mock court in the evening and laugh for hours at Lincoln's sense of the outrageous. Besides his friends Joshua Speed and David Davis (who became Lincoln's 1860 campaign manager, was later appointed to the Supreme Court, and after the war handled the Lincoln estate), Lincoln made perhaps his only adult friends on the circuit: Elihu B. Washburne, Leonard S. Swett, Ward Hill Lamon, Henry C. Whitney, and many others.[12]

Lincoln also thrived professionally on the circuit. He was at his best before a humble jury of decidedly ordinary citizens. He never talked down to them, and his careful dosing of technicalities with earthy humor made him enormously effective. It should also not be forgotten that circuit work was a professional advantage in two areas: in his law practice and in his political career. Lincoln's acute sense of the mood, potentialities, and prejudices of ordinary citizens in central Illinois came from long immersion in their ways. He came to grasp what they wanted and needed, which helped him consolidate his political career. A lot of votes were at stake. Circuit work in some ways gave Lincoln the chance to campaign half of every year for most of his adult life. New York Republicans were shortsighted (perhaps hoodwinked would be a better metaphor) when they saw him as little more than a favorite son in 1860. His renown throughout Illinois, based on twenty-five years of work among the people—of representing them honestly and thoroughly in remote corners of the state, of sleeping in their inns and eating at their tables, of gaining renown as a legendary storyteller before he was ever known for his views on the extension of slavery—was what his wise managers hoped to build on when they suggested Chicago as a "neutral" convention site in 1860.

One way to understand Lincoln's work as a lawyer is through his fees. He always earned a good income from the law, but usually his fees were quite small. A five-dollar payment was not uncommon, and most were between five and twenty dollars. It was the volume of his work that made it lucrative. Sometimes he even accepted payment in kind, such as firewood or subscription to a local newspaper. Lincoln never took advantage of his role as lawyer to acquire cheap land and other properties. In this he differed from many of his colleagues such as David Davis, Stephen T. Logan, and C. H. Moore, who amassed personal fortunes. Lincoln could be extraordinarily generous, as when he returned ten dollars of George Floyd's twenty-five-dollar payment for services rendered: "You must think I am a high-priced man," he told Floyd. "You are too liberal with your money. . . . Fifteen dollars is enough for the job." Still, Lincoln expected to be paid something and could be quite insistent with his clients. He felt in general that some if not all of the fee should be paid in advance; he noticed that he was not likely to hear from clients after their cases were settled. But in dealing with anyone over any fee, large or small, Lincoln never lost his sense of humor. "I have news from Ottawa," he wrote a circuit partner once, "that we *win* our Galatin & Saline county cases. As the dutch Justice said, when he married folk, 'Now, vere ish my hundred tollars.'" Similarly, he once asked another circuit partner to help him finish up a case for which he had already taken a fee. He disliked keeping the money without doing the work, he said, but he also hated to "disgorge."[13]

One fee Lincoln received has become quite famous. As lawyer for the Illinois Central Railroad after it was chartered in 1851, Lincoln handled some forty cases for the company. His most important by far was the McClean County tax case. In it Lincoln successfully argued that railroads should be exempt from county taxes as "public works" because they already paid state taxes. The decision was to have an enormous impact on railroad construction. Lincoln recognized the value of the case, but at first seemed uncertain what constituted a reasonable fee. He considered $2,000, but friends urged him to increase that amount considerably. In the end he charged $5,000, at which the company balked. So he sued the railroad company for the full amount, which he was awarded on June 23, 1857. The company, however, saw the payment, at least in part, as a kind of political payoff. In May 1857 (just prior to the uncontested court settlement) the Illinois Central's Chicago director wrote privately that Lincoln "proves to be not only the most prominent of his party, but the acknowledged special advisor of the Bissell Administration" (William H. Bissell was then Governor of Illinois). Most people agree Lincoln deserved the fee; it was a landmark case. In suing the Illinois Central, he was probably not consciously capitalizing on his political clout for his own material advantage. Still, no one as shrewd as Lincoln could be unaware of the connection. It seems he was more than a little conflicted about the fee. At the conclusion of the trial, the jury awarded him $5,000 but Lincoln's attorney, John M. Douglas, had to request immediately that the verdict be set aside and another jury called. This was done and a new judgment awarded for $4,800. It seems Lincoln "forgot" he had much earlier taken a $200 retainer fee.[14]

Several legal scholars have exhaustively examined Lincoln's activities as a lawyer. Much remains controversial, such as how "great" he was as a lawyer and what kinds of precedents he set. One of these studies—John P. Frank's *Lincoln the Lawyer*—has also stressed the development of Lincoln as a lawyer. "Perhaps the largest single difference," Frank wrote, "between the Lincoln of 1840 and the Lincoln of 1860 is in his self-confidence, his sense of personal assurance. . . . The tone changes. Diffidence is replaced by authority." Certain of Lincoln's human traits made him a good lawyer from the beginning: a personality that attracted clients; an aptitude for organizing materials to highlight the essential; a gift of selectivity; a restrained and effective verbal expression; an unusually retentive mind; and a capacity for hard work. Nevertheless, Frank felt he could clearly identify a young lawyer Lincoln and a mature lawyer Lincoln. In the early years, for example, Lincoln tended to brand the fellow on the other side a liar; the mature

Lincoln saw all people as seekers after truth. In his early practice Lincoln represented some flatboatmen suing a dam, which he showed obstructed a navigable river. He won eighty-five dollars for the defendants. Later, he shifted to the other side in the famous Rock Island Bridge case. Here he represented the bridge (and behind it the railroads that crossed the Mississippi on the bridge) against a boat that hit the bridge. If boats can go up and down the river, he essentially argued, why should trains not be allowed to go across it?[15]

Young lawyer Lincoln approached the law as a tricky game of variances, pleadings, niceties, and petty details. The law was a tool to use, something outside the self to foster prestige, bring in money, defeat opponents. Lincoln tended to focus on the details of his cases, to try to trip up witnesses, and to react indignantly to the lies of witnesses.

In his early years he was not a bad lawyer at all, but he was an ordinary one; nearly all the important cases with which his name is associated came in the second half of his career. The Lincoln Legal Project recently compiled a list of Lincoln's top ten cases, which may be a somewhat spurious task given the total number of five thousand. But even with such a list the point of the difference between the young and the more mature lawyer Lincoln seems validated. Of that list, only two cases occurred before 1850—and he lost both![16]

Lincoln found his way slowly in his chosen profession. It took time, as well as both experience *and* change in other areas, before he could work at his best—in Frank's terms, before law could become "an approach to life, a merger of engineering, surveying, economics, social wisdom, as well as precedent tightly analyzed."[17]

It will become all one thing, or all the other.

A. Lincoln, June 16, 1858

7

A HOUSE DIVIDED

Change came to the mature Lincoln both at home and in the political arena. It is clearest in his political development. He took positions on three major issues as a representative in the Thirtieth Congress (1847–49): He came out strongly against the Mexican War; he proposed to introduce a bill in Congress to abolish the slave trade in Washington, D.C.; and he worked against Henry Clay and for General Zachary Taylor in the 1848 presidential struggle. Lincoln was, in other words, antiwar, antislavery, and anti-Clay. In each case he either failed completely to accomplish his objective or met with only partial success. The country was joyfully militaristic, especially the South, and welcomed the huge acquisitions of the 1848 Treaty of Guadalupe Hidalgo with Mexico. In terms of his position against slavery, Lincoln only succeeded in identifying himself with extremists without altering the slave trade at all; he badly misjudged his support as well as the strength of the opposition. And in working against Clay, Lincoln managed to acquire the smell of a traitor without any offsetting advantage; Zachary Taylor, who beat Clay for the nomination and won the election, proved singularly unresponsive to Lincoln's requests for a position in the new administration. In each case, it seems Lincoln chose the wrong issue at the wrong time in the wrong place. It took years to undo the damage. It was a mark of Lincoln's greatness that he acknowledged to himself the extent of his failure as a congressman and pulled back gracefully to reflect, grow, and change for some five years. When his next opportunity came, in 1854, he was ready for the challenge. Neither he nor the country was ever again quite the same.

★★★

Lincoln introduced his "spot resolutions" in the House of Representatives on December 22, 1847. In legalistic language, Lincoln tried to force President Polk to admit that the actual spot where fighting began was in Mexico, not the United States; if true, that made the United States the aggressor. The first two of Lincoln's eight "interrogatories" respectfully directed President Polk to inform the House of Representatives, first, "Whether the spot of soil on which the blood of our *citizens* was shed, as in his messages declared, was, or was not, within the territories of Spain, at least from the treaty of 1819 until the Mexican revolution" and, second, "Whether that spot is, or is not, within the territory which was wrested from Spain, by the Mexican revolution."[1]

Lincoln over-lawyered himself in these interrogatories, which treated Polk as though he were a humble witness on the stand. The technique of asking detailed, probing questions to which only affirmative or negative answers can be given and then from those answers reconstructing a logically ordered chain of events is really only appropriate for the courtroom. In the complex world of parties and politics and the formalized tensions between Congress and the executive, the device Lincoln was using to unmask

Polk was inappropriate. Lincoln felt we were the aggressors in the Mexican War and that the whole venture was unjust and imperialistic. He should have said so in ways he uniquely could.[2]

It would be easy to chalk this up to inexperience. Lincoln was new to Congress and uncertain how best to mount an effective Whig response to Polk's war. He had little sense of his own support and even less appreciation of the resources of the executive. He was also not fully seasoned as a lawyer; he lacked a full grasp of when to use and when not to use legalistic devices. Nor had he fully developed his own political speaking style. His major speeches before 1848—the Young Men's Lyceum speech in 1838 and the Temperance Address in 1842—are windy pronouncements with little nuance, subtlety, or eloquence. Not quite forty in 1848, Lincoln seems young in every respect. He was a freshman congressman, a young lawyer, and a developing statesman.

Lincoln's opposition to the war was principled and determined; such were the concerns of Congressman Lincoln. As he said in another context, just two weeks after the resolutions were introduced and one week before a major anti-Polk speech he gave on January 12, 1848, "If we once yield to a wrong principle, that concession will be the prolific source of endless mischief." The interrogatories were an attempt to discredit President Polk and to prove to the world the aggressive intents of the United States against Mexico from the beginning. When his law partner disagreed with his position, Lincoln reacted angrily: "I regret this," Lincoln commented to Herndon, "not because of any fear we shall remain disagreed, after you shall have read this letter, but because, if *you* misunderstand, I fear other friends will also." Lincoln proclaimed to Herndon he would "stake his life" on the claim that if Herndon had been in his place he would have voted the same way. The vote on the floor had directly questioned the justice of the war. As a congressman Lincoln could hardly run from his responsibility to cast his vote. And surely he had to vote his conscience, "to tell the *truth* or tell a *lie*. I can not doubt which you would do."[3]

Lincoln's next letter to Herndon was a detailed response to a letter from Herndon (since lost) opposing Lincoln's position on the war in general political and constitutional terms. From Lincoln's response, it seems Herndon argued that the constitutional provision empowering the President to repel invasion justified Polk's unilateral action against Mexico. Lincoln got to the heart of the matter, pointing out that such a position went beyond even what the President or his supporters argued. "Their only positions," Lincoln continued, "are first, that the soil was *ours* where hostilities commenced, and second, that whether it was rightfully *ours* or not, *Congress had annexed it,* and the President, for that reason was bound to defend it." Both these positions, Lincoln felt, were manifestly wrong. The danger lay in the principle and the precedent: "Allow the President to invade a neighboring nation, whenever *he* shall deem it necessary to repel an invasion and you allow him to do so, *whenever he may choose to say* he deems it necessary for such purpose—and you allow him to make war at pleasure." And that was exactly what the framers of the Constitution sought to avoid. Kings had always made wars and impoverished their people; our Constitution was deliberately designed to preclude such action. Herndon's view, Lincoln concluded in his letter, would place our Presidents where kings have always stood.[4]

Lincoln's response to his law partner is a masterpiece of argument. It is subtle, clear, closely reasoned. As was his custom, Lincoln returned intelligently to the words and intent of the founders to clarify an important political issue in the present. But why did he bother to go through it all with Herndon? Perhaps Lincoln thirsted for reelection, and this letter was an attempt to enlist Herndon's considerable energies toward that goal and to stave off local opposition to his antiwar position. If this were true, the letter was clearly meant for public consumption. There are, however, several problems with this view. Lincoln never dealt with Herndon indirectly on anything; if he had *really* been writing the Whig establishment in the letter to Herndon and hoped his partner would know to circulate it, he would have said so. It is also not clear that Herndon was much of a political asset. He had a certain recognition, even clout, among young Whigs in the district, but he was hardly in a position of leadership to bring around someone like Stephen T. Logan to see the validity of Lincoln's position on the war. It is not even clear, for that matter, that local Whigs other than Herndon objected to Lincoln's antiwar position.[5] Furthermore, Lincoln was extremely sensitive to a complicated agreement he had affirmed before his election that rotated the Whig nomination among several contenders. Thus, unless the situation changed, he was committed to withdraw after one term. He was frankly ambivalent about the arrangement and essentially told Herndon that he would respond positively to a draft. ("I could not refuse the people the right of sending me again," he put it delicately.) But he was in no position to politick for renomination. His "word and honor" forbade such maneuvering.[6]

The only reasonable explanation for Lincoln's eloquent plea to Herndon is that Herndon was the only person listening. Lincoln's ambitions, indeed, his grandiosity, lay thinly disguised below the surface. His purpose in the interrogatories was to gloriously unmask Polk and force an acknowledgment of wrongdoing (whether Lincoln believed the damage by then could have been undone is another question). "Let him [Polk] answer [the interrogatories]," Lincoln thundered from the House floor, "fully, fairly, candidly. Let him answer with *facts,* and not with arguments. Let him remember he sits where Washington sat, and so remembering, let him answer, as Washington would answer. As a nation *should not,* and the Almighty *will* not, be evaded, so let him attempt no evasion—no equivocation."[7] The same evil genius, the dictator of the Lyceum speech a decade earlier, blended with the figure of Polk, only now the danger was real and present rather than potential. Polk had acted like a king, capriciously and independently, and deliberately dragged the country into war. The dictator so dreaded at the Lyceum seemed to have appeared. To disarm him was to slay him, to play a David to Polk's Goliath.

But Lincoln suffered the worst indignity of all: No one seemed to hear or care. The interrogatories themselves suffered the fate of inattention. Polk blandly ignored them and left it to prowar Democrats in the House to reply condescendingly to Lincoln's charges. Not one Whig rose to his support. Lincoln was isolated and alone with his righteous pretensions. He suffered in silence, though there are hints of a depression in his letter to Mary on April 16, 1848, which begins "In this troublesome world, we are never quite satisfied" and goes on to lament how much he hated to stay in his old room by himself directing documents. Lincoln had unleashed his wish for power, recognition, dominance, and fame. The forum had been the political arena, a public setting, where he had made an inauspicious showing. The resulting inattention Lincoln experienced was a blow of the first order. He responded in pained depression, quietly withdrawing from the fray. He only expressed his feelings to Mary, though to her the idiom was personal and private rather than public and political. The public and private were as yet separate, unintegrated.[8]

★★★

Lincoln's second major initiative as congressman was to attempt abolition of slavery in Washington. All sensitive observers, including some southerners, agreed that it was unseemly to allow slaves to be publicly traded in the nation's capital. There is no indication that Lincoln reacted in horror to the sight; indeed, there is no indication at all of his feelings on the matter. The bill he proposed to introduce on January 10, 1849, therefore, came as something of a surprise.

Lincoln's attitudes toward slavery and race before 1848 are quite murky and certainly lack the clarity given them by most later observers. It plays unjustly with the sources, for example, to quote from Lincoln's 1855 letter to Joshua Speed as evidence of Lincoln's early views on slavery and race. In that letter, Lincoln described strong feelings about slavery from as early as 1841. "You may remember," he told Speed, "as I well do, that from Louisville to the mouth of the Ohio there were, on board, ten or a dozen slaves, shackled together with irons. That sight was a continual torment to me." Lincoln's contemporary description of the same scene (interestingly enough, in a letter of August 1841, to Speed's sister, Mary) struck quite a different note. Lincoln introduced his description with a general, almost philosophical comment on what he had seen: "By the way," he wrote parenthetically in a paragraph that began with chatter about the "vexatious delays" in his trip, "a fine example was presented on board the boat for contemplating the effect of *condition* upon human happiness." A Kentucky gentleman had bought twelve slaves and was taking them by boat to his farm further south. Lincoln described in some detail the manner of their captivity:

> They were chained six and six together. A small iron clevis was around the left wrist of each, and this fastened to the main chain by a shorter one at a convenient distance from, the others; so that the negroes were strung together precisely like so many fish upon a trot-line.

This animal imagery, which occurred throughout Lincoln's thinking about blacks later, seemed to suppress the agonizing human experience of the slaves he saw. To compare the slaves with fish on a trotline was to see them as objects.⁹

But even as he distanced himself, Lincoln's empathy provided an insight: "In this condition they were being separated forever from the scenes of their childhood, their friends, their fathers and mothers, and brothers and sisters, and many of them, from their wives and children, and going into perpetual slavery where the lash of the master is proverbially more ruthless and unrelenting than any other where." It is significant that Lincoln was writing to the daughter of a slaveholding family. He may have expressed his real feeling of sorrow for these slaves being taken from their families more gently than he might have in another context. He also built in an implied contrast that was undoubtedly understood by Mary Speed—between the family togetherness of slaves in Kentucky, the scenes of their childhood, their fathers and mothers, brothers and sisters, and the cruelty of what they would encounter on the "farm in the south." Lincoln thus remained sensitive to Mary's feelings in describing a scene he found distressing, balancing his feelings for the slaves in tow against hers. Yet the conclusion of his description, which was really the point of the story, was that, despite the unhappy circumstances the slaves faced, "they were the most cheerful and apparently happy creatures on board. One, whose offense for which he had been sold was an over-fondness for his wife, played the fiddle almost continually; and the others danced, sung, cracked jokes, and played various games with cards from day to day. How true it is that 'God tempers the wind to the shorn lamb,' or in other words, that He renders the worst of human conditions tolerable, while He permits the best, to be nothing better than tolerable."¹⁰

A large measure of self-reference seemed to shape Lincoln's reaction to this scene. In September 1841, the month after he wrote to Mary Speed and the same year his engagement to Mary

Todd had been broken, he was in the midst of his most severe and extended depression. In fact, his visit to the Speeds in Kentucky was an artifact of that depression, an effort to restore his spirits and renew his close friendship with Joshua. Mary Speed knew well of Lincoln's "blues," which he discussed toward the end of this very letter. In some way, his description of the boat scene is a parable for himself. As the slaves display only happiness in great misery, so Lincoln, living in relatively happy conditions, feels only the agony of depression. This personal meaning of the passage in the letter seems entirely accessible to Lincoln, though one cannot be certain, for he failed to make the connection explicit. But whether or not it was conscious, Lincoln seemed unable to go beyond his own misery in reacting to the boat scene; he failed to distinguish his sense of dejection over his conflicted relationship with a woman who still loved him (Mary Todd) from the depths of sadness those slaves on the chain had reached. All human misery was only a mirror of his own unhappiness, and feigned gaiety (or suppressed misery) a behavior lesson for him to learn. That a part of himself knew better is apparent from his subsequent reconstruction of the scene in his 1855 letter to Joshua. By then there was no facile lesson to be learned, no Scripture quoted, just real feeling that sprang from empathy with people in a different and terrible situation: "That sight was a continual torment to me." Thus it seems Lincoln's memory of the scene changed over the years. If he felt torment for the slaves in 1841, it was a very personalized, largely unempathic, kind of misery. It is far more likely that he simply remembered the scene differently as his personal feelings and political convictions changed.

The only other direct source we have for Lincoln's views on slavery before 1848 provides a fascinating link with his aborted action on the slavery question in Washington as a United States congressman.[11] In 1837 the Illinois House, responding to resolutions on slavery passed by several southern legislatures, strongly condemned abolitionism, reaffirmed the constitutionally protected right to own slaves in slave states, and asserted that slavery could not be abolished in Washington without consent (and, presumably, compensation). Lincoln and Daniel Stone, another Illinois congressman from Springfield and a fellow Whig, objected to several particulars of the resolution and on March 3 entered their own protest in the Illinois House. Lincoln and Stone affirmed the resolutions in substance and objected only to a wording that made no moral judgment on slavery itself. The original resolution read: "That we highly disapprove of the formation of abolition societies, and of the doctrines promulgated by them." The Lincoln-Stone protest read: "They [that is, Lincoln and Stone] believe that the institution of slavery is founded on both injustice and bad policy; but that the promulgation of abolition doctrines tends rather to increase rather than to abate its evils."[12] This position was typically Lincolnesque: clear, even courageous, in statement of essential moral purpose but moderate in dealing with political realities. The Illinois winds obviously blew kindly over the slave states. Lincoln dissented, but gently. He went on record against both slavery and abolition, branding one morally evil and the other politically immoderate, which for Lincoln was another form of evil.

The Illinois House resolution and the Lincoln-Stone protest were to form the statement on slavery in Washington. Both affirmed the constitutional right of southerners to own slaves, but both also indicated that slavery might legitimately be abolished in Washington with the consent of its citizens. This 1837 position thus defined an agenda for Lincoln: Leave slavery alone where it existed; oppose abolitionism; demonstrate moral fiber by working politically to end slavery in Washington. This agenda gave Lincoln the kind of principled but delicate middle position he so enjoyed occupying.

After 1837 Lincoln appeared to drop the issue of slavery for more than ten years. He took no further political action on it in the Illinois House, where he served two more terms as Whig leader before retiring. He dealt, of course, with some legal matters that touched slavery, but it seems that before 1848 he seldom reflected on the issue of slavery itself (other than in his 1841 letter to Mary Speed). There are two exceptions worth noting. First, in his address to the Springfield Washington Temperance Society on February 22, 1842, Lincoln referred in passing to that happy day when "drunken bondage" will be broken, "a viler slavery, manumitted," and how proud the land will be "when there shall be neither a slave nor a drunkard on the earth." Second, in a letter to Williamson Durley on October 3, 1845, Lincoln went to some length to spell out his political principles. These included a recognition of how divisive slavery was for party unity; how abolitionists had been "wonderful" (Lincoln says sarcastically) in their opposition to Clay in 1845, which helped bring about the annexation of Texas; and how evil slavery was and yet how important it was to protect it in the South. He concluded with the hope that slavery would die out.[13]

The issue of slavery became a central concern of the Thirtieth Congress. The land acquired from Mexico in 1848 raised the constitutionally thorny issue of whether slavery could be extended into new areas. Opponents, including Lincoln, tried numerous times to pass the Wilmot Proviso, an amendment first offered in 1846 that would have prevented the expansion of slavery into any areas acquired from Mexico. Proponents of extension used increasingly intemperate language to defend the right to extend their peculiar institution. Furthermore, the spectacle of the slave trade in the heart of Washington probably did offend Lincoln. Whatever inclinations he felt toward abolition were undoubtedly encouraged by Joshua Giddings, another junior congressman who stayed at the same boarding house where Lincoln lived while in

Washington, Mrs. Sprigg's. It is important, however, not to put too much emphasis on the impact of abolitionists on Lincoln. He had always condemned them as extremists and felt decidedly uneasy when his own antiwar stand put him on their side.[14]

Lincoln's agenda in 1848 drew essentially on his formulation of slavery reform in 1837. He moved slowly but seldom forgot the past. He apparently drafted his measure sometime in the fall of 1848 with the support of others such as Joshua Giddings. He referred on the House floor to fifteen leading citizens who supported his measure, though when challenged for their names he chose not to produce them. The claim suggests Lincoln went to some trouble to line up support for his bill. It was also perhaps true that his support was more fragile than he realized. The measure went absolutely nowhere. Lincoln first read the bill to the House on January 10, 1849, as a "proposition" which he intended to submit. Three days later he gave further notice of his intention to introduce the bill, but afterward he never brought it up. The reason Lincoln gave later for quietly dropping the matter was that he lost the support of his former backers.[15]

Lincoln's original title of the bill was "an act to abolish slavery in the District of Columbia by consent of the free white people of said District, and with compensation to owners."[16] Lincoln proposed that no person then living in the District of Columbia nor anyone born there after January 10, 1849, should ever be held in slavery. But there were several qualifications: Children born to former slave mothers after January 1, 1850, would be "reasonably supported and educated" by their mothers' previous owners, to whom the children would owe "reasonable" service. He left open the age at which this debt would end. Lincoln's plan also called for government compensation to owners of slaves, but left it to the white owners to decide whether they wanted to enter such an agreement. If not, they could keep the slaves they then possessed.

It is difficult to imagine a more gradual emancipation plan. It made it optional for whites to participate and kept slave children in essential bondage until their maturity. Lincoln clearly thought in very long terms when he spoke of "gradual emancipation." Furthermore, the bill "empowered and required" authorities in Washington to return fugitive slaves. It was that clause which probably cost Lincoln his abolitionist support. Lincoln's aborted effort to introduce the bill reflected, of course, the devastating effects of the polarization on the issue of slavery that set in after 1848. Yet, oddly, he failed to read the political situation accurately, clinging instead to an agenda for action from his political youth in Illinois that proved irrelevant on a national level after the Mexican War.

★★★

Lincoln's political ideas took shape slowly in the late 1830s and the 1840s. From the beginning, he was a principled moderate. "There are few things *wholly* evil," he said in 1848, "or *wholly* good. Almost every thing, and especially governmental policy, is an inseparable compound of the two; so that our best judgment of the preponderance between them is continually demanded." Moderation meant tolerance, and nowhere was that more important in a revivalist age than in matters of religion. In the 1846 campaign for Congress, Lincoln was charged with openly scoffing at religion (his opponent, Peter Cartwright, was a minister). In response Lincoln issued a handbill to the voters in his district to clarify his position. He noted that he believed in God but was not a member of any church. His sense of religious fidelity was strikingly practical and rested on the convergence of his personal feelings with those of the community. He made it clear that he himself could not support a candidate who openly scoffed at religion. "Leaving the higher matter of eternal consequences, between him and his Maker," Lincoln said, "I still do not think any man has the right thus to insult the feelings, and injure the morals, of the community in which he may live."[17]

Lincoln's early sense of community bridged the gap between neighborhood and nation. Nothing done at the federal level, he thought, could be without some advantage to local communities. The navy, for example, which was founded and supported to defend the nation in time of war, also protects the merchant marine. For anyone in the twenty-first century this point is easy to recognize. But Lincoln argued just as strenuously that nothing is so "*local* as to not be of some *general* benefit." For example, the Illinois-Michigan canal considerably lowered the price of sugar from New Orleans for citizens of New York. This view went to the heart of the debate over "internal improvements" and the economic development of the nation that required federal initiative (and, usually, federal money), and implied a sense of national identity. It also expressed a sense of economic optimism, a faith that economic growth and development bring with them moral improvement.[18]

In those early years Lincoln's political style also emerged, one firmly grounded in attention to details. Politics among central Illinois Whigs in the 1840s were complicated by an agreement at Pekin in 1844 to rotate the party's congressional nomination. However, no two politicians seemed to have quite the same understanding of what was actually agreed to; and, besides, ambitions tended to cloud vision.[19] As Lincoln prepared for the 1846 congressional election, he watched closely how Whigs in his district were thinking about the Pekin agreement—and about him. It would seem he read an astounding number of local papers. "The Pekin paper," he wrote a friend who was presumably in a position to affect the Beardstown paper's editorial stand, "has lately nominated or suggested Hardin's name for Governor, and the Alton paper, noticing that, indirectly nominates him for Congress. I wish you would, if you can, see that, while these things are bandied about among the papers, the Beardstown paper takes no stand that may injure my chance, unless the conductor really prefers Genl. Hardin, in which case, I suppose it would be fair." Lincoln reaped great advantage from his close reading of the papers. He told Hardin (his opponent for the nomination) that it was unfair for him to think harshly of Lincoln because a paper friendly to Lincoln recommended Hardin for the governorship (thus proposing to remove Hardin as Lincoln's congressional opponent). Lincoln pointed out how little control one has in these matters, for "*what,* or *how,* ought I to think of you because of your paper at Jacksonville doing the same thing for *me* twice?"[20]

Lincoln watched everything closely. "I would rejoice to be spared the labour of a contest," he wrote a friend in 1846, "but 'being in' I shall go it thoroughly, and to the bottom." He then recorded a county-by-county analysis of his support that reflected a great deal of careful head-counting. This letter was part of an active campaign to garner support. His letters around this time were often marked confidential and suggest that many more such letters were written than have survived. There is throughout all this correspondence a healthy assertiveness, a fiercely competitive spirit, but one well within bounds. He defined a goal and then set to work aggressively to attain it. He felt wronged by Hardin's refusal to abide by the Pekin agreement but, rather than stew about it, he decided simply to take on the challenge and win. He succeeded.[21]

At the national level things were rather more complicated. It was impossible for Lincoln to control events in Congress as he could in central Illinois. He was only a freshman congressman and his party was weak, divided, leaderless. Henry Clay claimed few followers; he was old and discredited, generally regarded as something of a relic from the past. Lincoln seems never to have considered supporting Clay for the 1848 nomination. "Our only chance is with Taylor," he wrote in 1848. "I go for him, not because I think he would make a better president than Clay, but because I think he would make a better one than Polk, or Cass, or Buchanan, or any such creatures, one of whom is sure to be elected, if he is not." And, again, "Mr. Clay's chance for an election, is just no chance at all." Lincoln indeed was "decidedly" on Taylor's side and worked hard (and with some success) to bring Illinois around for the Mexican War hero.[22]

There were many things to consider in 1848. Once in Washington Lincoln probably realized quickly how weak Clay's base of support really was. In the aftermath of a war it was also desirable for the Whigs to have a military hero as standard-bearer. Furthermore, Taylor appeared to hold political views Lincoln could support. Lincoln could see enough flexibility in Taylor to allow for the implementation of Whig policies; he realized, however, that he could not be too sure. In a pro-Taylor speech given in Congress on July 27, 1849, Lincoln avoided defending Taylor and instead spent most of his time ridiculing the Democratic candidate, another general, Lewis Cass. Lincoln argued that Taylor at least had said he would support whatever proposal came to him from the people via their representatives in Congress. Taylor was willing to trust the people. Besides, "on the prominent questions of Currency, Tariff, internal improvements, and Wilmot Provision, Gen. Taylor's course is at least as well defined as is Gen. Cass'."[23]

Lincoln campaigned hard for Taylor and spent a good deal of time stumping Massachusetts, where he made a good impression. He argued strenuously that the central issue of the campaign was the extension of slavery. On this issue Taylor himself was perhaps vague, but the Whigs were clearly opposed to it; Cass and the Democrats supported extension. Thus both candidates in some ways lacked luster, but one leaned toward evil, the other toward essential Whig positions. Furthermore, it would be disastrous for Conscience Whigs and abolitionists to support Van Buren's third-party candidacy in the Free Soil Party: That would only draw off support from Taylor and insure the election of Cass. In the end Taylor won the election, including Massachusetts. Illinois, however, went for Cass, though Lincoln's district stayed with Taylor.[24]

Lincoln's stance against Clay and for Taylor reflected the sober realities of politics. Nevertheless, Lincoln's easy abandonment of Clay in 1848 represented a decided shift in his political loyalties. It seemed then—and later—that no one in antebellum America was a more devoted follower of Henry Clay's ideas than Abraham Lincoln. As George Fredrickson has noted, Lincoln "quoted Clay, paraphrased him, and at times virtually plagiarized from him, not merely for the practical political purpose of winning recalcitrant Whigs to the Republican cause but because he indeed thought of himself as taking up where Clay had left off."[25] Fredrickson was referring to Lincoln's statements during the 1850s, but Lincoln's fondness for Clay dated from the beginning of his career. He admired Clay's commitment to a national concept that transcended parochial, particularly southern, concerns. He held up as a model Clay's compromising moderation in the political process. And most of all he felt Clay's admittedly ambiguous position on slavery was the only reasonable stance to assume. It seemed that Clay epitomized all the virtues Lincoln so greatly valued: honesty, dignity, wisdom, vision, and a fierce devotion to the process of law in a fledgling republic. Clay defined the spirit and letter of compromise that Lincoln felt were essential to the preservation of the Union.

Lincoln's anti-Clay stance in 1848 seemed to make political sense. Yet his position took its psychological toll and left him with a sense of regret for precipitously abandoning his ideological idol. Clay died on June 29, 1852. One week later Lincoln delivered a moving eulogy to Clay in the Hall of Representatives of the Illinois state capitol. It is one of only four eulogies Lincoln ever delivered and certainly the only one with real emotion. The speech, which extended to some fifty-five hundred words, extolled Clay's "mighty mind," his "gallant heart," the "mighty sweep of that graceful arm," and the "magic of that eloquent tongue." In the speech Lincoln detailed the positions Clay took on crucial issues, particularly slavery. As Lincoln pointed out, Clay, an owner of slaves, detested the institution of slavery. It was this kind of ambiguity that Lincoln believed democracy had to tolerate. "Cast into life where slavery was already widely spread and deeply seated, [Clay] did not perceive, as I think no wise man has perceived, how it [slavery] could be at *once* eradicated, without producing a greater evil, even to the cause of human liberty itself." Lincoln concluded his speech with particularly effusive praise for the central place of Clay in our history. "But Henry Clay is dead. His long and eventful life is closed. Our country is prosperous and powerful; but could it have been quite all it has been, and is, and is to be, without Henry Clay? Such a man the times have demanded, and such, in the providence of God was given us. But he is gone. Let us strive to deserve, as far as mortals may, the continued care of Divine Providence, trusting that, in future national emergencies, He will not fail to provide us the instrument of safety and security."[26]

This fascinating document operates at several psychological levels. Most obviously, the speech placed Clay among the august political figures whom Lincoln invested with the full force of his idealizing needs, making Clay one of the glorious fathers who supplanted his own inadequate father. It is thus striking how close in time the eulogy was to the death of Thomas just six months earlier, in January 1851. Thomas was ignored while Lincoln heaped the greatest glory onto Clay. At the same time, Lincoln seemed to identify with Clay: "Mr. Clay's lack of a more perfect early education, however it may be regretted generally, teaches at least one profitable lesson; it teaches that in this country, one can scarcely be so poor, but that, if he *will,* he *can* acquire sufficient education to get through the world respectably."[27]

But the most interesting aspect of Lincoln's attitude toward Clay was that the eulogy seemed a kind of personal atonement for having opposed Clay politically for the Whig presidential nomination. Even in 1848 there were hints that Lincoln felt guilty for his abandonment of Clay. Certainly, Democrats charged Whigs with callous hypocrisy in their refusal to nominate Clay for the presidency. In his pro-Taylor speech of July 27, 1849, Lincoln noted that a "gentleman from Georgia" (Mr. Iverson) had accused the Whigs of deserting of all their principles and of having turned Henry Clay out "like an old horse to root." Lincoln seemed to take the charge personally. "This is terribly severe," he said. "It can not be answered by argument; at least I can not so answer it." Lincoln could only defensively turn the charge back on the Democrats. "I merely wish to ask the gentleman if the Whigs are the only party he can think of, who some times turn old horses out to root. Is not a certain Martin Van Buren, an old horse which your own party have turned out to root? and is he not rooting a little to your discomfort about now?"[28]

Ironically, Lincoln's support of Taylor turned out to be not even politically shrewd. When the election was over, Lincoln hoped for some reward. But as with everything else for Congressman Lincoln, there were unforeseen problems. The job he wanted was that of Commissioner of the General Land Office, a cabinet-level post. "In these days of Cabinet making," he wrote William Schouler on February 2, 1849, "we out West are awake as well as others. . . . the West is not only entitled to but is in need of, one member of the cabinet." Indeed, Lincoln was awake and under tremendous pressure from politicians back home about the job he himself coveted. He told David Davis on February 2 he had received three hundred letters about the Land Office Commissioner's job and that he felt he could get it for himself, but if he did he would have every man in the state snarling at him about it. On February 20 Lincoln used the same metaphor in a letter to Speed: "there is nothing about me which would authorize me to think of a first class office; and a second class one would not compensate me for being snarled at by others who want it for themselves. I believe that, so far as the Whigs in Congress, are concerned, I could have the Genl. Land office almost by common consent; but then Sweet, and Don: Morrison, and Browning, and Cyrus Edwards all want it. And what is worse, while I think I could easily take it myself, I fear I shall have trouble to get it for any other man in Illinois." At some point in late February it appears he decided to recommend Cyrus Edwards for the job. The other important Illinois Whig, Edward D. Baker, who had resigned his seat in Congress in 1846 to fight in the Mexican War and who had become something of a hero, recommended James L. D. Morrison for the post. The stage was set for some classic political jockeying.[29]

Lincoln and Baker each had his own candidate for the land office appointment but were themselves old friends (Lincoln's second son, Eddie, was named after Edward Baker). It seemed likely they could get together behind either Edwards or Morrison and secure the cabinet post for Illinois. Lincoln, however, was ambivalent about Edwards because he wanted the job himself— and felt he could have gotten it but for the clamor back home. Then, in late March, a genuine and apparently spontaneously organized group led by William B. Warren began to push Lincoln for the job. Lincoln was now treading on thin ice. He responded to the group that he could accept their nomination for the land office if that turned out to be the only way to keep it in Illinois.

In the meanwhile, he told them, he was bound to his commitment to recommend Cyrus Edwards and, that failing, to support Morrison (and conversely, he indicated, if the Morrison candidacy failed, Baker had agreed to support Edwards). "In relation to these pledges," Lincoln told Warren and the others, "I must not only be chaste but above suspicion." But Lincoln then hinted at the real issue, which was that by April he deeply regretted his coyness in February. For it turned out Baker had been eager all along to recommend Lincoln for the post and had turned to Morrison as a second choice. "Baker has at all times been ready to recommend me," Lincoln said, "if I would consent." Lincoln had played the reluctant bride and lost his chance. Now he was trying, ever so delicately, to get it back.[30]

The letter to the Warren group kept his own chances alive in Illinois. Lincoln then quickly turned his attention to the Taylor administration. He wrote the newly appointed Secretary of the Navy, William B. Preston, on April 10, stressing the need for the new administration to pay closer attention to its friends. He agreed with Taylor's refusal to turn out all public officials in true Jacksonian style just because the Whigs had won the election, but he urged strongly that the administration be careful to fill any vacancy that occurred naturally with a Whig. The support of his Whig friends for openings in his district was a task Lincoln was working on as he struggled for his own job. He had written numerous letters of recommendation in early April regarding various positions in Illinois and seemed to be following the situation closely. As of April 25, all of Lincoln's recommendations were in trouble. His influence in Washington seemed to be "broken down generally." Furthermore, an immensely complicated struggle had arisen between two men Lincoln had recommended for one minor office; somehow Lincoln himself was blamed for double-dealing, which made him feel stabbed in the back.[31]

The real worry, however, was further trouble in the land office position. For now Justin Butterfield of Chicago had suddenly become the front-runner. Lincoln was astounded. On April 25, he wrote a hurt letter to Josiah Lucas, a clerk in the land office in Washington. He noted that Butterfield was a personal friend and perfectly qualified for the job, "but of the quite one hundred Illinoisians, equally well qualified, I do not know one with less claims to it." Butterfield had worked strenuously for Clay and against Taylor; and Butterfield's sponsor, Lisle Smith, was also a Clay man who, despite Lincoln's "most earnest entreaties," had filled vacancies from Lincoln's district with Clay supporters at the Whig nominating convention in Philadelphia. "It will now mortify me deeply," Lincoln concluded self-righteously, "if Gen. Taylor's administration shall trample all my wishes in the dust merely to gratify these men."[32]

Lincoln had abandoned Clay for Taylor; now, oddly, those who had stayed with the Great Compromisor were triumphing over him for position in the government. Lincoln tried desperately during the next few weeks to save the situation. He complained to other cabinet members. He tried to reach those who might have Taylor's ear. He shot off letters to anyone, in fact, whom he thought could head off the Butterfield appointment. He even, finally, wrote President Taylor himself. It was all to no avail. The final irony was that his thirst for the office had become apparent to Cyrus Edwards, who now blamed Lincoln for never really advancing his name for the office. Edwards was so angry that he threw his weight behind Butterfield. Lincoln, hurt and confused, claimed that Edwards was wronging him very much. In the end, the Taylor administration offered Lincoln a consolation prize, the secretaryship of the Oregon Territory. He refused. The offer was then expanded to the position of governor. He again refused. He feared the isolation, it seems, and by then his pride was too wounded to take second-best. Besides, Mary objected to the Oregon job.[33]

Lincoln's three initiatives as congressman had all failed. He had never achieved adequate recognition either at home or in Washington for his antiwar position. He had erred in judgment on the slavery bill. And his political work against Clay and for Taylor brought shame without reward. Each of these failed initiatives haunted Lincoln. Stephen Douglas thundered out in the 1858 debates: "Whilst in Congress, he [Lincoln] distinguished himself by his opposition to the Mexican war, taking the side of the common enemy against his own country ([audience:] 'that's true') and when he returned home he found that the indignation of the people followed him everywhere, and he was again submerged or obliged to retire into private life, forgotten by his former friends. ('And will be again')." Lincoln's congressional stance on slavery later blended into his position after 1854, but the beginning of the charge against him as an abolitionist dated from 1848–49. And, finally, a feeling lingered that Lincoln had stabbed Clay in the back in 1848.[34]

In fact, Lincoln had not really failed in Congress. The scholarly consensus is that he performed reasonably well for a freshman congressman.[35] But his own sense was one of failure. He was profoundly depressed at his inability to perform up to the level of expectation of his grandiose ambitions. Unless one appreciates how much Lincoln expected of himself, his depression seems odd and misplaced. But it is in these terms—general and psychological rather than narrowly political—that Lincoln's statements to Herndon about committing political suicide in Washington make sense (and since these statements fall into the category in which Herndon is most reliable, they should be believed).[36] Lincoln's expansive ambitions had soared beyond his grasp. The perhaps inevitable frustration that resulted left Lincoln feeling empty and depleted.

His depression and studied withdrawal from politics after 1849 are not surprising.

In those private years between 1842 and 1854, Lincoln's one important foray into politics and the public world beyond the self was his term in Congress. His sense of failure in that effort must be measured against his absorption in the private concerns of his relationship with Mary, raising a family, building his career as a lawyer. It was a decade-long period of consolidation with sights focused intently inward. It seems he tried fleetingly to find a public self too soon. The public issues at that point were only marginally his own. There was no convergence, no merging, of public and private issues in 1848, only disjunction.

★★★

Ten years later, on June 16, 1858, the assembled members of the state Republican convention nominated Lincoln as their candidate for the United States Senate. Speaking in the sultry heat of the Illinois legislative chamber, Lincoln accepted the nomination and outlined his sense of current issues and future agendas.

The speech began with a rhetorical flourish—constituting some seven percent of its total—that has immortalized the speech in our political history:

> If we could first know *where* we are, and *whither* we are tending, we could then better judge *what* to do, and *how* to do it.
>
> We are now far into the *fifth* year, since a policy was initiated, with the *avowed* object, and *confident* promise, of putting an end to slavery agitation.
>
> Under the operation of that policy, that agitation has not only, *not ceased,* but has *constantly augmented.*
>
> In *my* opinion, it *will* not cease, until a *crisis* shall have been reached, and passed.
>
> "A house divided against itself cannot stand."

I believe this government cannot endure, permanently half *slave* and half *free*.

I do not expect the Union to be *dissolved*—I do not expect the house to *fall*—but I *do* expect it will cease to be divided.

It will become *all* one thing, or *all* the other.

Either the *opponents* of slavery, will arrest the further spread of it, and place it where the public mind shall rest in the belief that it is in course of ultimate extinction; or its *advocates* will push it forward, till it shall become alike lawful in *all* the States, *old* as well as *new*—*North* as well as *South*.[37]

The phraseology immediately captured people's imagination. The local Republican paper loudly voiced its approval, while Stephen Douglas (Lincoln's opponent in the senatorial race), other Democrats, and their local Springfield organ bemoaned Lincoln's radical message that seemed to call for war; at least, that was how they chose to interpret the speech. Because of Lincoln's increasing national prominence and the stature of his opponent in this election, the "house divided" speech received extensive coverage. From New York and Massachusetts to Illinois and the western territories, the evocative idea of a house divided against itself as a metaphor for the divisive ills of the nation struck a responsive political and religious chord.

In William Herndon's analysis, the apparently incendiary flavor of Lincoln's rhetoric in this speech later fused with the myth of the martyr. Herndon reports that Lincoln read him the speech a few days before delivery. Herndon was aghast at the tone of the opening salvo and wondered whether it would be politic to take such a radical stance. "I want to use some universally known figure [of speech]," Lincoln supposedly replied, "expressed in simple language as universally well-known, that may strike home to the minds of men in order to raise them up to the peril of the times. I do not believe I would be right in changing or omitting it, I would rather be defeated with this expression in the speech, and uphold and discuss it before the people, than be victorious without it." If his exaggerated and quite un-Lincolnesque response to Herndon seems distorted—the historian Don Fehrenbacher has noted that Herndon describes Lincoln here "as a man wrapped in passion like a Hebrew prophet"— there is no reason to doubt that Herndon did, in fact, raise objections to the rhetoric but that Lincoln stuck to his bold phrasing despite his partner's qualms. Since Lincoln lost the 1858 election to Stephen Douglas but went on to win the presidency in 1860, it has been an enduring myth that Lincoln intended such a scenario to unfold.[38]

The question here of Lincoln's motivation is central. Anyone who studies Lincoln's political activities in 1858 will conclude that he was concentrating all of his attention on his election to the Senate. Furthermore, even if Lincoln was thinking of the presidency in 1858, no one as shrewd as Lincoln would plan to lose a Senate race in his home state as a way of securing his party's presidential nomination two years later. One good discussion of the "house divided" speech examines its immediate Springfield context by a careful reading of the two local papers: one Republican, one Democratic; one strongly for Lincoln, the other just as strongly for Douglas.[39] This approach to the speech clarifies Lincoln's response to the incredibly complicated political situation that confronted him in the winter of 1858. For Douglas had effectively captured the support of large numbers of Republicans by opposing President Buchanan and the spuriously generated Lecompton Constitution for Kansas. Douglas, it seemed to loyal Republicans, had opposed political chicanery, given teeth to his doctrine of popular sovereignty, and supported the Free Soilers who made up the backbone of the Republican ranks. Better half a loaf than none at all, argued Republicans such as the influential Horace Greeley. Popular sovereignty was perhaps not an inadequate ideological foundation for Republicanism, but it seemed in the early months of 1858 that Douglas would support Free Soilers in the North, would be a vigorous supporter of railroads and the economic development of the country in general, and would agree to key Republican demands in return for their support in his future bid for the presidency. At the very least, argued the eastern leaders of the Republican party, Douglas was useful in the Senate because of his strong opposition to President Buchanan. That kept the Democrats divided, which served Republican interests. Lincoln should not be encouraged.

Lincoln watched Republicans make accommodations to the Douglas Democrats with growing alarm. For if Lincoln believed in anything by 1858, it was that Stephen Douglas was the principal spokesman for a disastrous set of policies dealing with the issues that the country faced. The founders, in Lincoln's view, had reluctantly accepted slavery as a southern institution. They recognized its existence and even validated its perpetuation with the three-fifths compromise; such constitutional protection had justified federal laws governing the return of fugitive slaves for more than half a century. It was thus illegal and unconstitutional to mobilize a national effort to end the South's peculiar institution. Lincoln hated the realities of tracking down fugitive slaves but reluctantly accepted the practice. He told Joshua Speed in 1855: "I also acknowledge *your* rights and my obligations, under the Constitution, in regard to your slaves. I confess I hate to see the poor creatures hunted down, and caught, and carried back to their stripes, and unrewarded toils; but I bite my lip and keep quiet."[40]

Nevertheless, Lincoln believed that the Constitutional recognition of slavery in the South by no means meant that the founders approved of an institution that excluded a whole race from the

Lincoln in 1854 (the second earliest photograph). He was then emerging from political obscurity to take on the major issue of the day—slavery's extension into the territories. Courtesy of Meserve-Kunhardt Collection.

benefits of the principles outlined in the Declaration of Independence. The only way the founders had to secure passage of the Constitution was to allow slavery to exist. But just as God defines ethical perfection, Lincoln continued, so the Constitution sets a standard for legal action. "If we cannot give freedom to every creature," Lincoln argued in the summer of 1858, "let us do nothing that will impose slavery upon any other creature." Slavery, Lincoln stated again and again in the 1850s, was morally wrong, a "monstrous injustice" as he called it in 1854. "I have always hated slavery," he proclaimed in 1858, "I think as much as any Abolitionist." Furthermore, this powerfully negative judgment of slavery, he argued, lay behind most of the founders' thinking when they accepted the three-fifths compromise. It took one hundred years of agitation, Lincoln once noted, to abolish the slave trade in Great Britain. Men such as Thomas Jefferson and George Washington were tied to slavery economically but were politically and morally opposed to it. Life as they knew it in the South seemed inconceivable without slaves, but all hoped for a better day when slaves could be freed and returned to Africa, and the ideals of life, liberty, and the pursuit of happiness genuinely engaged. Lincoln of course recognized the inconsistencies in this position but accepted the muddle as all too human. His great hero was Henry Clay, who could eloquently criticize those who would blow out the moral lights around us while sipping a mint julep served by a black house slave.[41]

Thus the heart of Lincoln's opposition to slavery was moral and Constitutional. The people of the South, he said, have an "immediate and palpable and immensely great pecuniary interest" in their institution, but for those in the North "it is merely an abstract question of moral right, with only *slight,* and *remote* pecuniary interest added." However, the "abstract" issue for Lincoln was not as far removed from political reality as the term might suggest. "When the white man governs himself that is self-government; but when he governs himself, and also governs *another* man, that is *more* than self-government—that is despotism." The moral issue was abstract only in that the Declaration of Independence defined a standard of equality that did not explicitly include Negroes. The founding documents defined republican institutions and established the criteria for assessing the ethics of political action in modern society. The documents, however, were complex, varied, contradictory—and human. Thus Lincoln argued vehemently after 1854 in favor of the abolitionists to the extent that they opposed the extension of slavery while he also argued for the return of fugitive slaves. "Stand with anybody that stands RIGHT," he thundered. "Stand with him while he is right and PART with him when he goes wrong. Stand WITH the abolitionist in restoring the Missouri Compromise; and stand against him when he attempts to repeal the fugitive slave law."[42]

Lincoln also had strong economic views on the poisonous effect of slavery on white workers. "As I would not be a slave," he wrote, "so I would not be a master. This expresses my idea of democracy." In general, Lincoln was a decided economic optimist. When he wrote about inventions or technological progress, he became almost boyish in his buoyant, hopeful, assertive enthusiasm. "All creation is a mine," he began his first lecture on discoveries and inventions, "and every man a miner." Lincoln went on to stress the uniqueness of man, who may work like an animal but, unlike animals, improves on his workmanship. Lincoln's view of technology was clearly optimistic; it was also somewhat naive. He seemed to believe unquestioningly that technological progress brought moral improvement. Slavery blocked that process: Keeping the slave apart from the just rewards for his labor degraded both him and his master and perverted democratic institutions. In Lincoln's view, our form of government as defined by the Constitution required free labor, which in turn brought opportunity, progress, hope. Slavery dashed all to the ground.[43]

Yet Lincoln's view of the evil of slavery coexisted in his mind with a mournful sense of racial inequality between white and black.[44] For there is no denying that at this point in his life Lincoln was convinced that blacks were inferior and did not deserve social or political equality with whites. He made that point often, though most vociferously at Charleston in 1858: "I am not, nor ever have been in favor of bringing about in any way the social and political equality of the white and black races." Lincoln would not make voters or jurors of blacks, nor qualify them to hold office, nor allow them to intermarry with whites. He believed that physical differences between the races would always keep them from living together on equal terms and that whites would always be superior. Just because he did not want a Negro woman to be his slave did not mean he wanted her for a wife; he could just leave her alone.[45]

These are not pleasant statements. As the historian Kenneth M. Stampp has put it, Lincoln's speech at Charleston represents Lincoln's "fullest and most explicit declaration of belief in white supremacy." Charleston, however, was not an isolated event in Lincoln's struggle with the issue of racial equality. Clearly, before that audience which leaned South in sentiment, Lincoln was rather more explicit in stating his white supremacist views. It has been frequently noted that Lincoln altered his emphasis on these matters, depending on which part of the state he found himself in; indeed, during the debates Stephen Douglas charged Lincoln with inconsistency on exactly this issue. But it would be naive to ignore the essential racism that informed Lincoln's thought wherever he spoke. In Peoria in 1854 he frankly acknowledged that his own feelings would not allow him to entertain the notion of political and social equality between the races. And, he added (as a shrewd politician), "if mine would, we well know that those of the great mass of white people will not." Even in Chicago, Lincoln stressed numerous categories of inequality between white and black in the same breath that he claimed the rights of life, liberty, and the pursuit of happiness for Negroes in America—a radical statement, for it was more than they enjoyed at the time. The Declaration of Independence, Lincoln noted in Springfield in 1857, never intended to assert that all men are equal in all respects; such a notion is patently absurd in any event. The Declaration simply defined basic rights and clarified a "standard maxim for free society" that, although never attained, could be admired, striven for, and, perhaps in time, approximated.[46]

The fact that Lincoln did not propose full equality for blacks does not necessarily cast doubt on the sincerity of his insistence that they be granted minimal rights described philosophically in the Declaration and more specifically guaranteed under the Constitution, especially in the first ten amendments. When Lincoln argued that the Declaration of Independence defined a standard for free society, he was nudging his fellow citizens toward giving blacks rights that they did not then possess. In the 1850s such an assertion had abolitionist overtones, the label that would most harm Lincoln politically and the one Stephen Douglas was most eager to pin on him. Lincoln made tortuous, indeed specious, distinctions after 1854, but he no longer thought of blacks as objects. They were people, albeit, at this point in what might be called his moral development, inferior in some almost incomprehensible way. Our sensibilities tend to emphasize the prejudices that remained in the man we generally admire as a paragon of American virtue. But in the 1850s, white supremacy was taken for granted; what was remarkable was that Lincoln had the courage to brand slavery wrong, oppose its extension into the territories on moral and political grounds, and risk association with abolitionism.

No one captured these contradictions better than Frederick Douglass, an ex-slave and a major intellectual of the nineteenth century, in a speech he gave after the war. Lincoln, said Douglass, was always devoted entirely to the welfare of whites. He was willing to postpone, deny, or sacrifice the rights of blacks. He came to the presidency opposed only to the spread of slavery, not its abolition. His patriotic dreams embraced only whites. He supported the Fugitive Slave Law and would have eagerly suppressed any uprising. Whites were his natural children; blacks were his only by adoption. And yet this "great and good man," measured by the "sentiment of his country," that is, by his times, was "swift, zealous, radical, and determined."[47]

It was not easy for Lincoln to resolve his genuine and growing hatred of slavery with his white supremacist views. Furthermore, to abolish slavery was not only unconstitutional but also impractical, for what would happen to the slaves? They would become unequal members of a society in which they could never fully participate. "If all earthly power were given me," he said in 1854, "I should not know what to do, as to the existing institution. My first impulse would be to free all the slaves, and send them to Liberia—to their own native land." Lincoln saw acutely that colonization of blacks would be expensive, dangerous, and time-consuming, but he also felt it might be the only viable solution. There seemed to be only two alternatives: Free the slaves and keep them in America as "underlings" or make them fully equal. Both alternatives seemed to him impossible from a white perspective. And so he toyed for years with colonization schemes, as absurd and offensive in retrospect as they seemed sensible and humane at the time. In 1852 he eulogized Clay's efforts since 1816 to return blacks to Africa: "May it indeed be realized! . . . If as the friends of colonization hope, the present and coming generations of our countrymen shall by any means, succeed in freeing our land from the dangerous presence of slavery; and, at the same time, in restoring a captive people to their long-lost father-land, with bright prospects for the future; and this too, so gradually that neither races nor individuals shall have suffered by the change, it will indeed be a glorious consummation." Lincoln himself was an active member of Springfield's Colonization Society, to which he spoke on January 4, 1855. When he talked of the "ultimate extinction" of slavery in the house divided speech, he may have had colonization in the back of his mind.[48]

The confusions, contradictions, and specious distinctions built into Lincoln's thought about the interrelated issues of slavery and racial equality in the 1850s reflected the fact that his primary concern lay elsewhere—with the preservation of the Union. For the political issue in slavery was not abolition but extension. And on that issue Lincoln saw the country hurtling toward civil war. The Constitution was vague regarding slavery in newly acquired territories. A sensibly worked out compromise in 1820 had seemed to settle the matter forever. However, the huge acquisitions from Mexico after 1848, and renewed tensions between North and South on a variety of other fronts, fatefully reopened the whole issue of slavery's spread. After much agony and near war, a second compromise was tried in 1850. It seemed secure at first but quickly fell apart under pressure from the man most responsible for putting it together—Stephen Douglas.

Douglas was an opportunist, inordinately ambitious, and very interested in the railroads. As chairman of the Senate Committee on the Territories, he wanted to push through a bill in 1854 that would quickly organize Kansas and Nebraska. Effective state government would then make possible the construction of a transcontinental railroad. In one blow Douglas hoped to solve the most vexing political issue of the day and, of course, assume leadership of the country in return for his labors. The key, he felt, lay in allowing the states to decide for themselves whether they would be free or slave. To justify this sidestepping of the issue of slavery, Douglas invoked the concept of popular sovereignty.

For Douglas, popular sovereignty was a convenient and perfectly legitimate evasion of the moral passions that inflamed the debate over slavery. He personally did not care whether slavery was voted "up or down," the phrase he used that now defines his historical memory. Let the people decide, he said, invoking the principle of democracy. For Lincoln, however, popular sovereignty was a grossly inappropriate concept for dealing with the question of slavery in the territories. The founders, he felt, never intended to allow slavery to extend beyond its original location in the states of the South. If left alone, it would in time wither away. But slavery must not be given a new lease on life in the territories. Thus the democratic principle of local self-government in the territories had to give way to the larger concern for legitimate government and the principles of the Declaration of Independence.

Lincoln knew immediately in 1854 that the issue of slavery's extension and its threat to the Union was his issue, one he could creatively engage and wrestle to the ground. A series of speeches that fall, especially one in Peoria on October 16, 1854, following remarks by Stephen Douglas, attests to his grasp of the deepest implications of the passage of the Kansas-Nebraska Act. And yet in formulating his position he struggled several years for an appropriate metaphor; until he found it, a certain groping, even indecision and confusion, characterized his thinking.

At first he tried two oddly inappropriate metaphors. In his Peoria speech Lincoln strove to explain why the founders were so circumspect in their treatment of slavery. He noted they had to strike a compromise and so included both recognition of and protection for slavery; but they did so reluctantly. The Constitution, Lincoln pointed out, never once actually used the word "slave."

Instead, the slave is spoken of as a "person held to service or labor." Similarly, the African slave trade is described as "The migration or importation of such persons as any of the States NOW EXISTING, shall think proper to admit." And Lincoln continued: "Thus, the thing is hid away in the constitution, just as an afflicted man hides away a wen [tumor or cyst] or a cancer, which he dares not cut out at once, lest he bleed to death; with the promise, nevertheless, that the cutting may begin at the end of a given time."[49] Lincoln here captured the defacement of the body politic by slavery but failed to enlarge on cancer's striking capacity to spread. The metaphor thus lost its most expressive and vital element.

He also stumbled around in the Peoria speech with animal imagery that compared slaves with hogs. "Equal justice to the south, it is said, requires us to consent to the extending of slavery to new countries. That is to say, inasmuch as you do not object to my taking my hog to Nebraska, therefore I must not object to you taking your slave. Now, I admit this is perfectly logical, if there is no difference between hogs and negroes." In this passage Lincoln made a connection between slaves and hogs in order to then refute it. He followed the metaphor with a curious reference to "snaky" contact with detested slave dealers. Elsewhere as well in 1854, animal metaphors pervaded his thinking. "The ant," Lincoln wrote in July, "who has toiled and dragged a crumb to his nest, will furiously defend the fruit of his labor, against whatever robber assails him. So plain, that the most dumb and stupid slave that ever toiled for a master, does constantly *know* he is wronged." The economic meanings of this comparison are readily apparent. But the metaphor also suggests that the slave is a kind of lowly animal who deserves at least the few crumbs it can drag to the nest.[50]

The rhetorical difficulty Lincoln faced was to express the meaning of the spread of slavery. That was the issue. In an editorial he wrote on September 11 for the *Journal* ("his" paper in Springfield) he again turned to animal imagery when he told a little parable:

> Abraham Lincoln has a fine meadow, containing beautiful springs of water, and well fenced, which John Calhoun had agreed with Abraham (originally owning the land in common) should be his, and the agreement had been consummated in the most solemn manner, regarded by both as sacred. John Calhoun, however, in the course of time, had become owner of an extensive herd of cattle—the prairie grass had become dried up and there was no convenient water to be had. John Calhoun then looks with a longing eye on Lincoln's meadow, and goes to it and throws down the fences, and exposes it to the ravages of his starving and famishing cattle. "You rascal," says Lincoln, "what have you done? what do you do this for?" "Oh," replies Calhoun, "everything is right. I have taken down your fence; but nothing more. It is my true intent and meaning not to drive my cattle into your meadow, nor to exclude them therefrom, but to leave them perfectly free to form their own notions of the feed, and to direct their movements in their own way!"[51]

This story strives to brand southern whites as hypocritical schemers, and it conveys that message by describing slaves as dumb, ravaging cattle set loose in a green meadow: The bountiful North is invaded by rapacious blacks let loose by scheming whites.[52]

These metaphors built logically on Lincoln's earliest experience on the frontier. In many respects his idiom remained agricultural. He talked of turkeys to express his deepest childhood memories. He joked endlessly about dogs, pigs, cows, and other beasts. His letters abound in references to the wild kingdom. When he was exhausted, Herndon said, Lincoln liked to lie down on the floor and "play with a little dog or kitten to recover."[53] James Gourley, a neighbor, noted that Lincoln tended his own cow and "loved his horse well."[54] And in a sense the once mighty but then defoliated oak trees, which symbolized the founders in Lincoln's Lyceum speech of 1838, became the timbers of the house divided twenty years later. It seems Lincoln often expressed the deepest and most complex meanings in the metaphors of his rural youth. Slavery's extension, however, was not an issue he could capture in these familiar ways. It was too immediate. Lincoln's profound sense of the nation's dilemma required a different metaphor.

After 1854 he sought a "right" formulation. He found it, gradually, in architectural imagery that likened the Union to a home, a house divided. The Biblical context of the "house divided" doctrine (Matthew 12:22–28; Mark 3:22–26; Luke 1:14–20) is curious. In Matthew, Jesus has just healed "one possessed with a devil, blind, and dumb." The people are amazed, but the Pharisees suspect Satanic magic. Jesus, knowing their thoughts, says to them, "Every kingdom divided against itself is brought to desolation; and every city or house divided against itself shall not stand." If Satan casts out Satan, Jesus continues, he is then divided against himself; his kingdom cannot stand. Jesus then asks the Pharisees rhetorically, if he casts out demons by the Devil's power, by whom do their sons cast them out? Jesus concludes: "But I cast out devils by the Spirit of God, then the kingdom of God is come unto you." Jesus' emphasis is on the source for healing; he wants to prove that his power to heal comes from the spirit of God. If from Satan, it is magical, disruptive, divisive. It turns the people against God's truth. If Satan casts out Satan, as Jesus puts it, he is divided against himself and therefore without power. The power of God alone must cast out demons.

The idea of a house divided, in its initial formulation, is a metaphor expressing complex sources of motivation. Jesus' concerns went beyond simple healing; that proved nothing. What he

Lincoln in the late 1850s.
Courtesy of Meserve-Kunhardt Collection.

sought to show the priests was that if God prompted his actions, his kingdom was upon them. If Satan were at work, the kingdom of God would be hopelessly rent asunder. That, he says, would be disastrous, for it would pit Satan against Satan, evil against itself, man against man. No kingdom can endure such tension; no house divided can stand. The message is intensely subjective and psychologically astute. It also takes for granted that a house divided against itself cannot stand and uses that image to clarify the source of Jesus' healing power.

Lincoln once drew on the "house divided" metaphor early in his career. It was in a Whig campaign circular of 1843 that argued, among other things, for the convention system to be adopted. Whigs generally had been outpaced by the Democrats because of their reluctance to use conventions, relying instead on selection by the state legislators or by local county convention. Lincoln clearly felt his party needed to adopt the system of state-wide nominating conventions to compete effectively against the Democrats, and he dwelt specifically on the most recent state election of 1842 in his argument. Lincoln proclaimed,

> Wherever in the counties the whigs had held Conventions and nominated candidates for the Legislature, the aspirants, who were not nominated, were induced to rebel against the nominations, and to become candidates, as is said, "on their own hook." And go where you would into a large whig county, you were sure to find the whigs, not contending shoulder to shoulder against the common enemy, but divided into factions, and fighting furiously with one another. The election came [and] what was the result? The Governor beaten, the whig vote being decreased many thousands since 1840, although the democratic vote had not increased any.

Thus he concluded that "union is strength" and "he whose wisdom surpasses that of all philosophers, has declared that 'a house divided against itself cannot stand.'"[55]

Lincoln probably suspected that this use of Jesus' words trivialized their meaning. In any event, he did not use the metaphor again until 1858. By then it had become a familiar expression through Daniel Webster's frequent use of it. It was a recognizable phrase for Lincoln to seize upon and imbue with a new meaning. He once came close to using it in an 1855 letter to George Robertson, whose collection of speeches Lincoln was praising. The letter was grimly pessimistic. Lincoln noted that, like Robertson, he had long hoped for a peaceful end to slavery, but unfortunately, the last thirty-six years had demonstrated that "there is no peaceful extinction of slavery in prospect for us. Henry Clay had failed miserably. The spirit of peaceful extinction apparently died along with the men of the Revolution." Colonization, he hinted, was no answer, for slave masters would never willingly give up their slaves. "Our political problem now is, 'Can we, as a nation, continue together *permanently—forever*—half slave, and half free?' The problem is too mighty for me. May God, in his mercy, superintend the solution."[56]

At last in 1858 Lincoln found his metaphor. He left behind the wens, cancers, hogs, cows, and horses, and turned instead to the concept of a house divided. This was what he had sought. It blended his private self to public concerns in a uniquely creative way. It was a metaphor with personal integrity.

With malice toward none; with charity for all; with firmness in the right, as God gives us to see the right, let us strive on to finish the work we are in; to bind up the nation's wounds; to care for him who shall have borne the battle, and for his widow, and his orphan —to do all which may achieve and cherish a just, and a lasting peace, among ourselves, and with all nations.

A. Lincoln, March 4, 1865

8

THE SHAPE OF A LEADER

A great "intensity of thought," Lincoln once counseled Joshua Speed, "will some times wear the sweetest idea thread-bare and turn it to the bitterness of death." No aspect of Lincoln's character has become more tangibly real in the literature than his sad, gloomy, melancholy appearance. "No man in this agony," Harriet Beecher Stowe wrote in 1864 after a visit with Lincoln, "has suffered more and deeper, albeit with a dry, weary, patient pain, that seemed to some like insensibility." One observer wrote in a letter dated February 25, 1865, that "his face denotes an immense force of resistance and extreme melancholy. It is plain that this man has suffered deeply." Lincoln's friend Ward Hill Lamon called him a "man of sorrows" who bore "a continued sense of weariness and pain" and attracted universal sympathy "because he seemed at once miserable and kind." He was, indeed, "the saddest and gloomiest man of his time." Toward the end of the war the artist Francis B. Carpenter spent about six months in the White House working on a painting of the signing of the Emancipation Proclamation. After the war Carpenter wrote a detailed memoir of his impressions. The book became an important source for the public's sense of the man whose "furrowed face" was the ultimate in sadness. "There were days when I could scarcely look into it without crying." In May of 1864, during the Battle of the Wilderness, Carpenter once saw Lincoln pacing, "his hands behind him, great black rings under eyes." The picture seemed so full of sorrow, care, and anxiety as would have "melted the hearts of the worst of the adversaries." Every time Carpenter looked up from his canvas, he seemed to see Lincoln looking haggard, weary, or with a "peculiar dreaminess of expression."[1]

Herndon described Lincoln's appearance as equally melancholy in the years before the war, and he used the same trite phrases. Lincoln's depression was "chiseled deep" in every line of his face; he was "dripping" with melancholy. Henry C. Whitney, who rode the eighth circuit with Lincoln in the 1850s, was struck by his shifting moods, particularly "when his whole nature was immersed in Cimmerian darkness." Whitney described a remarkable scene one night on the circuit:

> One morning [at Danville while sleeping in the same bed with Lincoln] I was awakened early—before daybreak—by my companion sitting up in bed, his figure dimly visible by the ghostly firelight, and talking the wildest and most incoherent nonsense all to himself. A stranger to Lincoln would have supposed he had suddenly gone insane. Of course I knew Lincoln and his idiosyncrasies, and felt no alarm, so I listened and laughed. After he had gone on in his way for say, five minutes, while I was awake, and I know not how long *before* I was awake, he sprang out of bed hurriedly washed, and jumped into his clothes, put some wood on the fire, and then sat in front of it, moodily, dejectedly, in a most sombre and gloomy spell, till the breakfast bell rang,

when he started, as if from sleep, and went with us to breakfast. Neither Davis nor I spoke to him; we knew this trait;
it was not remarkable for Lincoln.[2]

Retrospective observations on Lincoln's melancholy inevitably
suggest the legend of his Christlike martyrdom. He was shot on
Good Friday and died on Saturday; the next day, Easter Sunday
sermons hammered the outlines of this myth into place.[3] No one
since has escaped its influence. The picture of Lincoln's melancholy
figure fits well with the concept of a Christlike leader suffering
and dying for our sins. Furthermore, in the immediate postwar
period the "chiseled" features of Lincoln seemed to draw unto
themselves all the agonies of the war, the 600,000 dead in the
long series of dramatic battles. The funeral train back to Springfield
captured this sense of Lincoln's death as somehow symbolic of
the war itself. Thousands poured out along the way—in New
York, Buffalo, Cleveland, Chicago, and many points between—
to gaze at the elaborate black hearse. Whole houses were draped,
and in Springfield, the end of the line, the entire town seemed
covered with a shroud.

Throughout his life, Lincoln complained privately of his depression. His New Salem neighbors were unanimous in recalling
his deep sadness when Ann Rutledge died in 1835, and the next
year he told Mary Owens that some mysterious things "have con-
spired and have gotten my spirits so low, that I feel that I would
rather be any place in the world than here." He asked Owens to
write back "as soon as you get this, and if possible say something
that will please me, for really I have not [been] pleased since I
left you. This letter is so dry and [stupid] that I am ashamed to send
it, but with my pres[ent feel]ings I can not do any better."[4] The
following year, in Springfield, one of Lincoln's first letters was to
Mary. "This thing of living in Springfield is rather a dull business

after all," he wrote. "I am quite as lonesome here as [I] ever was anywhere in my life." Lincoln went on to lament that no one talked to him and that he feared going to church because he would not know how to behave himself.[5] Subsequently, of course, Lincoln experienced devastating depression in January 1841; his letter to his wife in 1848 suggests feelings of emptiness and sadness; and reports by contemporaries such as Conkling clearly substantiate that Lincoln's melancholy was at the core of his personality. Twice, it seems—after the death of Ann Rutledge and the broken engagement with Mary Todd—he was even suicidal.

Depression, however, has many causes and takes many forms. In Lincoln's case it came most obviously in response to the deaths of those he loved. He deeply mourned the death of his young son, Edward, in 1850, and even more so the death of his beloved Willie in 1862. His responses to these deaths have been obscured somewhat by Mary's collapse after the deaths of her boys. But the effects on Lincoln were powerful and enduring. The death of any close friend also could cause Lincoln pain and depression. John Hay noted in his diary on October 22, 1861: "This has been a heavy day. Last night Col. [Edward] Baker was killed at Leesburg at the head of his brigade. McClellan & the Pres' talked sadly over it." The war itself soon absorbed these personal feelings into an expanding web of carnage. Harriet Beecher Stowe noted Lincoln's "heavy eyes and worn and weary air" after Fredericksburg. It is possible that he came to see his own death as imminent: He always refused to take precautions against assassination and once interpreted a dream as forecasting his own death at the beginning of a second term in office.[6]

Real loss in the present becomes exquisitely painful largely because it evokes the parallel experiences of a lost and often buried childhood. In this sense the evocative meaning of a parent's death can require lifelong mourning. But death and its lingering hold can be variously symbolized by even trivial situations of separation and loss. For example, Lincoln's separation from Mary Owens in 1836 may well have prompted feelings of sadness that lingered from the death of Ann Rutledge the year earlier. Lincoln's more radical break with Speed and Mary Todd in 1841 brought him near disaster. Circuit life with all its separations from family seemed to evoke a chronic melancholy in Lincoln. And so it went. Lincoln's response to symbolized encounters with death seemed to derive from an association of loving and death that led him to assure Speed gratuitously in 1842 that if Speed did not love his fiancée, although he "might not wish her death," he "would most calmly be resigned to it."[7]

Lincoln's depressions were not restricted to his encounters with death or its symbolized equivalents in situations of separation and loss. He also seemed particularly vulnerable to issues of self-esteem. Political defeat could devastate Lincoln. Before the Civil War he was an experienced loser in Illinois politics. He lost his first election to the state legislature in 1832 (noting, however, in his autobiography that those who actually knew him in the New Salem precinct voted in his favor 277 to 7). Twice during the 1850s he lost races for the United States Senate: in 1855, to Lyman Trumbull, and in 1858, to Stephen Douglas. There is no indication of what Lincoln felt about his first defeat in 1832, but his conscious "withdrawal" from active politics in 1849 suggests a depressive response to his sense of the failure of his political ambitions after his term as United States congressman. In 1855 Lincoln seemed resigned to his defeat by Trumbull. There is some evidence that in 1858 Lincoln was distraught at the loss to Douglas; on the evening of the defeat he told his friend Henry C. Whitney that his life had been "an abject and lamentable failure." Whitney reported: "I never saw any man so radically and thoroughly depressed, so completely steeped in the bitter waters of hopeless despair."[8]

In these cases, the depression came from Lincoln's sense of failure to realize his ambitions and ideals. The grandiose young man of the Lyceum speech of 1838 gave way to a politician in the 1850s who tackled one of the nation's leading political figures, Stephen Douglas, on his own turf. Lincoln became a man unafraid to interpret the founding fathers to a country hurtling toward war. He was unabashedly majestic in the "house divided" speech. And when he left Springfield he saw himself as facing a challenge equal to, if not greater than, that dealt with by the founders. Yet his personal and political performances kept falling short. He seemed unable to match his own expectations, and failure at the polls dramatized the enormity of the gap between expectation and performance.

Lincoln also lived in a world of other people on whom he depended for love, support, interaction, and the maintenance of his complicated needs. In periods of vulnerability these needs were most apparent. For example, he wrote Mary Owens in 1837: "I want in all cases to do right, and most particularly so, in all cases with women. I want, at this particular time, more than any thing else, to do right with you." And to Speed, Lincoln once poured out his soul on the devastating effect of his broken engagement in 1841: "But before I resolve to do the one thing or the other, I must retain my confidence in my own ability to keep my resolves when they are made. In that ability, you know, I once prided myself as the only, or at least the chief, gem of my character; that gem I lost—how and when, you too well know." Losing Mary seemed to evoke childhood memories of his mother; but perhaps even more importantly, it cut Lincoln off from the one person in his life who could potentially anchor him psychologically. Speed substituted briefly and helped Lincoln find his way back to her.[9]

The key issue for Lincoln in these intensely personal struggles was to maintain his self-esteem in his relationships with others.

Just before leaving Springfield in 1861, Lincoln grew a beard,
supposedly in response to a letter from a young girl
but probably because he wanted to look more "presidential"
for his arrival in Washington. Courtesy of
Louis A. Warren Lincoln Library & Museum,
Fort Wayne, Indiana.

Psychologically, however, the "other" in this kind of encounter
is not separate but is included in the conception of the self. For
Lincoln, the political analogue of this private world of meanings
was the stability and cohesion of the political process itself. His
choice of career and his early political affinities reflected an abiding commitment to order and stability in the community. In the

1850s his use of the founders' thoughts grew out of a respect for the sources of healthy continuity in the country, yet he had to watch in horror as it all unraveled. In this regard his uncharacteristic paranoia in the "house divided" speech in 1858 makes some sense: It described a violent disruption that he felt was external but which he experienced psychologically as part of his inner life.

Lincoln's psychological uncertainty continued during the chaos of the early months of the war. Badly prepared, the army suffered a series of defeats. Many of its best generals defected to the South. The northern states were disunited, and the border states on the verge of leaving the Union. The administration was young and halting, its relations with Congress in doubt. John Hay, one of Lincoln's two secretaries, noted in his diary on April 24, 1861: "This has been a day of gloom and doubt. Everybody seems filled with a vague distrust and recklessness." And later that summer, on July 28, Orville Browning, Lincoln's old friend and now senator from Illinois, recorded in his diary that during an extended conversation at the White House Lincoln "seemed very melancholy; admitted he was so, but said he knew of no special cause for it."[10]

Lincoln's equilibrium seemed to hinge on the emotional supplies served up by both intimate and formalized encounters with others. In this sense, the irresistible appeal of politics was its potential for providing recognition and admiration. "Every man is said to have his peculiar ambition," Lincoln wrote in a circular for his very first campaign in 1832. "Whether it be true or not, I can say for one that I have no other so great as that of being truly esteemed of my fellow man, by rendering myself worthy of their esteem." Lincoln once described himself as "too *thin-skinned*" and, at times during the war, expressed a fear that he possessed no administrative ability. A law lecture he once prepared began: "I am not an accomplished lawyer. I find quite as much material

Springfield campaign rally, August 8, 1860.
Courtesy of Chicago Historical Society.

for a lecture in those points wherein I have failed, as in those wherein I have been moderately successful."[11]

And yet there were many rewards for Lincoln in law, politics, and government service. His election as a captain in the Black Hawk War was an event of great emotional significance; no other success in his life until 1860 "gave him so much satisfaction." During the 1830s he played a prominent role in the Illinois legislature and rose to the leadership of the Whig party. He loved the rough-and-tumble of politics and never seemed to regard speech-making as tedious. A master politician, he could exert enormous influence behind the scenes without demeaning his own stature. He worked hard as a lawyer to make a respectable income and strove vigorously for high political office. As David Donald has reminded us, a statesman is a politician who succeeds in getting elected. The hard-working, shrewd, resourceful Lincoln became such a statesman. Even during his political "retirement" from 1849 to 1854, he remained active in Whig politics. During the 1850s, it is true, he twice lost campaigns for the Senate, but he was also the leading figure in a complex alliance of Whigs and other smaller groups who began calling themselves Republicans. He was mentioned often for the governorship, but he was not interested, though he was something of an *eminence grise* in the Bissell administration of the late 1850s. Then at last, in 1860, he was elected President and, in 1864, reelected.[12]

Such success went a long way to build Lincoln's confidence and ease his transition into the presidency. In fact, after the dark early days, Lincoln seemed newly capable of leading the North to victory. "The Tycoon is in a fine whack," wrote John Hay on August 7, 1863. "I have rarely seen him more serene and busy. He is managing the war, the draft, foreign relations, and planning a reconstruction of the Union, all at once." Except for Lincoln's despair during the first few months of the war, Hay almost always seemed to encounter a cheery, confident, and competent President. On October 17, 1861, Lincoln and Nicolay had found a topic of discussion "vastly amusing." On July 11, 1863, Hay reported, "The President seemed in a specially good humor today." On July 19, 1863, "The Tycoon was in a very good humor. Early in the morning he scribbled this doggerel and gave it to me." On August 9, 1863, "Lincoln was in very fine spirits." On November 23, 1863, Hay noted that Lincoln had been "a little despondent abt Grant" but cheered again with the news of Grant's advance on Chattanooga and Thomas's success. On July 11, 1864, "The President is in a very good feather this evening." The next day, "The President seemed in a pleasant and confident humor today." Lincoln's visit to the front on June 23, 1864, exhausted him but also left him "refreshed and cheered." And nowhere is there a more charming description of Lincoln than Hay's account of a midnight visit from him in the spring of 1864:

> A little after midnight as I was writing those last lines, the President came into the office laughing, with a volume of Hood's works in his hands, to show Nico and me the little caricature "An Unfortunate Beeing," seemingly utterly un-conscious that he with his short shirt hanging above his long legs & setting out behind like the tail feathers of an enormous ostrich was infinitely funnier than anything in the book he was laughing at. What a man it is! Occupied all day with matters of vast moment, deeply anxious about the fate of the greatest army of the world, with his own fame & future hanging on the events of the passing hour, he yet has such a wealth of simple bonhommie & good fellowship that he gets out of bed & perambulates the house in his shirt to find us that we may share with him the fun of one of poor Hood's queer little conceits.[13]

Hay's testimony is reliable and contemporary, and no one worked more closely with Lincoln for a longer period of time and kept a diary. Hay is observant, articulate, and witty. His regular entries in his diary capture the bustling activities of the White House but also Lincoln's calm, reassuring leadership. Hay at first seemed ambivalent toward Lincoln, referring jocularly to him as "The Tycoon" (thirty-eight times), "the Ancient" (twice), and "the old man" (once). But by the middle of the war Hay became deeply devoted to Lincoln and his style. "There is no man in the country," Hay wrote in 1863, "so wise, so gentle and so firm. I believe the hand of God placed him where he is."[14] But Hay only seldom referred to Lincoln's melancholy and never noted that it inhibited Lincoln's work. In Hay's diaries Lincoln emerges as a warm, inspiring, very hard-working, subtly competent adminis-trator, a statesman, and a military strategist.

How, one asks, could Lincoln have combined such effective leadership with recurring, often devastating depression? The theologian Elton Trueblood has noted that "Lincoln's was the kind of mind which did not reach its true magnitude except in experiences of sorrow and strain."[15] Still, Lincoln's emotional vulnerabilities remained throughout his life. But his competence, his easy, confident style, his warmth and kindness, all suggest a large measure of transcendence of his debilitating conflicts. Freud's theories of psychology help explain what made Lincoln so susceptible to separation, loss, death, and disturbances in the maintenance of his self-esteem. But the classical psychoanalytic model falls short of providing clues to his transcendence. One needs a way of understanding what provides cohesion, integrity, flexibility, growth, and change within a personality. Here the work of psychoanalyst Heinz Kohut can be enormously helpful, especially his thoughts on the cohesiveness of the self. The criteria Kohut enumerates for evaluating the potential for healthy psychological growth are ultimately simple and obvious: humor, empathy, creativity, and wisdom.[16] For Lincoln, these become the vehicles to transcend the core conflicts within his personality.

Humor needs no definition. Freud once wrote a whole book on why a joke "works," but Kohut's interest is in the psychological flexibility inherent in someone who can tolerate the self-reflection and regression in joking. Humor in this sense excludes biting sarcasm or joking that targets someone else as the butt. Part of the appeal of Lincoln's humor is the self-deprecation of so many of his jokes. He loved to tell of a stranger who once came up to him on the circuit and said, "Excuse me, sir, but I have an article in my possession which belongs to you." "How is that?" Lincoln asked with some surprise. The stranger took a knife out of his pocket and said it had been given to him some years ago with the order "that I was to keep it until I found a man *uglier* than myself. I have carried it from that time to this. Allow me *now* to say, sir, that I think *you* are fairly entitled to the property." Another favorite anecdote, in which Lincoln ridiculed his own modest habits, told of a friendly Kentuckian he once rode with in a carriage. The man offered Lincoln a chew of tobacco, then a cigar, and finally a sip of brandy from a flask. Each offer Lincoln politely declined. As they were parting the Kentuckian said good-humoredly: "See here, stranger, you're a clever but strange companion. I may never see you again, and I don't want to offend you, but I want to say this: My experience has taught me that a man who has no vices has damned few virtues. Good-day."[17]

Recently it has been argued that the true spirit of Lincoln's humor was one of anger and cruelty. Michael Burlingame, in fact, has put Lincoln's supposed anger at the center of his psychological portrait of Lincoln, *The Inner World*. In this book, Burlingame includes an entire chapter that links Lincoln's humor with anger and cruelty and compiles a vast array of quotes and references to prove his point.[18] But Burlingame in general lacks critical judgment and proportion. Certainly Lincoln could be sharp with people, and at times in his youth he was edgy. In the political arena, he often harnessed his keen sense of the absurd to ridicule his opponents. But if there is a man in our political history who lacked anger and cruelty, it has to be Abraham Lincoln. And it is exactly the range, depth, and complexity of his humor that provides a measure of insight into the complex workings of his soul.

Lincoln had a delicious sense of understated irony. The effusive Herndon once told Lincoln of his impression of Niagara Falls with its "mad rush of water, the roar, the rapids, and the rainbow." When he asked Lincoln for his opinion of Niagara Falls, Lincoln replied: "The thing that struck me most forcibly when I saw the Falls was, where in the world did all that water come from?" In fact, Lincoln had written rather extensive notes to himself on

Niagara Falls after visiting them in 1849: "It calls up the indefinite past. When Columbus first sought this continent—when Christ suffered on the cross—when Moses led Israel through the Red Sea—nay, even, when Adam first came from the hand of his Maker—then as now, Niagara was roaring here."[19] The interesting point about the contrast between what Lincoln told Herndon and what he really felt is what it suggests about their relationship. Lincoln was clearly the senior partner, remote, distant, and "shut-mouthed." Herndon would not be let in.[20]

A week before his death, Lincoln visited the Confederate capital, Richmond, which had been captured by federal troops. In the party was the French aristocrat Adolphe de Chambrun, who described in a letter to his wife how a band came up to the presidential steamer to play a few tunes. Afterward Lincoln asked the band to play the *Marseillaise* (which was forbidden in the Third Republic) and turned to Chambrun with a twinkle in his eye: "You have to come to America to hear it."[21]

Lincoln told his friend Ward Hill Lamon that he "lived by his humor, and would have died without it." When he told a story, the fun danced in his eyes and played over every feature. The mirth "seemed to diffuse itself all over him, like a spontaneous tickle." In the White House, Francis Carpenter once came across Lincoln telling a story to Nicolay and Hay late in the evening, "laughing and talking with the hilarity of a schoolboy." Herndon remarked on how much Lincoln enjoyed his own telling of stories: "His little gray eyes sparkled; a smile seemed to gather up, curtain like, the corners of his mouth; his frame quivered with suppressed excitement; and, when the point—or 'nub' of the story, as he called it—came, no one's laugh was heartier than his." Lincoln had a dread of people who could not appreciate humor, and said once of a cabinet member (probably the dour Edwin Stanton) that "it required a surgical operation to get a joke into his head."[22]

As Lincoln told all kinds of jokes in every conceivable context, his fame as a storyteller spread far and wide. "Men quoted his sayings, repeated his jokes, and in remote places he was known as a story-teller before he was heard of either as lawyer or politician." As President, Lincoln often related the story of the Irishman who had foresworn liquor but told the bartender he was not averse to having a spot added to his lemonade, "so long as it's unbeknownst to me." David Donald feels this anecdote expressed the way Lincoln wrapped his pragmatism, even opportunism, in a cloak of passivity. His humor was generally "clean" and the kind of American tall tale that would not have been out of place in a ladies' drawing room. But not always. His bawdy humor was a special delight for the small group of lawyers following the eighth circuit. Moses Hampton wrote to him in a lighthearted vein on March 30, 1848, asking for a favor: "Do you remember the story of the old Virginian stropping his razor on a certain member of a young negro's body which you told?" Herndon, who was a bit of a stuffed shirt and a great reader of "heavy" texts, once asked Lincoln if he believed in heredity. Lincoln mused for a moment and replied, yes, he had no doubt that personality traits were passed from one generation to another; for example, old so-and-so from his New Salem days had fathered five boys. Well, Lincoln continued, "I know that ———— suffered terribly in the old days from chronic diarrhea, and you know for a fact that every one of the boys has turned out to be a perfect shitass!"[23]

Lincoln's bawdy humor was mostly anal, and typical of its time. He once handed a bailiff in a Springfield court the following piece of foolery:

> He said he was riding *bass-ackwards* on a *jass-ack,* through a *pattoncotch,* on a pair of *baddle-sags,* stuffed full of *binger-gred,* when the animal *steered* at a *scump,* and the *lirrup-streather* broke, and throwed him in the *forner* of the *kence* and broke

his *pishing-fole*. He said he would not have minded it much, but he fell right in a great *tow-curd;* in fact, he said it give him a right smart *sick of fitness*—he had the *molera-corbus* pretty bad. He said, about *bray dake* he came to himself, ran home, seized up a *stick of wood* and split the *axe* to make a light, rushed into the house, and found the *door* sick abed, and his *wife* standing open. But thank goodness she is getting right *hat* and *farty* again.

Another story that Herndon says he heard Lincoln tell "often and often" described a man of audacity: At a party "not far from here" (which, of course, puts it anywhere) a fine table was set and everyone was having a grand time. Among the guests was our man of audacity, who was confident, self-possessed, and never off his guard. After some dancing, promenading, flirting, and so forth, dinner was served and the man of audacity was placed at the head of the table to carve. With everyone surrounding the table the man whetted the blade and set to work. But he expended too much energy, for he let go a large fart. Everyone heard it and was shocked. Silence reigned. But the audacious man was cool and self-possessed. He calmly took off his coat, rolled up his sleeves, put his coat deliberately on a chair, spat on his hands and rubbed them together, squared his shoulders, and picked up his knife, all without a smile or a movement of the muscles in his face. "Now, by God," he said, starting to carve the turkey again, "I'll see if I can't cut up this turkey without farting."[24]

Even Lincoln's vulgar jokes usually had a purpose. If it was "merely a ribald recital" he had no use for it. Often the purpose was political. For example, in 1848 Lincoln gave a pro-Taylor speech in the United States House of Representatives during his term as a congressman. His goal in the speech was to debunk the spurious military record of Taylor's opponent, General Cass. To accomplish that, he recalled his own record:

By the way, Mr. Speaker, did you know that I am a military hero? Yes sir; in the days of the Black Hawk war, I fought, bled, and came away. Speaking of Gen: Cass' career, reminds me of my own. I was not at Stillman's defeat, but I was about as near it, as Cass was to Hulls surrender; and, like him, I did not break my sword, for I had none to break; but I bent a musket pretty badly on one occasion. If Cass broke his sword, the idea is, he broke it in de[s]peration; I bent the musket by accident. If Genl Cass went in advance of me in picking huckleberries, I guess I surpassed him in charges upon the wild onions. If he saw any live, fighting indians, it was more than I did; but I had a good many bloody struggles with the musquetoes; and, although I never fainted from loss of blood, I can truly say I was often hungry. Mr. Speaker, if I should ever conclude to doff whatever our democratic friends may suppose there is of black cockade federalism about me, and thereupon, they shall take me up as their candidate for the Presidency, I protest they shall not make fun of me, as they have of General Cass, by attempting to write me into a military hero.[25]

The device of lacing political speeches with anecdotes became a Lincoln hallmark. In the early years of his career some found this trait offensive. On November 23, 1839, Springfield's Democratic paper, the *Register,* chided Lincoln for his "assumed clownishness" and warned that "this game of buffoonery convinces the mind of no man, and is utterly lost on the majority of his audience. We seriously advise Mr. Lincoln to correct this clownish fault before it grows upon him." In time, however, even the *Register* conceded, in reporting a Lincoln speech on October 6, 1854, that he began with jokes, "the character of which will be understood by all who know him, by simply saying they were Lincolnisms." He joked endlessly with law clients to put them at ease, sometimes repeating a story several times in the course of one day. Each time he laughed harder at his own jokes. Even Herndon, who had to listen to these stories over and over, was forced to laugh because he "thought it funny that Mr. Lincoln enjoyed a story so repeatedly told." In the White House, Lincoln used anecdotes cleverly to ward off supplicants or angry politicians demanding action on some crucial measure. Charles Sumner, who had no sense of humor, found conversation with Lincoln "a constant puzzle" and asked Carl Schurz "with an air of innocent bewilderment" whether Schurz knew what the President meant.[26]

Lincoln's was a raucous, infectious, charming humor, a bubbling over of story, joke, anecdote, and tale that became a part of his every action and experience. It defined his style in law, politics, and in personal relationships. No subject escaped his humor, not even his own famous tendency to pardon soldiers for desertion, cowardice, or failure to perform adequately in the army. A number of witnesses such as Carpenter have described Lincoln's acts of pardon in saccharine terms, noting his sad eyes and melancholy appearance. But two of Hay's diary entries are also worth pondering. On July 18, 1863, Lincoln told Hay he was averse to using the death penalty for desertion and cowardice because "it would frighten the poor devils too terribly, to shoot them." He also told Hay the government should let alone a boy who had escaped after his conviction for desertion: "We will condemn him as they used to sell hogs in Indiana, as they run." And despite his deep commitment to the necessity of fighting the Civil War, Lincoln recognized that politics dictates the support of any country's war. To illustrate the point, he once told Seward of a politician he knew in Illinois, Justin Butterfield, who was asked why he supported the Mexican War when it was known he opposed it. "I opposed one war," Butterfield replied; "that was enough for me. I am now perpetually in favor of war, pestilence and famine."[27]

If humor was a central part of Lincoln's personality, it was also necessary. Henry C. Whitney, Lincoln's friend on the circuit, quoted him as saying, "I laugh because I must not weep—that's all, that's all." The actual origin of the line is Lord Byron's *Don Juan,* a poem Lincoln knew well: "And if I laugh at any mortal thing, tis that I may not weep." To laugh to keep from weeping expresses the dynamic relationship between Lincoln's humor and his depression. Contemporary observers were quite aware of the connection. Harriet Beecher Stowe felt Lincoln possessed "a never-failing fund of patience" that lay beneath his deep melancholy and periodically rose to the surface in some "droll, quaint saying, or story, that forced a laugh, even from himself." David Davis, the judge on the eighth circuit who was Lincoln's campaign manager in 1860 and a dear friend, said Lincoln's stories were intended primarily "to whistle off sadness." Herndon stressed the rapid alternation of Lincoln's moods from gloom to joy—and back. Chambrun also noted this alternation of mood. "He willingly laughed either at what was being said or at what he himself was saying. Then, suddenly, he would retire himself and close his eyes, while his face expressed a melancholy as indescribable as it was deep. After a few moments, as though by an effort of the will, he would shake off his mysterious weight and his generous and open disposition again reasserted itself. I have counted, in one evening, more than twenty of such alternations of mood." And everyone noted his hearty laugh and sparkling eyes. "That laugh," noted Carpenter, "has been the President's life-preserver."[28]

Humor served therapeutic purposes for Lincoln, though it also relaxed his clients, helped keep political opponents in their place, won many friends and much influence, and facilitated his leadership as President. Humor seemed to provide a kind of vitality for Lincoln, a zest that kept his depression at bay. More hypothetically, it also seems that the effectiveness of his humor helped him to tolerate the regressive pulls of depression and thereby enabled him to stop fearing his melancholy, as he probably did in his childhood and as he certainly did in his youth. Humor never completely eliminated his depression—he was gloomy to the end. But it helped ease his radical shifts in mood and gave him confidence that he need not disintegrate in his depression. Thus at the start of analysis a gloomy patient may wrap himself in a shroud of desperate isolation to avoid experiencing the pulls of the transference. Years later, at the termination of analysis, this same patient might still become depressed, but if his analysis has worked out tolerably well, he will be able to shift easily into other moods and see some humor in his earlier fears.

As Lincoln matured and confronted increasingly complex responsibilities and challenges, his humor changed. He generally avoided cruel satire and biting sarcasm. But as a young man, when he was more confused and needy, his humor at times lost its empathic glow. He was a youth in Indiana when he wrote the angry satire, the "Chronicles of Reuben," to get back at the Grigsbys, his sister's in-laws, who he felt were indirectly responsible for her death in childbirth in 1828. The poem describes in mock-Biblical style a wedding-night confusion after the joint wedding of Reuben's two sons, when the wrong parties end up in bed together. Then in the early 1840s, Lincoln helped Mary Todd and Julia Jayne write the "Rebecca Letters," three tales satirizing the blustering James Shields. Lincoln wrote only one of the three tales (the best one, from a literary point of view), but he willingly assumed responsibility for all three when Shields demanded to know the author. To Lincoln's horror, Shields challenged him to a duel. Lincoln reportedly suggested as weapons that they use cow-dung at five paces. Shields was not amused, and the two had to proceed with all the silly rituals of seconds exchanging notes, challenges, and counter-challenges. At the last minute battle was prevented, but Lincoln never forgave himself for getting into such a situation and refused ever to talk about it; nor did he develop a repertoire of duel jokes. Still, even in this serious and, for Lincoln, shameful experience, he managed some humor. His final choice of weapons was broadswords at ten paces; Lincoln was a full foot taller than Shields.[29]

★★★

"It really hurts me very much," Lincoln said during his debates with Stephen Douglas in 1858, "to suppose that I have wronged anybody on earth." Such sentiments expressed Lincoln's need for support and esteem from those around him. But they also express his sensitivity to others and his empathic relatedness to those from whom he sought esteem. "He was modest, quiet and unobtrusive in his manner," wrote Whitney of Lincoln before 1860, but also "sympathetic and cordial in social contract. . . . His sad countenance aroused universal sympathy, his *bonhomie,* geniality and humor drew all men involuntarily to him." Judge Holt, who implemented Lincoln's wartime reprieves for soldiers, called him "without exception the most tender-hearted man I ever knew." Such characterizations contain an element of ambiguity, however, for someone with a "tender" heart is also "soft-hearted," a pushover. Lincoln, on the contrary, rose above the petty jealousies and compulsive ritualizations of our culture to deal honestly and empathically with personal and political issues. There is no reason to question his genuine feeling for the thousands of terrified young soldiers who proved to be cowards. He managed, however, to cover his kindness politically, by allowing the Secretary of War, Edwin Stanton, virtually free reign in repealing his reprieves. "I want to oblige everybody when I can," Lincoln once said, "and Stanton and I have an understanding that if I send on an order to him which cannot be consistently granted, he is to refuse it. This he sometimes does."[30]

Perhaps the most famous example of Lincoln's empathy was his letter to Mrs. Lydia Bixby on November 21, 1864 (though it may have been written by John Hay[31]). "I have been shown," he began, "that you are the mother of five sons who have died gloriously on the field of battle." Lincoln notes how "weak and fruitless" any words from him must be to comfort her on the loss. "But I cannot refrain from tendering to you the consolation that may be found in the thanks of the Republic they died to save." In conclusion Lincoln essentially joins in prayer with Mrs. Bixby to help her mourn such a terrible loss: "I pray that our Heavenly Father may assuage the anguish of your bereavement, and leave you only the cherished memory of the loved and lost, and the solemn pride that must be yours, to have laid so costly a sacrifice upon the altar of Freedom. Yours, very sincerely and respectfully, A. Lincoln."[32] The invocation of God here and the rather extravagant imagery of the "altar of Freedom" is a good example of Lincoln slipping into the kind of language and metaphor that he suspected would prove most understandable to his reader. In the same way, he could move easily between folksy, sometimes vulgar humor with illiterate clients on the circuit and exalted, noble statements on the ultimate meaning of the war that spoke quite consciously to history. No one had an ear more finely tuned to his audiences.

One of the wonders of Lincoln's style was the way it changed and adapted to new environments. The presidency nourished Lincoln's strengths and gave him renewed confidence. His depression ebbed. He took complete charge of his cabinet and greater control of military affairs. He brushed aside the unrelenting criticism. And he carefully shaped his own heroic image. It was not simply that he was ambitious to the point of arrogance; Lincoln nourished a heroic style as the one best suited to a country emerging from a terrible civil war. The shaping of that style drew on his greatest empathic strengths. He knew better than anyone the deep yearnings for greatness in a war-torn nation. The style he developed fitted exactly.

Empathy also carries within it forgiveness. Lincoln, it can be fairly said, never held a grudge ("It doesn't pay," he said). Like most lawyers, he could leave a bitter courtroom battle without an ounce of enmity. He never seemed to feel petty anger toward anyone, tolerating even Mary's lifelong hatreds toward others. Where possible he simply adjusted his behavior to meet her demands, while refusing to identify with her feelings. For example, he yielded to her dislike of his law partner Herndon by never having him in his home; but for all those years, from 1844 to 1861, he never questioned the permanence of their partnership. The most important example of Lincoln's forgiveness is in the public rather than the private sphere—his attitude toward the South's responsibility for causing the war. "Both parties deprecated war," he noted in his Second Inaugural Address, "but one of them would *make* war rather than let the nation survive; and the other would *accept* war rather than let it perish. And the war came." Neither side anticipated the scale of war that resulted or that the "*cause* of the conflict might cease with, or even before, the conflict itself should cease." Both sides, he said, read the same Bible and pray to the same God; "but let us judge not that we be not judged. The prayers of both could not be answered; that of neither has been answered fully."[33]

★★★

One of the wonders of Lincoln's creative impulse is that, superficially, it seems to have come from nowhere. As a child he read intently, but he had relatively few books at his disposal and the few "blab" schools he attended were hardly model institutions of learning. Many close to Lincoln were struck by how "desultory" his reading was, even when he was an adult. Herndon made a comment with characteristic bombast that is off-base but captures something important: "Beyond a limited acquaintance with Shakespeare, Byron, and Burns, Mr. Lincoln, comparatively speaking, had no knowledge of literature. He was familiar with the Bible . . . [but] he never in his life sat down and read a book through."[34]

Lincoln says he began reading law in 1834 with the encouragement of John T. Stuart. A contemporary later noted: "He borrowed all the Law Books he could . . . get hold of." It is not clear what he read in those years, because the oral history accounts mention only his reading law books, but it would seem he must have read something else. Herndon has left us a vivid description of Lincoln stretched out on his couch, reading aloud from the newspaper "to catch the sound with both senses." The daily newspaper was the most important literary item in Lincoln's life; he absorbed newspapers and everything they had to say about contemporary political affairs. Sarah Lincoln told Herndon that her stepson began reading newspapers closely in Indiana in the late 1820s. In New Salem Lincoln was interested in becoming postmaster largely because it gave him the opportunity to read the incoming newspapers free of charge. In Springfield he took an avid interest in the affairs of the *Journal*, writing many stories for it over the years and becoming close friends with the editor. He even owned a share of a German-language newspaper. The notebook that he carried with him to the debates with Douglas in 1858 consisted largely of newspaper clippings. He even joked about his fascination with newspapers. He once told John E. Rosette, an attorney in Springfield, about a subscription to a new newspaper: "When the paper was brought to my house, my wife said to me, 'Now are you going to take another worthless little paper?'"[35]

The notion that Lincoln's simple literary tastes barely went beyond the newspaper (except, of course, for the Bible) draws largely on the myth that Lincoln's genius was effortless and imparted directly from God. In fact, Lincoln was quite a bookish fellow (in this, Randall and many others have it wrong). Roy P. Basler examined some of the textbooks Lincoln used as a boy and felt that he "probably had a more thorough training in formal rhetoric than the average college graduate of the present." That, of course, says something about both Lincoln and our recent college graduates. What Lincoln did read, from Parson Weems's *Life of Washington* to the Bible and the newspaper, he completely absorbed, often memorizing whole passages. He was able to recite long poems and knew much of his beloved Shakespeare by heart.[36]

Nothing is more striking about Lincoln's creative style than the Biblical tone of his prose. At times he seems to be another Old Testament prophet. Elton Trueblood, a theologian, has given us the most complete discussion of this aspect of Lincoln's thought. By the time of his maturity, Lincoln had absorbed not only the contents of the Bible but its style and unique use of language. In his "house divided" speech Lincoln noted the superiority of a living dog to a dead lion, a reference to Ecclesiastes 9:4. The Gettysburg Address, with its heavy use of monosyllables, reads like the Twenty-third Psalm, which Lincoln could recite from memory. Of the 272 words in the Gettysburg Address, 194 have only one syllable; the Twenty-third Psalm has a similar proportion with its total of 118 words, 92 of which have one syllable. Even in personal letters Lincoln evoked the Bible. He wrote to Ward Hill Lamon: "As to the inclination of some Republicans to favor Douglas that is one of the chances I have to run and which I intend to run with patience." This phrasing evokes the beginning of the twelfth chapter of Hebrews in an "oblique and subtle" way.[37]

The Bible, however important, was not alone in shaping Lincoln's creative style. Two literary critics, William K. Wimsatt and Cleanth Brooks, make the astute point that Lincoln was profoundly influenced by the oratorical tradition that began with the

Greek sophists. This "Ciceronian ideal" is that "of rational man reaching his noblest attainment in the expression of an eloquent wisdom. Necessary steps in the attainment of this ideal are careful drill in the poets followed by a program of encyclopedic scope directed to the forensic end of political power." Basler has noted the technical devices that characterize Lincoln's rhetoric—repetition, grammatical parallelism, and antithesis—devices that Garry Wills has analyzed in the Gettysburg Address. Lincoln strove always for emphasis and simplicity. The Gettysburg Address repeats "we" ten times, "here" eight times, and nearly half of all the words in the speech are repetitions. Lincoln tended to read everything aloud —law, papers, and poetry—much to the annoyance of Herndon. His explanation was that he remembered it better when he heard *and* read it. Lincoln also wanted to hear what he read because he knew that his important, mature thoughts would be spoken.[38]

The word, creatively used, is an instrument of enormous power. As a boy Lincoln tested his father by talking first to strangers. After church he stood on a stump and mimicked the preacher's sermon. Later, as a young man, he struck out in anger with the satirical poem "The Chronicles of Reuben," and again with his "Rebecca Letters." In time he learned to direct his power with words more productively. In his law practice he was simple, direct, and forceful; and his law practice brought him an entirely respectable life. But the most important achievement of his creative use of the word was to secure political power. At first he groped, as in the awkward Lyceum speech in 1838, which is confused in places: "Thus, then, by the operation of this mobocratic spirit, which all must admit, is now abroad in the land, the strongest bulwark of any Government and particularly of those constituted like ours, may effectually be broken down and destroyed—I mean the *attachment* of the People." As he matured, however, Lincoln sharpened his skills. His long struggle with Stephen Douglas from

1854 to 1860 forced him to find clearer, simpler, more effective ways of repeatedly saying the same thing. With Lincoln each repetition became more eloquent. By the time of his inauguration in 1861, Lincoln could turn a phrase that mobilized a nation. Consider, for example, these two drafts for the closing paragraph of his First Inaugural Address that William Seward presented to Lincoln.

> However unusual it may be at such a time to speak of sections or to sections, yet in view of the misconceptions and agitations which have strained the ties of brotherhood so far, I hope it will not be deemed a departure from propriety, whatever it may be from custom, to say that if in the criminations and misconstructions which too often imbue our political contests, any man south of this capital has been led to believe that I regard with a less friendly eye his rights, his interests, or his domestic safety and happiness, or those of his State, than I do those of any other portion of my country, or that I would invade or disturb any legal right or domestic institution in the South, he mistakes both my principles and feelings, and does not know me. I aspire to come in the spirit, however far below the ability and wisdom, of Washington, of Madison, of Jackson, and of Clay. In that spirit I here declare that in my administration I shall know no rule but the Constitution, no guide but the laws, and no sentiment but that of equal devotion to my whole country, east, west, north, and south.

> I close. We are not, we must not be, aliens or enemies, but fellow-countrymen and brethren. Although passion has strained our bonds of affection too hardly, they must not, I am sure they will not, be broken. The mystic chords which, proceeding from so many battlefields and so many patriot graves, pass through all the hearts and all hearths in this broad continent of ours, will yet again harmonize in their ancient music when breathed upon by the guardian angel of the nation.

And compare them with the final draft Lincoln developed from them:

> I am loth to close. We are not enemies. Though passion may have strained, it must not break our bonds of affection. The mystic chords of memory, stretching from every battle-field, and patriot grave, to every living heart and hearth-stone, all over this broad land, will yet swell the chorus of the Union, when again touched, as surely they will be, by the better angels of our nature.[39]

No writer appealed to Lincoln more than Shakespeare. Some of the plays—*King Lear, Richard III, Henry VIII, The Merry Wives of Windsor, Hamlet,* and his favorite, *Macbeth*—he knew virtually by heart. He was fond of talking with the actor James H. Hackett of the subtle meanings of different characters and passages. John Hay noted on December 13, 1863, that a conversation between Lincoln and Hackett "at first took a professional turn, the Tycoon showing a very intimate knowledge of those plays of Shakespeare where Falstaff figures." Hay also noted a few days later that Lincoln went to Ford's theater with him, Nicolay, and Swett to see Hackett in *Henry IV.* Lincoln thoroughly enjoyed the performance (though he disputed Hackett's interpretation of one line). It seems clear that Lincoln turned repeatedly to Shakespeare for the depth of his insight into human motivation, the cleverness of his wit, and, perhaps, most of all, for the aesthetic appeal of his language. Lincoln continually sought to chasten and perfect his style; in Shakespeare, and probably nowhere else, he found a master whose own creativity provided a model.[40]

What several commentators have found psychologically interesting about Lincoln's fascination with Shakespeare is his attraction to the plays in which ambitious and envious men kill their brothers and other members of their families to gain and keep power.

Lincoln in 1865, not long before his death and
the end of the war. This photograph evokes the lines
in the Second Inaugural Address:
"With malice toward none; with charity for all."
Courtesy of Illinois State Historical Library.

These men—Macbeth, Hamlet, and various princes and kings
in the histories—reflect on their guilt but still carry forward
plans of aggression and murder. In *Hamlet,* Lincoln was struck
most of all by Claudius's soliloquy, "O, my offence is rank," which
he felt surpassed Hamlet's "To be or not to be." Nowhere, however, are issues of guilt and ambition clearer than in *Macbeth.*
"I think nothing equals Macbeth," Lincoln told Hackett. "It is
wonderful." Lincoln turned to *Macbeth* often, but once most dramatically at the very end of his life. Richmond was liberated,
the war all but over. Lincoln had traveled by steamer to visit the
Confederate's fallen capital. He stared "a long while" at the battle-

fields, "absorbed in thought," Chambrun reported to his wife the next day. And he read *Macbeth*. On Sunday, April 9, "Mr. Lincoln read aloud to us for several hours. Most of the passages he selected were from Shakespeare, especially *Macbeth*. The lines after the murder of Duncan, when the new king falls a prey to moral torment, were dramatically dwelt on. Now and then he paused to expatiate on how exact a picture Shakespeare here gives of a murderer's mind when, the dark deed achieved, its perpetrator already envies his victim's calm sleep. He read the scene over twice."[41]

Lincoln's fascination with these themes in Shakespeare suggests a large measure of unconscious guilt. This has prompted some to interpret Lincoln's plans for a rapid and gentle reconstruction of the Union as a kind of absolution for what he might have felt as responsibility in causing the war. Don Fehrenbacher develops a rather larger view of Lincoln's "apparent guilt" (for there is no direct evidence that Lincoln felt guilty about anything): "Yet his responsibilities as President must have weighed as heavily as the guilt of any assassin, and the latest casuality lists must have seemed like accusations." Fehrenbacher concludes dramatically: "It is not altogether unlikely that in the gloom of some sleepless night he too beheld blood upon his hands or found a prayer faltering on his lips."[42]

More recently, George B. Forgie interprets Lincoln's attraction to *Macbeth* in terms of Lincoln's murderous hate and jealousy of Douglas during their titanic struggle for power in the 1850s. Lincoln only achieved power by finally conquering his opponent. This political victory, which meant the symbolic death of Douglas (who in fact died shortly after Lincoln's inauguration), seemed to bring with it large doses of guilt that the war soon absorbed and enlarged. Lincoln's identification with conscience-stricken murderers in some of Shakespeare's plays, Forgie argues, derived from this guilt. If Fehrenbacher draws attention to the events of the war itself as the basis for Lincoln's guilt, Forgie argues that the formative political struggles of the 1850s were the arena in which Lincoln's guilt was molded.[43]

Guilt, however, is rooted psychologically and developmentally in childhood experiences. Later, guilt will attach itself to many different but derivative experiences. Events in the present, in other words, provide the material for our guilty thoughts, but the repressed, unconscious experiences from childhood generate the guilt itself. Both Fehrenbacher and Forgie miss this point: The war and the struggle with Douglas were perhaps the kind of psychological experiences that prompted the appearance of Lincoln's guilt. But they hardly created it. For one thing, their essential evidence is Lincoln's strong attraction to certain aspects of Shakespeare's writings. But Lincoln, as contemporaries unanimously agreed, was "a close and appreciative reader of many of the plays during his mature years in Springfield." Furthermore, he probably first encountered Shakespeare as a child in passages selected for grammar books such as one we know he used, William Scott's *Lessons in Elocution*. The famous soliloquies and other familiar passages were excerpted in books like Scott's. It is likely Lincoln first memorized these disjointed parts of Shakespeare and later, as an adult, fitted them into the complete plays.[44]

Roy Basler has taken a fruitful approach to Lincoln's fascination with Shakespeare's plays. Lincoln's lifelong devotion to Shakespeare, Basler argues, assumed new meaning during the war, for Lincoln came to see himself as the nation's poetic hero. He aimed to "identify himself, by words and in relationship to his contemporaries, as a representative, symbolic identity." During the war Lincoln became a kind of Shakespearian figure, a tragic and symbolic hero, as much by his words as by his actions. And, further, as Basler suggests, Lincoln quite consciously created his image, shaping it as opportunity arose "with his mind's eye on the ultimate scene of the ultimate act." The fact that Lincoln also seemed like an Old Testament prophet by no means contradicts this point. The apocalyptic vision, as Edmund Wilson once noted, imposed itself.[45]

AFTERWORD

————————•—————————

Lincoln's quest for union found expression in many directions. At first, the issues were purely personal; at the end, the public realm swallowed up the self. In between—where this study concentrates—public and private concerns blended in creative ways.

The story of Lincoln's personality and character has its own special interest. The personal lives of few historical figures have, in fact, attracted so much attention. In that story, generations of Americans have tried to find themselves. There was adversity in Lincoln's poverty and lack of opportunity. There was conflict with his father, with sexuality and intimacy, within himself. There was sadness in his struggle with death and a lifelong pattern of depression. There was determination and hard work. There was unaccountable skill as the young boy defined his separateness from his rural environment and as the man grew in stature after each defeat. There was wonderful humor. There was empathy. There was creativity.

Lincoln's childhood issues merged with adult concerns of love and work. The young man juggled many roles before finding cohesion and integrity in his identity as a lawyer and politician. He worked hard at loving, first in courtship, then in a deeply satisfying but complicated relationship with his wife, Mary. Over the course of a decade he tried to find a viable role as husband and father. But his closeness alternated with inner demands for being apart, separate, and idealized. Mary in turn gave much, perhaps most of all the confirmation that he could love genuinely and father children. But their close relationship and enclosed home held deep divisions. Their intimacy, one might say, was always potentially explosive.

After 1854 Lincoln discovered, remarkably enough, that his private concerns found reflection in the country as a whole. His own ambivalent quest for union—with his dead mother, his bride, his alienated father—gave meaning to the nation's turbulence as it hurtled toward civil war. It took time for Lincoln to bridge the public and private spheres exactly. He needed the right metaphor. In the idea of a house divided, Lincoln found a way of creatively enlarging his private concerns to fill the public space. When he found it, there was resonance.

Until the presidency, however, Lincoln hardly spoke for the nation. He defined the issues of union—and disunion—but until late in the 1850s he was in many respects only a midwestern politician dwarfed by Stephen Douglas in his own state, even in his own town. In retrospect the extent to which Lincoln had his finger on the pulse of the nation after 1854 is much clearer. Lincoln expressed then the deep and underlying issues for everyone in the troubled country. It was a confusing time, when few were touched, as Lincoln put it in his First Inaugural Address, by the better angels of their nature.

Lincoln the president rose to new heights as he led the North toward victory and, as soon as that was secured, began to lay the groundwork for healing the wounds of war. He died, of course, before Reconstruction, which makes it futile to speculate what he might have done. But it is not frivolous to guess that he purposely shaped his heroic image to fit a nation longing for unity and greatness. The image he shaped dissolved struggles over father, fatherhood, and founders. It put him in touch with God. And it gave America its greatest hero.

Notes

————◆————

Preface

1. Charles B. Strozier, "Disciplined Subjectivity and the Psychohistorian: A Critical Look at the Work of Erik Erikson," *The Psychohistory Review*, 5 (1976): 28–31. Disciplined subjectivity as the working method of psychohistory, as Erikson describes it, builds on the psychoanalytic notion of empathy. See Heinz Kohut, "Introspection, Empathy, and Psychoanalysis: An Examination of the Relationship between Mode of Operation and Theory," in *The Search for the Self: Selected Writings of Heinz Kohut, 1950–1978,* ed. Paul H. Ornstein, 2 vols. (New York: International Universities Press, 1978), 1: 205–32. It is worth pointing out that not everyone in psychohistory agrees with this emphasis on "disciplined subjectivity." See Fred Weinstein and Gerald Platt, *Psychoanalytic Sociology: An Essay on the Interpretation of Historical Data and the Phenomenon of Collective Behavior* (Baltimore: Johns Hopkins University Press, 1973), 1.

2. Charles B. Strozier, *Heinz Kohut: The Making of a Psychoanalyst* (New York: Farrar, Straus & Giroux, 2001).

3. James G. Randall, *Lincoln the President: Springfield to Gettysburg,* 2 vols. (Peter Smith: Glouchester, Mass.: 1976), 1: vii.

4. William H. Herndon and Jesse W. Weik, *Life of Lincoln,* ed. Paul M. Angle (Cleveland: World Publishing, 1930), 1–2. Note also Herndon to Weik, January 22, 1887, and Herndon to Truman H. Bartlett, September 22, 1887, Herndon/Weik Collection, microfilm, Illinois State Historical Society Library. The most important material in the Herndon/Weik Collection has been published in Douglas L. Wilson and Rodney O. Davis, *Herndon's Informants: Letters, Interviews, and State-*

ments about *Abraham Lincoln* (Urbana: University of Illinois Press, 1998). Wilson and Davis are working on a second volume of Herndon's letters, especially to Weik but also to Ward Hill Lamon and others. Until that is published, one can also consult a much less well-edited book for these letters, Emanuel Hertz, ed., *The Hidden Lincoln* (New York: Viking Press, 1938), though it is always worthwhile to check the original on microfilm.

5. David Donald, *Lincoln's Herndon: A Biography* (New York: Alfred A. Knopf, 1948), 343.

6. David Donald, *Lincoln Reconsidered: Essays on the Civil War Era* (New York: Alfred A. Knopf, 1956), 304, 305.

7. Ibid., 347.

8. Paul Angle, in Herndon and Weik, *Life of Lincoln,* xi.

9. See, for example, my discussion of the Drake letter in chapter 2, note 42.

10. Albert J. Beveridge, *Abraham Lincoln, 1809–1858,* 2 vols. (Boston: Houghton Mifflin, 1928), 1: 49.

11. Things, however, are changing, influenced in small part, I would like to believe, by my work. Note especially John Y. Simon, "Abraham Lincoln and Ann Rutledge," *Journal of the Abraham Lincoln Association* 11 (1990), and Douglas L. Wilson, *Honor's Voice: The Transformation of Abraham Lincoln* (New York: Alfred A. Knopf, 1998).

12. Seminar at Sangamon State University in Springfield, Illinois, April 16, 1979. His earlier comments on Sandburg are in Roy P. Basler, *The Lincoln Legend: A Study in Changing Conceptions* (Boston: Houghton Mifflin, 1935), 25–26.

Chapter 1

1. Herndon and Weik, *Life of Lincoln,* 2–3. Note also three Herndon letters to Ward Hill Lamon, February 28, 1869, February 25, 1870, and March 6, 1870, published in Hertz, *Hidden Lincoln,* 59, 62–69, 69–72.

2. *The Collected Works of Abraham Lincoln,* ed. Roy P. Basler, 8 vols. (New Brunswick, N.J.: Rutgers University Press, 1953), 4: 59–61. For Leonard Swett's comments, see Allen Thorndike Rice, *Reminiscences of Abraham Lincoln by Distinguished Men of His Time* (New York: North American Review, 1889), 457.

3. Carl Sandburg, *Abraham Lincoln: The Prairie Years,* 2 vols. (New York: Harcourt Brace, 1926), 1: 11–12; Louis A. Warren, *Lincoln's Parentage and Childhood: A History of the Kentucky Lincolns Supported by Documentary Evidence* (New York: Century, 1926); William E. Barton, *The Life of Abraham Lincoln,* 2 vols. (Indianapolis: Bobbs-Merrill, 1925), and his *The Lineage of Lincoln* (Indianapolis: Bobbs-Merrill, 1929).

4. The best recent genealogical work on the Hanks family has been done by Paul Verduin: "New Evidence Suggests Lincoln's Mother born in Richmond County, Virginia, giving Credibility to Planter-Grandfather Legend," *Northern Neck of Virginia Historical Magazine* 38 (December 1988): 4354–4589, and "Lincoln's Tidewater Virginia Heritage: The Hidden Legacy of Nancy Hanks Lincoln" (unpublished address to the Lincoln Group of the District of Columbia, October 17, 1989).

5. Donald, *Lincoln's Herndon,* 357; and David Donald, *Lincoln* (New York: Simon & Schuster, 1995), 20.

6. Herbert Guttman, *The Black Family in Slavery and Freedom, 1725–1915* (New York: Pantheon Books, 1976). Frederick Douglass's story is probably the best known: *Narrative of the Life of Frederick Douglass: An American Slave, Written by Himself,* ed. Benjamin Quarles (Cambridge: Harvard University Press, 1960 [1845]).

7. Catherine Beecher, *Treatise on Domestic Economy, for the use of Young Ladies At Home and At School* (Boston: T. H. Webb, 1842), Barbara Welter, "The Cult of True Womanhood: 1820–1860," *The American Family in Social-Historical Perspective,* ed. Michael Gordon, 2nd ed. (New York: St. Martin's Press, 1978), 313–34; Nancy F. Cott, "Notes Toward an Interpretation of Antebellum Childrearing," *The Psychohistory Review* 6 (1978): 4–20; Nancy F. Cott and Elizabeth H. Pleck, eds., *A Heritage of Her Own: Toward a New Social History of American Women* (New York: Simon & Schuster, 1979); Carl Degler, *At Odds: Women and the Family in America, From the Revolution to the Present* (New York: Oxford University Press, 1980).

8. Kathryn Kish Sklar, "Victorian Women and Domestic Life: Mary Todd Lincoln, Elizabeth Cady Stanton, and Harriet Beecher Stowe," in *The Public and Private Lincoln: Contemporary Perspectives,* ed. Cullom Davis, Charles B. Strozier, Rebecca Veach, and Geoffrey C. Ward (Carbondale: Southern Illinois University Press, 1979), 20–37.

9. Charles Friend to Herndon, August 20, 1889, Wilson and Davis, *Herndon's Informants,* 674–676; Barton, *Life of Lincoln,* 20.

10. Beveridge, *Lincoln,* 1: 15.

11. Herndon to Ward Hill Lamon, February 25, 1870, Hertz, *Hidden Lincoln,* 63–64.

12. Herndon to Ward Hill Lamon, March 15, 1870, Hertz, *Hidden Lincoln,* 79.

13. Herndon to Jesse Weik, January 19, 1888, Hertz, *Hidden Lincoln,* 138. Compare a similar account of Herndon's in a letter to Weik, September 30, 1887, Hertz, *Hidden Lincoln,* 340–41. The Donald quote is from *Lincoln's Herndon,* 357.

14. Herndon to Ward Hill Lamon, March 6, 1970, Hertz, *Hidden Lincoln,* 74.

15. Ibid., 63.

16. Sandburg, *The Prairie Years,* 1: 13.

17. *Collected Works,* 4: 61.

18. Dennis F. Hanks to Herndon, June 13, 1865, Wilson and Davis, *Herndon's Informants,* 35–43; William Woods's statement to Herndon, September 15, 1865, Wilson and Davis, *Herndon's Informants,* 123–125; John Hanks's statement to Herndon, n.d., Wilson and Davis, *Herndon's Informants,* 43–45. Compare Nathaniel Grigsby to Herndon, September 12, 1865, Wilson and Davis, *Herndon's Informants,* 111–115.

19. Herndon to Jesse Weik, January 19, 1886, Hertz, *Hidden Lincoln,* 139.

20. Sandburg, *The Prairie Years,* 1: 26. Dennis Hanks reported that "Lincoln's mother [Nancy] learned him to read the Bible." See Dennis F. Hanks's statement to Herndon, June 13, 1865, Wilson and Davis, *Herndon's Informants,* 35–43.

21. Elton Trueblood, *Abraham Lincoln: Theologian of American Anguish* (New York: Harper and Row, 1973), 50.

22. Barton, *Life of Lincoln,* 14; Beveridge, *Lincoln,* 1: 15; Herndon to Truman H. Bartlett, October 1887, Herndon/Weik Collection; Hertz, *Hidden Lincoln,* 208.

23. This specific connection between the quality of the infantile empathic environment and the shape of the adult personality was first noted by Kohut, "Forms and Transformations of Narcissism," in *Search for the Self,* 1: 118.

24. *Collected Works,* 1: 118.

25. Dennis F. Hanks to Herndon, June 13, 1865, Wilson and Davis, *Herndon's Informants,* 35–43.

26. Herndon to Ward Hill Lamon, February 25, 1870, Hertz, *Hidden Lincoln,* 63; Charles Friend to Herndon, July 31, 1889, Wilson and Davis, *Herndon's Informants,* 673–674; Herndon's notes to himself, n.d., Hertz, *Hidden Lincoln,* 393–94.

27. Herndon to Jesse Weik, January 1, 1886, Hertz, *Hidden Lincoln,* 118–19; Herndon's notes to himself, n.d., Hertz, *Hidden Lincoln,* 393.

28. Herndon's notes to himself, n.d., Hertz, *Hidden Lincoln,* 393. For years Herndon wrestled with the issue of the exact timing of castration but never doubted the reality of the event. He never seemed to note the distinction between castration and induced sterility from mumps. See Herndon to Truman H. Bartlett, September 30, 1887, Herndon/Weik Collection; Hertz, *Hidden Lincoln,* 205–207.

29. Nathaniel Grigsby to Herndon, September 12, 1865, Wilson and Davis, *Herndon's Informants,* 111–115.

30. Beveridge, *Lincoln,* 1: 5; Herndon and Weik, *Life of Lincoln,* 12; Ward Hill Lamon, *The Life of Abraham Lincoln: From His Birth to His Inauguration as President* (Boston: James E. Osgood, 1872), 75; and Josiah G. Holland, *The Life of Abraham Lincoln* (Springfield, Mass.: Gurdon Bill, 1866), 22–23, 28.

31. Warren, *Lincoln's Parentage,* 47; Harry E. Pratt, *The Personal Finances of Abraham Lincoln* (Springfield, Ill.: Abraham Lincoln Association, 1943), 4.

32. Herndon's note on his visit to the Lincoln farm in Kentucky, September 14, 1865, Hertz, *Hidden Lincoln,* 359.

33. Dennis F. Hanks to William Herndon, June 13, 1865, Wilson and Davis, *Herndon's Informants,* 35–43.

34. Benjamin Thomas, *Abraham Lincoln: A Biography* (New York: Alfred A. Knopf, 1952), 5; Herndon and Weik, *Life of Lincoln,* 13; Warren, *Lincoln's Parentage,* 122–23.

35. *Collected Works,* 1: 280.

36. Barton, *Lineage of Lincoln,* 83.

37. Thomas, *Lincoln,* 134.

38. Lincoln retained a disdain for symbols of ignorance. He once asked Herndon to handle a letter from Louis W. Chandler because he was "bored more than enough about it; not the least of which annoyance is his cursed, unreadable, and ungodly handwriting." *Collected Works,* 1: 445. The "bunglingly" quote is *Collected Works,* 4: 61, and the family history quote is *Collected Works,* 1: 456.

39. Dennis F. Hanks's to Herndon, June 13, 1865, Wilson and Davis, *Herndon's Informants,* 35–43; Sarah Lincoln to Herndon, September 8, 1865, Wilson and Davis, *Herndon's Informants,* 106–109.

40. Beveridge, *Lincoln,* 1: 3.

41. Sarah Lincoln to Herndon, September 8, 1865, Wilson and Davis, *Herndon's Informants,* 106–109; John Hanks to Herndon, n.d. [1865–1866], Wilson and Davis, *Herndon's Informants,* 453–458; Beveridge, *Lincoln,* 1: 45.

42. Alexis de Tocqueville, *Democracy in America,* ed. Richard D. Heffner (New York: New American Library, 1956), 243–47.

43. *Collected Works,* 4: 61; Warren, *Lincoln's Parentage,* 154.

44. *Collected Works,* 2: 94.

45. Ibid., 3: 511; 4: 61.

46. Dennis F. Hanks to Herndon, June 13, 1865, Wilson and Davis, *Herndon's Informants,* 35–43; Beveridge, *Lincoln,* 1: 33 (note also the discussion of the slavery issue in Benjamin Quarles, *Lincoln and the Negro* [New York: Oxford University Press, 1962], 16); *Collected Works,* 4: 61–62.

47. *Collected Works,* 4: 62.

48. Dennis F. Hanks to Herndon, June 13, 1865, Wilson and Davis, *Herndon's Informants,* 35–43.

49. Roy P. Basler, *A Touchstone for Greatness: Essays, Addresses, and Occasional Pieces about Abraham Lincoln* (Westport, Conn.: Greenwood Press, 1973), 57. Note also Wilson, *Honor's Voice,* 55–62, 331.

50. Sarah Lincoln to Herndon, September 8, 1865, Wilson and Davis, *Herndon's Informants,* 106–109; John Hanks to Herndon, n.d. [1865–1866], Wilson and Davis, *Herndon's Informants,* 453–458.

51. Sarah Lincoln to Herndon, September 8, 1865, Wilson and Davis, *Herndon's Informants,* 106–109.

52. John Romine to Herndon, September 14, 1865, Wilson and Davis, *Herndon's Informants,* 118 (compare Herndon and Weik, *Life of Lincoln,* 38, that changed the quote in many particulars).

53. Herndon to Weik, December 29, 1885, Hertz, *Hidden Lincoln,* 116; Donald, *Lincoln's Herndon,* 128; Herndon and Weik, *Life of Lincoln,* 258, 268, 272.

54. Herndon to Weik, November 12, 1885, Hertz, *Hidden Lincoln,* 99; Herndon to Cyrus O. Poole, January 5, 1886, Hertz, *Hidden Lincoln,* 120; Sarah Lincoln's statement to Herndon, September 8, 1865, Wilson and Davis, *Herndon's Informants,* 106–109. Compare Matilda Moore to Herndon on the same day, Wilson and Davis, *Herndon's Informants,* 109–110.

55. Louis A. Warren, *Lincoln's Youth: Indiana Years, Seven to Twenty-One, 1816–1830* (New York: Appleton-Century-Crofts, 1959), 84.

56. Herndon's notes to himself, n.d., Hertz, *Hidden Lincoln,* 422–24. In his book with Weik, the "thigh" became the "ankle"; see Herndon and Weik, *Life of Lincoln,* 31. Oddly, Matilda in her one written statement says "foot"; see Matilda Moore to Herndon, September 8, 1865, Wilson and Davis, *Herndon's Informants,* 109–110. The best one can say with certainty, it seems, is that the ax cut Matilda somewhere in the lower half of her body. I have chosen the "thigh" version because it is the most complete account. Weik probably censored Herndon for the book, though the conflict between Herndon's notes and Matilda's statement is unexplained. Herndon perhaps missed the sexual meaning of the story because he focused too intently on the theme of honesty, an aspect of the story given emphasis by the ax that connects Lincoln to Washington and the cherry tree (personal communication, John Patterson, Springfield, Illinois).

57. Dennis F. Hanks to Herndon, June 13, 1865, Wilson and Davis, *Herndon's Informants,* 35–43.

58. Sarah Lincoln to Herndon, September 8, 1865, Wilson and Davis, *Herndon's Informants*, 106–109.

59. Sandburg, *The Prairie Years*, 1: 50; Justin G. Turner and Linda Levitt Turner, eds., *Mary Todd Lincoln: Her Life and Letters* (New York: Alfred A. Knopf, 1972), 464–65; Joshua Fry Speed, *Reminiscences of Abraham Lincoln and Notes of a Visit to California: Two Lectures* (Louisville: John P. Morton, 1884), 11–17; Lamon, *Life of Lincoln*, 463; Sarah Lincoln to Herndon, September 8, 1865, Wilson and Davis, *Herndon's Informants*, 106–109; *Collected Works*, 4: 62.

60. In Freud's early papers on hysteria he reported with absolute conviction that early childhood sexual trauma (by which he meant seduction by the parent of the opposite sex) lay behind every adult case of hysteria; see Sigmund Freud, "Heredity and the Aetiology of the Neuroses" (1896), *The Standard Edition of the Complete Psychological Works of Sigmund Freud*, ed. James Strachey, 23 vols. (London: Hogarth Press, 1962), 3: 153; "Further Remarks on the Neuro-Psychoses of Defence" (1886), 3: 163, and "The Aetiology of Hysteria" (1896), 3: 199. By the fall of 1897, Freud came to feel that his infantile seduction theory was implausible; see Sigmund Freud to Wilhelm Fliess, September 21, 1897, *The Origins of Psycho-Analysis: Letters to Wilhelm Fliess, Drafts and Notes: 1877–1902*, ed. Marie Bonaparte, Anna Freud, and Ernst Kris, trans. Eric Mosbacher and James Strachey (New York: Basic Books, 1954), 215–16. What mattered, clearly, was fantasy rather than reality. That idea led to the theory of infantile sexuality; see "Three Essays on the Theory of Sexuality" (1905), *Standard Edition*, 7: 125–245.

61. Sigmund Freud, "Screen Memories" (1899), *Standard Edition*, 3: 301–22.

62. One must be highly selective in discussing this literature, for it is enormous. The orienting theoretical statement on mourning and loss generally remains the first: Sigmund Freud, "Mourning and Melancholia" (1917 [1915]), *Standard Edition*, 14: 239–58. George Pollock extended Freud's insights to include the adaptive aspects of mourning; see George Pollock, "Mourning and Adaptation," *International Journal of Psychoanalysis* 42 (1961): 341–61. Pollock has also worked on the specific meanings of childhood parental loss; see "Childhood, Parent, and Sibling Loss in Adult Patients," *Archives of General Psychiatry* 7 (1962): 295–305; and "Mourning and Childhood Loss," *Bulletin of the Association of Psychoanalytic Medicine* 5 (1966): 51–54. Note also Jeanne Lample-de-Groot, "Mourning in a 6-Year-Old Girl," *Psychoanalytic Study of the Child* 31 (1976): 273–81; Joshua M. Perman, "The Search for the Mother: Narcissistic Regression as a Pathway of Mourning in Childhood," *Psychoanalytic Quarterly* 48 (1979): 448–64 (note Perman's excellent bibliography for additional references); and the third volume of John Bowlby's impressive *Attachment and Loss, Loss: Sadness and Depression* (New York: Basic Books, 1980). For insight into the relationship between childhood parental loss and adult suicide, see T. L. Dorpat, "Suicide, Loss, and Mourning," *Life-Threatening Behavior* 3 (1973): 213–24. Heinz Kohut's work provides a different perspective on these issues; see *The Analysis of the Self: A Systematic Approach to the Psychoanalytic Treatment of Narcissistic Personality Disorders* (New York: International Universities Press, 1971); *The Restoration of the Self* (New York: International Universities Press, 1977); and *Search for the Self*. The most useful source, however, for interpreting mourning and loss specifically from a self-psychological point of view are the cases of Mr. E and Mr. M in *The Psychology*

of The Self: A Casebook, written with the Collaboration of Heinz Kohut, ed. Arnold Goldberg (New York: International Universities Press, 1978), 263–96, 121–64.

63. *Collected Works,* 4: 62.

64. The turkey story seems part of family legend. Dennis F. Hanks added the detail of his mother loading the gun: "Lincoln saw a wild turkey near the camp on the second day after landing [in Indiana], and Mrs. Lincoln, Abe's good mother, loaded the gun. Abe poked the gun through the crack of the camp and accidentally killed one, which he brought to the camp house." Dennis F. Hanks to Herndon, June 13, 1865, Wilson and Davis, *Herndon's Informants,* 35–43.

65. Don E. Fehrenbacher, *Lincoln in Text and Context: Collected Essays* (Stanford: Stanford University Press, 1987), 225, calls this my "wild turkey hypothesis." He does, however, bring to my attention the fact that prior to my book Fawn M. Brodie and Michael Rogin had both noted that the turkey story had some psychological significance, though I would have to say with few of the meanings or little of the elaboration that I bring to it. See Fawn M. Brodie, "Hidden Presidents," *Harper's Magazine* 254 (1977), 71, and Michael Paul Rogin, "The King's Two Bodies: Abraham Lincoln, Richard Nixon, and Presidential Self-Sacrifice," *Massachusetts Review* 20 (1979), 573. Fehrenbacher in his footnote 38 on page 331 makes a snide reference to the fact that I "revealed" in one of my footnotes that I first got the essential outlines of my interpretation of the turkey story from an undergraduate thesis at Harvard, as though that diminishes the source. In fact, then, as now, I want to acknowledge that I first heard about Lincoln and turkeys from Paul Dry, when he was writing his undergraduate thesis at Harvard University in 1966, "With Charity Toward All: A Study of Lincoln's Political Moratorium and Re-Emergence," under the direction of Erik Erikson.

66. *Collected Works,* 4: 62.

67. J. D. Wickizer to Herndon, November 25, 1866, Wilson and Davis, *Herndon's Informants,* 423–424; Mary S. Vineyard to Herndon, July 22, 1866, Wilson and Davis, *Herndon's Informants,* 262–263.

68. Herndon to Jesse Weik, December 1, 1888, Hertz, *Hidden Lincoln,* 227; see also Herndon and Weik, *Life of Lincoln,* 58.

69. Herndon and Weik, *Life of Lincoln,* 23; *Collected Works,* 4: 64; Nat Grigsby to Herndon, September 12, 1865, Wilson and Davis, *Herndon's Informants,* 111–115.

70. This sentence occasioned Michael Burlingame, *The Inner World of Abraham Lincoln (Urbana: University of Illinois Press, 1994),* 107, to say that even I label my theory "fanciful," which suggests that he has trouble reading, and then to call on the authority of Fehrenbacher, *Text and Context,* 223–227. Fehrenbacher is quite respectful of my book in general but does disagree rather strenuously with what I say about Lincoln and the turkey in what follows. So be it; we cannot all agree.

71. *Collected Works,* 1: 378.

72. Ibid., 1: 367–70; 1: 378–79; 1: 386–89.

73. Beveridge, *Lincoln,* 1: 39.

74. *Collected Works,* 1: 388–389.

Chapter 2

1. W[illiam] D[ean] Howells, *Life of Abraham Lincoln* (Springfield, Ill.: Abraham Lincoln Association, 1938), 32–33. Minutes from the New Salem Debating Society no longer exist, but the Illinois State Historical Library does have the minutes from the debating society in Petersburg. Memberships in the societies overlap, and the range of topics discussed was quite similar. One can therefore infer the nature of the New Salem Debating Society with some confidence from these records.

2. Russell Godby told William Herndon in 1865 that he once hired Lincoln to do some farm work but to his surprise found him sitting on a woodpile reading a book. Godby asked Lincoln what he was reading: "I'm not reading," he answered, "I'm studying." "Great God Almighty!" Godby exclaimed and walked on. See *Life of Lincoln*, 92. One should note, however, the literary quality of Charles James Fox Clarke's letters to his mother and brother from the village in the 1830s. See Charles R. Clarke, "Sketch of Charles James Fox Clarke with Letters to his Mother," *Journal of the Illinois State Historical Society* 22 (January 1930): 559–81. Jack Kelso quoted Shakespeare and Burns, with or without encouragement, and Mentor Graham was sufficiently educated to assist Lincoln when he needed to learn some mathematics quickly. Finally, Dr. Allen, as mentioned above, was a graduate of Dartmouth.

3. The best recent discussion of Lincoln in New Salem is Wilson, *Honor's Voice*, though John Y. Simon was the first to re-evaluate that love story in "Abraham Lincoln and Ann Rutledge," *Journal of the Abraham Lincoln Association* 11 (1990). Note as well John Evangelist Walsh, *The Shadows Rise: Abraham Lincoln and the Ann Rutledge Legend* (Urbana: University of Illinois Press, 1993). The best narrative history of the town itself is Benjamin P. Thomas, *Lincoln's New Salem: Its History, Its Influence on Lincoln, Its Lincoln Legends, and the Story of Its Restoration*, new and rev. ed. (1834; Chicago and Lincoln's New Salem: Lincoln's New Salem Enterprises, 1973). Most of the New Salem stories about young Lincoln can be found in Wilson and Davis, *Herndon's Informants* and then recast in Herndon and Weik, *Life of Lincoln*.

4. Lincoln left his father's house on the Sangamon River near Decatur after the harsh winter of 1830–1831. Thomas and Sarah Lincoln then settled in Coles County, Illinois, some seventy miles from Springfield.

5. *Collected Works*, 1: 510; "'I was out of work,' he [Lincoln] said to me [Herndon] once, 'and there being no danger of more fighting, I could do nothing better than enlist again.'" Herndon and Weik, *Life of Lincoln*, 82.

6. *Collected Works*, 4: 64–65.

7. Ibid., 4: 65.

8. Thomas, *Lincoln's New Salem*, 102–103.

9. Harry E. Pratt, *The Personal Finances of Abraham Lincoln* (Springfield, Ill.: Abraham Lincoln Association, 1943), 13. Compare Thomas, *Lincoln's New Salem*, 111–12.

10. *Collected Works*, 4: 65.

11. Ibid., 1: 25, 4: 65; Thomas, *Lincoln's New Salem*, 95–97; Howells, *Life of Lincoln*, 32–33.

12. *Collected Works*, 3: 16.

13. After Lincoln's death, Dummer told Herndon that "Lincoln used to come to our office—Stuart's and mine —in Springfield from New Salem and borrow law books." Herndon and Weik, *Life of Lincoln*, 145n.; *Collected Works*, 3: 16, 4: 65; Thomas, *Lincoln's New Salem*, 101.

14. Paul Simon, *Lincoln's Preparation for Greatness: The Illinois Legislative Years* (Norman: University of Oklahoma Press, 1965), 277–78, 232–36.

15. Kohut, "On the Adolescent Process as a Transformation of the Self," in *Search for the Self*, 2: 659–62. See also Kohut, *Analysis of the Self*, 43–44, 55, 70, 76–77, 119, 139, 261, 312–13, 321; and *Restoration of the Self*, 5, 6, 131, 272. Note also Kenneth Kenniston, "Youth as a Stage of Life," *Youth and Dissent* (New York: Harcourt Brace Jovanovich, 1960), 3–21. The most extensive thoughts on identity are in the writings of Erik Erikson. Note especially *Childhood and Society*, 2nd ed. (New York: W. W. Norton, 1963); *Identity: Youth and Crisis* (New York: W. W. Norton, 1968); *Insight and Responsibility* (New York: W. W. Norton, 1964); and *Young Man Luther* (New York: W. W. Norton, 1958).

16. Lincoln's relationship with Ann Rutledge was brought into completely new focus with the work of Simon, "Abraham Lincoln and Ann Rutledge," 13–33. Note also Wilson, *Honor's Voice*, and John Evangelist Walsh, *The Shadows Rise: Abraham Lincoln and the Ann Rutledge Legend* (Urbana: University of Illinois Press, 1993). The literature is summarized by Richard Taylor, "Review Essay: Telling Lincoln's Story," *Journal of the Abraham Lincoln Association* 21 (2000): 44–68. The tradition against which this revisionist literature argues was most clearly established by Randall, *Lincoln the President*, 2: 321–42.

17. Wilson, *Honor's Voice*, 114–118 (which also notes the many New Salem sources that testify to the romance); Simon, "Abraham Lincoln and Ann Rutledge."

18. Robert B. Rutledge to Herndon, c. November 1, 1866, Wilson and Davis, *Herndon's Informants*, 383; Elizabeth Abell to Herndon, February 15, 1867, Wilson and Davis, *Herndon's Informants*, 557; Henry McHenry to Herndon, January 8, 1866, Wilson and Davis, *Herndon's Informants*, 156; and Robert L. Wilson to Herndon, February 10, 1866, Wilson and Davis, *Herndon's Informants*, 205.

19. Herndon and Weik, *Life of Lincoln*, especially 105, but also throughout the text, makes the case that Lincoln never really recovered from the loss of Ann Rutledge. Wilson, in *Honor's Voice*, disputes Herndon in this regard but surprisingly (121–22) accepts the generally discredited testimony of Isaac Cogdal, on which Herndon heavily relied. The one thing Randall was right about was to question the reliability of Cogdal; see Randall, *Lincoln the President* 2: 333–35.

20. L. M. Greene to Herndon, May 3, 1866, Wilson and Davis, *Herndon's Informants*, 250; Johnson Gaines Greene to Herndon, [1866], Wilson and Davis, *Herndon's Informants*, 530; and Mentor Graham to Herndon, April 2, 1866, Wilson and Davis, *Herndon's Informants*, 243. Compare Thomas, *Lincoln*, 56.

21. *Collected Works*, 1: 78–79.

22. Ibid., 1: 94–95.

23. Mary S. Vineyard [Owens] to Herndon, May 23, 1866, Wilson and Davis, *Herndon's Informants*, 255–256; Herndon quoted the entire letter in his book; see Herndon and Weik, *Life of Lincoln*, 119.

24. *Collected Works*, 1: 118–119.

25. James C. Conkling to Mercy Levering, September 21, 1840, Illinois State Historical Library.

26. Turner and Turner, *Mary Todd Lincoln*, 21.

27. *Collected Works*, 1: 78.

28. Ruth Painter Randall, *The Courtship of Mr. Lincoln* (Boston: Little, Brown, 1957), 125. Note also Randall's earlier book, *Mary Lincoln: Biography of a Marriage* (Boston: Little, Brown, 1953), 47–51, 64, 70–71; Herndon and Weik, *Life of Lincoln*, 162–82.

29. Randall, *Mary Lincoln*, 64.

30. *Abe Lincoln Laughing: Humorous Anecdotes from Original Sources by and about Abraham Lincoln,* ed. P. M. Zall, with an introduction by Ray Allen Billington (Berkeley: University of California Press, 1982), 136, Number 263. Zall is the authoritative source on Lincoln's humor. I have slightly recast the story in a way that seems reasonable, given that it is at best second-hand.

31. Elizabeth Wirt Edwards to Herndon, July 27, 1887, *Herndon's Informants,* 622–23; Herndon to Ward Hill Lamon, February 25, 1870, Hertz, *Hidden Lincoln,* 68; Herndon and Weik, *Life of Lincoln,* 304; Edmund Wilson, *Patriotic Gore: Studies in the Literature of the American Civil War* (New York: Oxford University Press, 1962), 118–19.

32. Harriet A. Chapman to Herndon [1886–1887], Wilson and Davis, *Herndon's Informants,* 646; Elizabeth Keckley, *Behind the Scenes; Or Thirty Years a Slave and Four Years in the White House* (New York: G. W. Carleton, 1868), 230, is the source for Baker's story in Turner and Turner, *Mary Todd Lincoln,* 84–85.

33. Turner and Turner, *Mary Todd Lincoln,* 18.

34. Abner Y. Ellis wrote Herndon on March 24, 1866, Wilson and Davis, *Herndon's Informants,* 238: "I had it from good authority that after Mr. L. was engaged to be Married to his wife Mary. That She a Short time before they were Married backed out from her engagement with him." Besides being second-hand ("I had it from good authority"), it is not even clear what time period Ellis is talking about. There was, after all, a twenty-two-month gap between the broken engagement and the marriage. Is that the "Short time" of which Ellis speaks?

35. Turner and Turner, *Mary Todd Lincoln,* 26.

36. Jean Baker, *Mary Todd Lincoln: A Biography* (New York: W. W. Norton, 1987), 142; the narrative of the courtship is 83–91.

37. Burlingame, *Inner World,* 349n, 331, has found a couple of obscure 1936 articles on this subject with two additional references to Matilda, but one source is not even named, and another is a distant Todd relative (Burlingame also quotes an irrelevant source about a Julia Evans in Indiana in 1827). But the number of very tangential references to Matilda proves nothing. As I argue below, it is clear there was gossip in town about Lincoln and Matilda, and I suspect the idea of Matilda winning Lincoln's heart might have been something of an official Todd family story. The task of the historian is to sort out the real story from the gossip, not to swallow the myth just because it comes to us from many angles.

38. Joshua Speed to Herndon [1865–1866], Wilson and Davis, *Herndon's Informants,* 474–477; James H. Matheny to Herndon, May 3, 1866, Wilson and Davis, *Herndon's Informants,* 251; Wilson, *Honor's Voice,* 242, which in turn quotes Browning's

interview with Herndon, June 17, 1865, published in Michael Burlingame's *Oral History of Abraham Lincoln: John G. Nicolay's Interviews and Essays* (Carbondale and Edwardsville: Southern Illinois University Press, 1996), 2.

39. Elizabeth Todd Edwards to Herndon [1865–1866, though in a footnote the editors suggest it was most likely on January 10, 1866] Wilson and Davis, *Herndon's Informants*, 443–444; and Elizabeth and Ninian W. Edwards to Herndon, July 27, 1887, Wilson and Davis, *Herndon's Informants*, 622–623. Note that in Ninian's first interview he felt Matilda may have been a factor: Ninian W. Edwards to Herndon, September 22, 1865, Wilson and Davis, *Herndon's Informants*, 133.

40. Herndon and Weik, *Life of Lincoln*, 169–169. It is impossible not to add that Lincoln's distinguished biographer, David Donald, *Lincoln*, 84–87, accepts my reading of the documents in his narrative of the courtship.

41. Another piece of Wilson's argument is that Mary suddenly put on weight in the late fall of 1840, thus turning off Lincoln's affections. The evidence for the weight gain, however, may be the weakest link in his argument. See Wilson, *Honor's Voice*, 221.

42. Herndon to Jesse Weik, January 1891, Hertz, *Hidden Lincoln*, 259–60. Wilson, *Honor's Voice*, 127–128, gives the full account of the source. I have always felt the supposed syphilis was connected to Lincoln's lost letter to Dr. Daniel Drake, though that is supposition. See Joshua Speed to Herndon, November 30, 1866, Wilson and Davis, *Herndon's Informants*, 430–431, and December 6, 1866, Wilson and Davis, *Herndon's Informants*, 498–500.

43. Wilson, *Honor's Voice*, 127.

44. Milton H. Shutes, *Lincoln's Emotional Life* (Philadelphia: Dorrance, 1957), 68–69.

45. Erikson, *Childhood and Society*, 263–264.

46. Speed, *Reminiscences*, 16–17.

47. Joshua F. Speed, "Incidents in the Early Life of A. Lincoln," memorandum to Herndon, n.d. [by 1882], Joshua Speed Collection, Illinois State Historical Library, and Wilson and Davis, *Herndon's Informants*, 588–591.

48. Herndon to Ward Hill Lamon, February 25, 1870, Hertz, *Hidden Lincoln*, 65–66. This personal letter is consistent with Herndon's treatment in Herndon and Weik, *Life of Lincoln*, 150–51, and with Speed's memorandum to Herndon, Wilson and Davis, *Herndon's Informants*, 588–591. All commentators who have worked with this evidence agree that Lincoln therefore slept with Speed from 1837 to late December 1840. Note Randall, *The Courtship*, 122; and Gary Lee Williams, "James and Joshua Speed: Lincoln's Kentucky Friends" (Ph.D. diss., Duke University, 1971), 15–29. I agree with this reconstruction of events. However, it should be noted that Herndon contradicted himself in two letters to Jesse Weik. In Herndon to Weik, Springfield, January 15, 1886, Hertz, *Hidden Lincoln*, 134, Herndon wrote: "Lincoln came to this city in 1837, and Joshua F. Speed gratuitously took him into his room, gave him bed and house room, etc. William Butler was a man of some wealth for the time . . . he took Lincoln to his house, gave him a bed, sleeping room, and boarded him from 1837 to 1842, when Lincoln got married to Miss Todd." The next day Herndon wrote again to Weik: "I intended to say that, in the Butler note, Butler gratuitously, freely, and without charge boarded Lincoln from 1837 to 1842,

when Lincoln got married." In these letters to Weik, Herndon was of course contradicting his own dating elsewhere as well as all the other evidence. The explanation seems to me to be, first, Herndon's concern in those two letters to Weik was with Butler, not the establishment of accurate dates, and since it was long after the event, he probably was simply confused; and second, Lincoln probably did stay with Butler after January 1841, that is, after he left Speed's store. In other words, Lincoln stayed from 1837 to December 1840, with Speed and from sometime in early 1841 to November 1842, with Butler. Herndon simply collapsed the two in his 1886 letters to Weik, even though elsewhere he correctly dated Lincoln's stay with Speed. The importance of this question will become obvious later in my discussion.

49. Speed, *Reminiscences of Lincoln,* 23; Randall, *The Courtship,* 11–17; and Herndon and Weik, *Life of Lincoln,* 150–51.

50. In the first edition of this book, I called Speed Lincoln's "only" intimate friend. Susan Krause, "Abraham Lincoln and Joshua Speed, Attorney and Client," *Illinois Historical Journal* 89 (1996): 36, chides me for overstatement. She is right. Robert J. Johnson, a Ph.D. student working partly under my direction on Lincoln the lawyer, has reiterated this point in an unpublished paper, "The Education of Abraham Lincoln."

51. Lamon, *Life of Lincoln,* 483.

52. Leonard Swett once described how he stumbled into Davis's hotel room in Danville and found Davis and Lincoln in a pillow fight. See Leonard Swett to Herndon [1887–1889], Wilson and Davis, *Herndon's Informants,* 731–732.

53. Herndon to Jesse Weik, January 22, 1887, Hertz, *Hidden Lincoln,* 159.

54. *Collected Works,* 1: 269.

55. Herndon wrote that "on the love question alone Lincoln opened to Speed possibly the whole." Herndon to Jesse Weik, January 22, 1887, Hertz, *Hidden Lincoln,* 159.

56. Randall, in *The Courtship,* variously characterizes Speed as "the frequent lover" (42); as having a "pleasing personality" (12); as "apt to fall in love with practically every pretty girl he encountered" (12); as having a "handsome Byronic face" (12); and as "that Don Juan of Springfield, Joshua Speed" (43). To call Speed a "frequent lover" and a "Don Juan," however, confuses mild flirtations with sexually consummated relationships. All the evidence indicates the former. Note Mary Todd to Mercy Ann Levering, Springfield, December 15, 1840, in Turner and Turner, *Mary Todd Lincoln,* 20; Lincoln to Speed, January 3, 1842, in *Collected Works,* 1: 266; and the two references to Sarah Rickard in Lincoln to Speed, February 3, 1842, in *Collected Works,* 1: 268, and Lincoln to Speed, March 27, 1842, in *Collected Works,* 1: 282. As I argue here, Speed seemed to have the same kind of sexual conflicts as Lincoln, which in part explains their friendship.

57. Speed memorandum to Herndon, November 30, 1866, Wilson and Davis, *Herndon's Informants,* 430–431.

58. Note Robert H. Wiebe, "Lincoln's Fraternal Democracy," *Abraham Lincoln and the American Political Tradition,* ed. John L. Thomas (Amherst: University of Massachusetts Press, 1986), 19–28. My argument about male society in this period is nicely complemented by the fascinating article by Carroll Smith-Rosenberg, "The Female World of Love and Ritual: Relations between Women in Nineteenth-

Century America," *Signs: Journal of Women in Culture and Society* 1 (Autumn 1975): 1–29.

59. Paton Yoder, *Taverns and Travelers: Inns of the Early Midwest* (Bloomington: Indiana University Press, 1969), 146–47.

60. Henry Clay Whitney, *Life on the Circuit with Lincoln* (Caldwell, Idaho: Caxton Printers, 1940), 62–63; William G. Greene to Herndon, May 30, 1865, Wilson and Davis, *Herndon's Informants,* 17–21.

61. S. A. Crawford to Herndon, January 4, 1866, Hertz, *Hidden Lincoln,* 287.

62. Mary Todd wrote to Mercy Ann Levering in June 1841: "Mr. Speed, our former most constant guest has been in Kentucky for some weeks past, will be here next month, on a visit perhaps, as he has some idea of deserting Illinois, his mother is anxious he should superintend her affairs, he takes a friend's privilege, of occasionally favouring me with a letter, in his last he spoke of his great desire of once more inhabiting this region & of his possibility of soon returning—." Turner and Turner, *Mary Todd Lincoln,* 27.

63. Speed wrote Herndon on September 17, 1866, Wilson and Davis, *Herndon's Informants,* 342: "I sold out to Hurst 1 Jany 1841. And came to Ky in the spring," Also note the weekly announcements in the *Sangamo Journal,* beginning January 8, 1841; "The co-partnership heretofore existing between Jas. Bell and Joshua F. Speed is this day dissolved by mutual consent . . . January 1, 1841." A separate announcement noted the formation of the partnership of Bell and Charles R. Hurst, as of January 1, 1841. Wilson curiously argues in *Honor's Voice,* 356n.5, and note also his "Abraham Lincoln and 'That Fatal First of January,'" *Lincoln Before Washington: New Perspectives on the Illinois Years* (Urbana: University of Illinois Press, 1997), that this evidence fails to prove Lincoln and Speed separated; Wilson says categorically there is "no evidence" to this effect (and concludes they stayed together after January 1). But Wilson ignores the obvious implication of the sale: namely that Speed had to move from a place he no longer owned (besides the evidence, admittedly indirect, in note 46). Probably more importantly, the phrasing of Herndon's account of Lincoln's depression in January 1841, following the break (Herndon and Weik, *Life of Lincoln,* 170) clearly suggests Lincoln had his own room after January 1: He was confined to "his bed" and his friends needed to gather around to remove his razors when he became suicidal, which would not have been a problem in the dormitory setting above Speed's store. I would also note a contradiction in Wilson's argument about the "fatal first": Wilson argues to not much effect but at great length that the engagement was actually broken in November. He makes at least a reasonable case; but if true, we are left without an explanation for Lincoln's own crucial reference to "that fatal first of Jany. '41," which even Wilson calls "eye-catching" (*Honor's Voice,* 229). If Wilson is correct about the chronology of the broken engagement, Lincoln in this famous phrase could only be referring to his break with Speed. I actually doubt that. I suspect Lincoln broke his engagement with Mary Todd on January 1 in the wake of his confusion over the separation from Speed but always experienced that day as "fatal" because of the pain it caused Mary and the intensity of his own loss. Such a conclusion is consistent with a balanced read of the evidence and takes into account the full range of Lincoln's emotional confusions.

64. It has often been noted that Lincoln did not take to his bed until January 13 and that it was only between the 13th and the 19th that his name failed to appear in any roll call of the legislature; see *Day by Day,* 1: 152. Some would conclude from this sequence that his depression could not be a reaction to events on January 1, but such an interpretation is psychologically naive. Depression and collapse often can be delayed, pending important affairs; in fact, it is not uncommon to need a period of time to process despair before reacting.

65. *Collected Works,* 1: 282.

66. See letters of Anson G. Henry to his wife, February 17 and 18, 1863; April 12, 1863; December 18, 28, and 30, 1864; January 2, 9, and 16, 1864; February 8, 1864; March 9, 13, and 21, 1864, Illinois State Historical Library; Simon, *Lincoln's Preparation for Greatness,* 239; Herndon to Isaac Arnold, November 20, 1866, Hertz, *Hidden Lincoln,* 37; *Collected Works,* 1: 282, 2: 31, 46, 68–69.

67. See Lincoln's thank-you note to Speed's half-sister, Mary, *Collected Works,* 1: 259–61; Mary Todd to Mercy Ann Levering, June 1841, Turner and Turner, *Mary Todd Lincoln,* 27.

68. *Collected Works,* 1: 266.

69. Ibid., 1: 269.

70. *Collected Works,* 1: 265–266, 267, 269, 280.

71. Ibid., 1: 280–281.

72. Ibid., 1: 270.

73. John Hanks's statement to Herndon [1865–1866], Wilson and Davis, *Herndon's Informants,* 453–458; Herndon to James H. Wilson, September 23, 1889, Herndon/Weik Collection; Sarah Lincoln's statement to Herndon, September 8, 1865, Wilson and Davis, *Herndon's Informants,* 106–109.

74. Herndon and Weik, *Life of Lincoln,* 385–86. Wilson, in *Honor's Voice,* 348n.36, accepts my interpretation and yet at the same time feels we should believe Lincoln visited prostitutes, which "would seem not only consistent with such a fear but possibly further evidence of it." I think more hinges on this issue. If Lincoln visited prostitutes, he would have been familiar with sex. The February 25, 1842, letter to Speed concerns only one issue; if Beardstown girls and five-dollar whores had been a part of Lincoln's experience, the tension in the letter makes little sense.

75. Ibid., 1: 303.

76. *Collected Works,* 1: 389–91 and 320–23.

77. Ibid., 1: 289, 319, 389–91; 2: 320–323; Herndon and Weik, *Life of Lincoln,* 385–386.

78. Ibid., 1: 389–391, 2: 17.

Chapter 3

1. Erik Erikson, *Gandhi's Truth: On the Origins of Militant Nonviolence* (New York: W. W. Norton, 1968), 123.

2. Charles H. Coleman, *Abraham Lincoln and Coles County, Illinois* (New Brunswick, N.J.: Scarecrow Press, 1955), 24, 25, 37; *Collected Works,* 1: 261; Sarah Lincoln's statement to Herndon, September 8, 1865, Wilson and Davis, *Herndon's Informants,* 106–109.

3. Herndon to Jesse Weik, December 1, 1885, Hertz, *Hidden Lincoln,* 109.

4. *Collected Works,* 1: 282.

5. Harry E. Pratt, *The Personal Finances of Abraham Lincoln* (Springfield, Ill.: Abraham Lincoln Association, 1943), 73–75.

6. John D. Johnston for Thomas Lincoln to Abraham Lincoln, December 7, 1848, quoted in Coleman, *Abraham Lincoln and Coles County,* 73.

7. *Collected Works,* 2: 15.

8. Ibid., 2: 98–99.

9. Earl Schenck Miers, William Baringer, and C. Percy Powell, eds., *Lincoln Day by Day: A Chronology, 1809–1865* (Washington, D.C., Lincoln Sesquicentennial Commission, 1960), 2: 46–47.

10. Coleman, *Abraham Lincoln and Coles County,* 139; Turner and Turner, *Mary Todd Lincoln,* 464–465; Lamon, *Life of Lincoln,* 463.

11. The importance of idealization is central in the work of Heinz Kohut. See most notably, *Analysis of the Self.* For a complete discussion of Kohut's work, see my biography, *Heinz Kohut: The Making of a Psychoanalyst* (New York: Farrar, Straus & Giroux, forthcoming).

12. Rush Welter, *The Mind of America, 1820–1850* (New York: Columbia University Press, 1975), 190–218; David Donald, *Liberty and Union* (Lexington, Mass.: D. C. Heath, 1978), 3–51; Henry Clay, "The American System," *The American Whigs,* ed. Daniel Walker Howe (New York: John Wiley and Sons, 1973), 34–35; George B. Forgie, *Patricide in the House Divided: A Psychological Interpretation of Lincoln and His Age* (New York: Norton, 1979), 35–53.

13. Thomas F. Schwartz has researched the lyceum movement in Springfield and discussed the immediate context of Lincoln's speech in "The Springfield Lyceums and Lincoln's 1838 Speech," *Illinois Historical Journal* 83 (1990), 45–49. Compare Donald M. Scott, "The Popular Lecture and the Creation of a Public in Mid-Nineteenth-Century America," *Journal of American History* 66 (1980): 791–908.

14. All the following references to the Lyceum speech are in *Collected Works,* 1: 108–15. In what follows, the revision of my original text draws heavily on my paper, "On the Verge of Greatness: Psychological Reflections on Lincoln at the Lyceum," *Civil War History: A Journal of the Middle Period* (1990) 36: 137–47.

15. John Y. Simon, Commentary at the Symposium of the Abraham Lincoln Association, Springfield, 1984, later published in *Papers of the Abraham Lincoln Association* 6 (1984): 25–27.

16. George W. Fredrickson, "The Search for Order and Community," in Davis et al., *Public and Private Lincoln,* 86–90.

17. *Collected Works,* 1: 279.

18. Wilson, *Patriotic Gore,* 107–108.

19. Dwight G. Anderson, *Abraham Lincoln: The Quest for Immortality* (New York: Alfred A. Knopf, 1982).

20. Fehrenbacher, *Text and Context,* 222–223; Richard N. Current, "Lincoln After 175 Years: The Myth of the Jealous Son," *Papers of the Abraham Lincoln Association* 6 (1984): 15–24.

21. *Collected Works,* 3: 522–550.

22. Ibid., 4: 190; Herbert Mitgang, ed., *Abraham Lincoln, A Press Report: His*

Life and Times from the Original Newspaper Documents of the Union, the Confederacy and Europe (Chicago: Quadrangle Books, 1971), 225.

23. *Collected Works*, 7: 17–18.

24. Trueblood, *Theologian*, 75; Mitgang, *A Press Report*, 378.

25. *Collected Works*, 8: 332–33.

Chapter 4

1. Elizabeth Norris to Emilie Todd Helm, January 12, 1895, Illinois State Historical Library.

2. Herndon to Jesse Weik, January 16, 1886, Hertz, *Hidden Lincoln*, 137.

3. Katherine Helm, *The True Story of Mary, Wife of Lincoln* (New York: Harper and Brothers, 1928), 81.

4. Turner and Turner, *Mary Todd Lincoln*, 15.

5. Ibid., 20–21.

6. Ibid., 15.

7. Ibid., 22.

8. Mrs. John T. Stuart in *Chicago Tribune*, December 2, 1900, Louis A. Warren Library and Museum, Fort Wayne, Indiana.

9. Randall, *Mary Lincoln*, 77.

10. E. H. Merryman, "A Story of the Early Days in Springfield—And A Poem," *Journal of the Illinois State History Society* 16 (1912): 141–46.

11. Turner and Turner, *Mary Todd Lincoln*, 25, 27.

12. Norris to Helm, January 12, 1895, Illinois State Historical Library.

13. The first complete and satisfying account of the duel ever written is Wilson, *Honor's Voice*, 265–283.

14. Randall, *Mary Lincoln*, 23–24; Helm, *The True Story*, 53.

15. Keckley, *Behind the Scenes*, 228–29; Randall, *Mary Lincoln*, 28–29; Dennis Hanks interview, *St. Louis Globe-Democrat*, January 4, 1887, Louis A. Warren Library and Museum, Fort Wayne, Indiana.

16. William H. Townsend, *Lincoln and the Bluegrass: Slavery and Civil War in Kentucky* (Lexington: University of Kentucky Press, 1955), 26–59.

17. Ibid., 27.

18. Ibid., 48.

19. Turner and Turner, *Mary Todd Lincoln*, 37.

20. Randall, *Mary Lincoln*, 22.

21. Norris to Helm, January 12, 1895, Illinois State Historical Library.

22. Ibid., 27.

23. Herndon to Jesse Weik, January 16, 1886, Hertz, *Hidden Lincoln*, 137.

24. Anson G. Henry to his wife, February 18(?), 1963, Illinois State Historical Library; Helm, *The True Story*, 140; Randall, *Mary Lincoln*, 81–82, 93; Turner and Turner, *Mary Todd Lincoln*, 523.

25. Robert Todd asked Lincoln to handle some of his legal matters in Illinois and, later, to probate his will.

26. Turner and Turner, *Mary Todd Lincoln*, 536.

27. Henry E. Pratt, *The Personal Finances of Abraham Lincoln* (Springfield, Ill.: Abraham Lincoln Association, 1943), 63–66.

28. Randall, *Mary Lincoln,* 95–96.

29. Turner and Turner, *Mary Todd Lincoln,* 293. Herndon, of course, amply supported Mary's point. See Herndon to Jesse Weik, February 9, 1887, and to Truman Bartlett, September 22, 1887, Hertz, *Hidden Lincoln,* 69, 204. See also Herndon and Weik, *Life of Lincoln,* 342.

30. Herndon to Jesse Weik, January 23, 1886, Hertz, *Hidden Lincoln,* 141.

31. *Day by Day,* 2: 244; Turner and Turner, *Mary Todd Lincoln,* 53; *Collected Works,* 2: 391.

32. James Gourley to Herndon [1865–1866], Wilson and Davis, *Herndon's Informants,* 451–453.

33. Herndon to Jesse Weik, December 1, 1885, January 8 and 16, 1886, and to Isaac N. Arnold, November 20, 1865, Hertz, *Hidden Lincoln,* 37, 109, 129, 137.

34. Herndon and Weik, *Life of Lincoln,* 166.

35. Donald, *Lincoln's Herndon,* 151–53.

36. Herndon to Jesse Weik, January 5, 1889, Hertz, *Hidden Lincoln,* 233.

37. Ibid., 248.

38. Wilson, *Patriotic Gore,* 130.

39. *Collected Works,* 1: 466.

40. Herndon to Jesse Weik, January 1887, Hertz, *Hidden Lincoln,* 160–62. Compare Randall's view of the story, *Mary Lincoln,* 123–25.

41. Herndon to Jesse Weik, January 11 and 23, 1886, Hertz, *Hidden Lincoln,* 133–34, 149–141; *New York Times,* February 6, 1938, Louis A. Warren Library and Museum, Fort Wayne, Indiana; James Gourley's statement to Herndon [1865–1866], Wilson and Davis, *Herndon's Informants,* 451–453.

42. Herndon to Jesse Weik, February 5, 1887, Hertz, *Hidden Lincoln,* 166; Lamon, *Life of Lincoln,* 482; Frank Fuller, *A Day with the Lincoln Family* (New York, n.d.), pamphlet, Illinois State Historical Library; *Chicago Tribune,* January 1, 1921, Louis A. Warren Library and Museum, Fort Wayne, Indiana.

43. Turner and Turner, *Mary Todd Lincoln,* 60–61, 251. Note also that in a letter written in 1860 Lincoln commented on his son, Robert, who "promises very well, considering we never controlled him much." *Collected Works,* 4: 82. See Herndon to Chauncey F. Black, September 17, 1873, Hertz, *Hidden Lincoln,* 42.

44. Herndon to Jesse Weik, January 8, 1886, Hertz, *Hidden Lincoln,* 128. See also Lamon, *Life of Lincoln,* 472–73.

45. *Collected Works,* 1: 466 and 477.

46. Randall, *Mary Lincoln,* 118; *Collected Works,* 1: 139.

47. Turner and Turner, *Mary Todd Lincoln,* 632; Miers et al., Miers, Baringer, and Powell, *Day by Day,* 2: 27; Octavia Roberts, *Lincoln in Illinois* (Boston: Houghton Mifflin, 1918), 67; Randall, *Mary Lincoln,* 141.

48. Turner and Turner, *Mary Todd Lincoln,* 57–58, 59, 64.

49. Ibid., 632–34.

50. *Collected Works,* 1: 495; Turner and Turner, *Mary Todd Lincoln,* 42; Villard, *Lincoln on the Eve of '61,* 63; James Gourley's statement to Herndon [1865–1866], Wilson and Davis, *Herndon's Informants,* 451–453.

51. Turner and Turner, *Mary Todd Lincoln,* 475.

52. Sklar, "Victorian Women and Domestic Life," in Davis et al., *Public and Private Lincoln,* 30–31.

53. Jean Baker, *Mary Todd Lincoln: A Biography* (New York: W. W. Norton, 1987), 116–117, says categorically that it is a mistaken idea to imagine the separate bedrooms had anything to do with the Lincolns' sexual relationship (though she has no footnote to my work, I am of course the writer against whom she is arguing). Baker says separate bedrooms were common then as a "tangible token of the nineteenth century's emphasis on the divided spheres of men and women" and as an expression of the prosperity the Lincolns had then reached. No one (certainly not I) would disagree that the separate bedrooms had many social meanings for the Lincolns. But besides the reasonable ones she mentions, how can she be so certain that this basic fact of their living space after 1856 had nothing to do with the nature of their intimate relations? I am not claiming I *know* anything more about the Lincolns' sex life than she does; I am only making what I think is a rather interesting historical argument that pieces together various strands of evidence in fresh ways. One of those strands is the meaning of the separate bedrooms. Perhaps I am wrong, but it is definitely not the stretch Baker makes it to suggest that separate bedrooms may well have served to assist the Lincolns in what appeared to be their self-imposed abstinence. And speaking of context, separate bedrooms was probably for the Lincolns, as it was for many other contemporary Americans, an upper-middle-class form of contraception.

54. Turner and Turner, *Mary Todd Lincoln,* 46–49.

55. Villard, *Lincoln on the Eve of '61,* 63; Isaac N. Arnold, *The Life of Abraham Lincoln* (Chicago: Jansen, McClurg, 1885), 83; Randall, *Mary Lincoln,* 158; Turner and Turner, *Mary Todd Lincoln,* 56.

56. Walter Barlow Stevens, *A Reporter's Lincoln* (St. Louis: Missouri Historical Society, 1916), 48; Turner and Turner, *Mary Todd Lincoln,* 66; Gustave P. Koerner, *Memories of Gustave Koerner; Life Sketches Written at the Suggestion of His Children,* ed. Thomas J. McCormack, 2 vols. (Cedar Rapids, Iowa: Torch Press, 1909), 2: 66–67.

57. Randall, *Mary Lincoln,* 30–31; Baker, *Mary Todd Lincoln,* 143–145, 147–149, 152–153, 160–162; Roy P. Basler, "Lincoln, Blacks, and Women," in Davis et al., *Public and Private Lincoln,* 38–56; Townsend, *Lincoln and the Bluegrass,* 72–80.

58. *Collected Works,* 2: 323; Turner and Turner, *Mary Todd Lincoln,* 46.

59. Brooks, *Washington in Lincoln's Time,* 281; Randall, *Mary Lincoln,* 258 (compare Anson G. Henry's view of Hay in the letter to his wife, March 13, 1865, Illinois State Historical Library); John Hay, *Lincoln and the Civil War in the Diaries and Letters of John Hay,* ed. Tyler Dennett (Westport, Conn.: Nego Universities Press, 1972), 41.

60. Turner and Turner, *Mary Todd Lincoln,* 176, 188–89; Marquis Adolphe de Chambrun, *Impressions of Lincoln and the Civil War: A Foreigner's Account* (New York: Random House, 1952), 76.

61. Keckley, *Behind the Scenes,* 128; Turner and Turner, *Mary Todd Lincoln,* 79; de Chambrun, *Impressions,* 21–23.

62. Keckley, *Behind the Scenes,* 116–17; Noyes W. Miner, *Mrs. Abraham: A Vindication,* n.d., manuscript, Illinois State Historical Library, 2–3; Randall, *Mary Lincoln,* 299.

63. Keckley, *Behind the Scenes,* 131; Turner and Turner, *Mary Todd Lincoln,* 71, 87–98, 140; Randall, *Mary Lincoln,* 193.

64. Turner and Turner, *Mary Todd Lincoln,* 183, 447; Basler, "Lincoln, Blacks, and Women," 43.

65. Anson G. Henry to his wife, February 17, 1863, Illinois State Historical Library; *Collected Works,* 7: 34, 5: 492; Turner and Turner, *Mary Todd Lincoln,* 159.

66. Randall, *Mary Lincoln,* 372–75; Adam Baday, *Grant in Peace: From Appomattox to Mount McGregor, A Personal Memoir* (Hartford, Conn.: S. S. Scranton, 1887), 356–65. Baker, *Mary Todd Lincoln,* 238–240, struggles mightily to salvage Mary's reputation from the episode by glossing over some of the established details.

67. De Chambrun, *Impressions,* 84; Randall, *Mary Lincoln,* 382; Turner and Turner, *Mary Todd Lincoln,* 114.

68. Anson G. Henry to his wife, February 17, 1863, Illinois State Historical Library.

69. Elizabeth Edwards to Julia Edwards, April 1, 1862, Illinois State Historical Library.

70. Turner and Turner, *Mary Todd Lincoln,* 130–131, 189.

71. Elizabeth Edwards to Julia Edwards, March 1, 2, and 12, 1862, Illinois State Historical Library.

72. Ibid., April 1, 9, 19, and 26, 1862, Illinois State Historical Library.

73. Keckley, *Behind the Scenes,* 104–105; Baker, *Mary Todd Lincoln,* 212–213. This issue came up in the making of a television documentary by David Grubin that was first aired by PBS in February 2001. Baker in her interview questioned the authenticity of the famous Keckley story, as she does in her book. Sarah Colt, Grubin's assistant, consulted with Matthew Gilmore, the reference librarian at the Martin Luther King Library, Washingtonian Division. Gilmore was able to show, using contemporary maps, including a United States Geological Survey topographic map and Washington street maps, that St. Elizabeth's (or, as it was originally named, the Government Hospital for the Insane) was easily visible from the White House at the time. Gilmore's research was confirmed by that of Gail Redman, reference librarian at the Historical Society of Washington, D.C. As Colt notes in her detailed memorandum on this question dated March 24, 1999, St. Elizabeth's is approximately four miles from the White House as the crow flies. The White House is 50 feet above sea level and St. Elizabeth's is 150 feet above sea level on the eastern bank of the Anacostia River. Today, looking southeast from the White House, the Jefferson Memorial obscures the view of St. Elizabeth's; in the 1860s there was no Jefferson Memorial. The Washington Monument, in turn, was only half built in the 1860s and too far south in any event to block a view of the hospital.

74. Turner and Turner, *Mary Todd Lincoln,* 525.

75. *Collected Works,* 8: 223; Keckley, *Behind the Scenes,* 121–22; Helm, *The True Story,* 226–27.

76. Turner and Turner, *Mary Todd Lincoln,* 89, 125–126, 161–162.

77. Hay, *Diaries,* 234; Turner and Turner, *Mary Todd Lincoln,* 179, 180, 321; Keckley, *Behind the Scenes,* 85.

78. Anson G. Henry to John Williams, May 1, 1865, Illinois State Historical Library; Anson G. Henry to his wife, May 8, 1865, Illinois State Historical Library; de Chamburn, *Impressions,* 175.

79. Turner and Turner, *Mary Todd Lincoln,* 303–304, 315.

80. Ibid., 228, 228–29, 236, 257, 258, 260, 263, 264, 269, 289, 302, 311–12.

81. Ibid., 265, 268, 284, 319; see also 393, 454–55.

82. Ibid., 269–71.

83. Randall, *Mary Lincoln,* 431; *Chicago Tribune* and *Chicago Inter-Ocean,* May 19, 1875, Illinois State Historical Library; Turner and Turner, *Mary Todd Lincoln,* 316, 366, 460.

84. Turner and Turner, *Mary Todd Lincoln,* 265–266, 547.

85. *Chicago Tribune* and *Chicago Inter-Ocean,* May 19, 1875, Illinois State Historical Library; Turner and Turner, *Mary Todd Lincoln,* 261, 306.

86. Leonard Swett to David Davis, May 24, 1875, Illinois State Historical Library.

87. *Chicago Tribune* and *Chicago Inter-Ocean,* May 19, 1875, Illinois State Historical Library.

88. Robert Lincoln to Elizabeth Edwards, January 17, 1876, vol. 3, 382, of Robert Lincoln's manuscript correspondence, 46 vols., Illinois State Historical Library; Rodney A. Ross, "Mary Todd Lincoln, Patient at Bellevue Place, Batavia," *Journal of the Illinois State Historical Society* 63 (1970): 5–34; Leonard Swett to David Davis, May 24, 1875, Illinois State Historical Library. Baker, *Mary Todd Lincoln,* 277–278, 295, 313, 316–338, essentially argues that Mary was simply unhappy, the trial a set-up from start to finish, Robert greedy, the jury all-male, the press malicious, the reports of her hallucinations mere gossip, and even the suicide attempt a false tale told in a newspaper owned by Robert's former law partner. Baker is not very historical, but she is consistent.

89. Miner, *Mrs. Abraham Lincoln,* 6–7.

Chapter 5

1. *Collected Works,* 2: 506.

2. Ibid., 1: 448; 1: 490–491, 497, 496, 489, 499; 2: 489; 4: 190.

3. Ibid., 1: 305; James C. Conkling to his wife, April 8, 1843, Illinois State Historical Library.

4. Brooks, *Washington in Lincoln's Time,* 64–66; Keckley, *Behind the Scenes,* 104.

5. Herndon to Jesse Weik, February 5, 1887, Hertz, *Hidden Lincoln,* 166.

6. *Collected Works,* 2: 15, 111, 112, 113, 194–95, 203–204; Herndon to Jesse Weik, December 1, 1885, Hertz, *Hidden Lincoln,* 109. Weik in *The Real Lincoln: A Portrait* (Boston: Houghton Mifflin, 1922), 54, corrected Herndon's dates. See also Randall, *Mary Lincoln,* 134.

7. Turner and Turner, *Mary Todd Lincoln,* 55, 59.

8. *Day by Day,* 1: 207, 2: 77.

9. Herndon and Weik, *Life of Lincoln,* 249; Herndon to Jesse Weik, February 2, 1887, Hertz, *Hidden Lincoln,* 178; Whitney, *Life on the Circuit,* 62; David Davis's letters to his wife, 1843–1860, Illinois State Historical Library.

10. Burlingame, *Inner World,* 352n.382, says that *Day by Day* fails to support the conclusions I draw from it because the book does not indicate where Lincoln was every single day. It is a strange criticism. My method was to laboriously count

the days when Lincoln was at home and away, and tabulate them, for every other year between 1842 and 1860. In my analysis, I then examine the patterns that emerged. I chose every other year to simplify what was already a rather tedious task. There are, of course, days when the editors of *Day by Day* did not know where Lincoln was, but the impression one has in reading it is the remarkable completeness of their account. Whatever days are missing surely do not compromise the general picture.

11. *Collected Works,* 2: 327, 344, 394; Herndon to Wendell Philips, August 4, 1857, Blagdon Collection, Houghton Library, Harvard University.

12. The fact that few letters have survived does not, of course, prove he never wrote any. However, Mary seemed to save letters, and in her expansive old age she never referred to letters of any kind from Lincoln.

13. *Collected Works,* 1: 465.

14. Ibid., 1: 477.

15. Ibid., 1: 496.

16. Ibid., 4: 190.

17. Mrs. George C. Beal, *New York Times,* February 6, 1938, Louis A. Warren Library and Museum, Fort Wayne, Indiana; Miner, *Mrs. Abraham Lincoln,* 9; Lamon, *Life of Lincoln,* 472.

18. Frances Wallace newspaper interview, "Lincoln's Marriage," Springfield, September 2, 1895 (privately printed, 1917), Illinois State Historical Library; unidentified newspaper clipping, Louis A. Warren Library and Museum, Fort Wayne, Indiana.

19. Herndon and Weik, *Life of Lincoln,* 344; Herndon to Jesse Weik, November 19, 1885, and February 18, 1887, Hertz, *Hidden Lincoln,* 105, 176–77; Donald, *Lincoln's Herndon,* 191, explains the confused story of Herndon's 1866 interview with Mary. The barely legible notes themselves are in the Herndon/Weik Collection. For Herndon's published version of the interview, see "Mrs. Lincoln's Denial and What She Says," Massachusetts Historical Library.

20. Herndon to Jesse Weik, January 18, 1886, Hertz, *Hidden Lincoln,* 129; Herndon to Jesse Weik, January 8, 1886, Hertz, *Hidden Lincoln,* 129; Herndon to Jesse Weik, November 10, 1885, Hertz, *Hidden Lincoln,* 104–5.

21. *Collected Works,* 1: 496.

22. Ibid., 1: 319, 325, 328.

23. Ibid., 1: 391.

24. Ibid., 1: 466.

25. Robert Todd Lincoln, autobiographical statement for the 1864 *Harvard Class Book,* Harvard University Archives, 1; Walter Barlow Stevens, *A Reporter's Lincoln* (St. Louis: Missouri Historical Society, 1916), 72.

26. Robert Todd Lincoln, autobiographical statement, 3.

27. Robert Todd Lincoln to David H. Bates, June 22, 1907, Correspondence of Robert Todd Lincoln, vol. 40, 145, Illinois State Historical Library; John S. Goff, *Robert Todd Lincoln: A Man in His Own Right* (Norman: University of Oklahoma Press, 1968), 30–33; Robert Lincoln to James Schouler, December 27, 1907, Correspondence of Robert Todd Lincoln, vol. 40, 468, Illinois State Historical Library.

28. Goff, *Robert Todd Lincoln,* 215.

29. Robert Todd Lincoln, autobiographical statement, 99.

30. Robert Todd Lincoln to John Hanna, April 29, 1884, Correspondence of Robert Todd Lincoln, vol. 11, 151, Illinois State Historical Library.

31. Goff, *Robert Todd Lincoln,* 223.

32. Robert Todd Lincoln to J. C. Jankins, March 6, 1884, Correspondence of Robert Todd Lincoln, vol. 10, 526, Illinois State Historical Library; Robert Todd Lincoln, autobiographical statement, 1; Robert Todd Lincoln to Miss Harriett Henton, October 17, 1902, Correspondence of Robert Todd Lincoln, vol. 36, 118, Illinois State Historical Library.

33. Robert Todd Lincoln to E. A. Buck, January 7, 1887, to Mrs. Wyatt Eaton, June 4, 1900, and to W. Ewing Hill, July 28, 1887, Correspondence of Robert Todd Lincoln, vol. 3, 891, vol. 34, 260, and vol. 3, 983, Illinois State Historical Library; David C. Mearns, *The Lincoln Papers,* 2 vols. (Garden City, N.Y.: Doubleday, 1948), 1: 134.

34. Robert Todd Lincoln to William H. Reed, May 5, 1884; to Isaac N. Arnold, January 28, 1883; to Hon. H. M. Teller, June 23, 1883; Correspondence of Robert Todd Lincoln, vol. 11, 171, vol. 8, 273, and vol. 9, 184, Illinois State Historical Library.

35. Robert Todd Lincoln to Joseph Deuell, January 9, 1900, Correspondence of Robert Todd Lincoln, vol. 34, 115, Illinois State Historical Library.

36. Robert Todd Lincoln to Samuel H. Bishop, January 29, 1900, and to J. W. Wartmann, June 5, 1882, Correspondence of Robert Todd Lincoln, vol. 34, 148–49 and vol. 7, 4, Illinois State Historical Library.

37. Goff, *Robert Todd Lincoln,* 247; Turner and Turner, *Mary Todd Lincoln,* 440; Robert Todd Lincoln, autobiographical statement, 2.

38. Robert Todd Lincoln to Le Grand Van Valkenburgh, May 26, 1913, Correspondence of Robert Todd Lincoln, Illinois State Historical Library.

39. Robert Todd Lincoln to J. H. Orne, June 1, 1875, cited in Katherine Helm, *The True Story of Mary, Wife of Lincoln* (New York: Harper and Brothers, 1928), 295–96.

40. Herndon to Jesse Weik, January 15, 1889, to Truman Bartlett, December 20, 1889, to Jesse Weik, March 7, 1890, and to Jesse Weik, February 7, 1891, Hertz, *Hidden Lincoln,* 238, 244, 249, 260–61; Goff, *Robert Todd Lincoln,* 196.

41. *Chicago Tribune,* January 1, 1921, Louis A. Warren Library and Museum, Fort Wayne, Indiana; Turner and Turner, *Mary Todd Lincoln,* 463.

42. Keckley, *Behind the Scenes,* 103; Elizabeth Todd Grimsley, "Six Months in the White House," Illinois State Historical Library.

43. Grimsley, "Six Months," 13, gives a nice example from the wartime period of how close Lincoln was to Willie.

Chapter 6

1. Speed, *Reminiscences of Abraham Lincoln,* 20–21. Speed was not only a friend to Lincoln but also used him often as a lawyer and had a good sense of his professional abilities. See the detailed study by Susan Krause, "Abraham Lincoln and Joshua Speed, Attorney and Client," *Illinois Historical Journal* 89 (1996): 35–50.

2. Herndon notes on an interview with David Davis [1866], Wilson and Davis,

Herndon's Informants, 529; John P. Frank, *Lincoln as a Lawyer* (Urbana: University of Illinois Press, 1961), 10–11; Herndon and Weik, *Life of Lincoln,* 271–272; *Collected Works,* 2: 327, 3: 344, 3: 535, 4: 121; John J. Duff, *A. Lincoln, Prairie Lawyer* (New York: Holt, Rinehart, 1960), 16; Albert A. Woldman, *Lawyer Lincoln* (Boston: Houghton Mifflin, 1936), 22–23. Elizabeth W. Matthews of the Lincoln Legals Project in Springfield, Illinois, has published for the project *Lincoln as a Lawyer: An Annotated Bibliography,* which is available on its web site. Note also the complete law cases of Lincoln from the Legals Project, as presented on a disk that I have consulted courtesy of Cullom Davis.

3. "Introduction," Lincoln Legals Project; Dan Bannister, *Lincoln and the Supreme Court* (Springfield: published privately, 1992); William D. Beard, "Abraham Lincoln in Illinois," *Illinois History* 40 (1987): 98–100; "Lincoln Legal Briefs," *Quarterly Newsletter of the Lincoln Legal Papers* 44 (1997) and 46 (1998); "An Emerging Reappraisal of Lawyer Lincoln" (1999), online at www.fgi.net/lincolnlegalpapers.

4. Whitney, *Life on the Circuit,* 232–33; Herndon notes on his interview with David Davis, September 19, 1866, Wilson and Davis, *Herndon's Informants,* 347; Herndon and Weik, *Life of Lincoln,* 268ff; my article, "The Lives of William Herndon," *Journal of the Abraham Lincoln Association* 14 (1993): 1–14; Woldman, *Lawyer Lincoln,* 94–95; Beveridge, *Lincoln,* 1: 549; Sandra K. Lueckenhoff, "A. Lincoln, a Corporate Attorney and the Illinois Central Railroad," *Missouri Law Review* 61 (1996): 393–428.

5. Benjamin Quarles, *Lincoln and the Negro* (New York: Oxford University Press, 1962), 23–24; Donald, *Lincoln,* 103–104.

6. Herndon to Wendell Philips, May 12, 1857, Blagdon Collection, Houghton Library, Harvard University; Herndon to Jesse Weik, January 11, 1886, Hertz, *Hidden Lincoln,* 133–34.

7. *Collected Works,* 2: 80–82; 218–219; Herndon and Weik, *Life of Lincoln,* 225; "Lincoln Legal Briefs," *Quarterly Newsletter of the Lincoln Legal Papers* 46 (1998).

8. Frank, *Lincoln as a Lawyer,* 17; *Collected Works,* 2: 81–82.

9. Herndon to Wendell Philips, April 7, 1857, Blagdon Collection, Houghton Library, Harvard University.

10. Frank, *Lincoln as a Lawyer,* 16. Interestingly, the Lincoln Legals Project offers the lower figure of "several dozen" such affiliations. Perhaps they are only considering more established legal relationships. The key point is that Lincoln worked within a complex web of lawyers throughout the state.

11. Whitney, *Life on the Circuit;* Frank, *Lincoln as a Lawyer,* 21–25; Herndon and Weik, *Life of Lincoln,* 248.

12. Lamon, *Life of Lincoln,* 478; Herndon and Weik, *Life of Lincoln,* 248, 283; Herndon to Jesse Weik, November 13, 1885, Hertz, *Hidden Lincoln,* 101.

13. *Collected Works,* 1: 204, 1: 290, 1: 345, 2: 106, 2: 191, 2: 332–333; "Lincolniana Notes," *Journal of the Illinois State Historical Society* 53 (1960): 70.

14. *Collected Works,* 2: 398.

15. *Collected Works,* 2: 415–22; Frank, *Lincoln as a Lawyer,* 42, 44–96.

16. Frank, *Lincoln as a Lawyer,* 44–96; "Lincoln Legal Briefs," *Quarterly Newsletter of the Lincoln Legal Papers* 46 (1998).

17. Frank, *Lincoln as a Lawyer,* 98.

Chapter 7

1. There is an old view (which began with Herndon) that Congressman Lincoln honorably but foolishly opposed the Mexican War, lost the support of his central Illinois constituency, and was forcibly retired to circuit work in 1849; Herndon and Weik, *Life of Lincoln*, 219–36; compare *Collected Works*, 1: 51n.9. Nearly every detail of this interpretation has been shown wrong. It was a good Whig position from Maine to Illinois to oppose the war, though the party was divided on the issue. See Mark Neely, "Lincoln and the Mexican War. An argument by Analogy," *Civil War History* 24 (1978): 5–24; see also Brian C. Walton, "Elections of the 30th Congress," *Journal of Southern History* 35 (1969): 186–87. There is also no indication beyond Herndon's own complaint to Lincoln that Whigs in the district back home took offense at his opposition to the war, and if they did, it failed to register in newspapers, letters, or diaries that have survived. Only the stridently Democratic press made that charge. See Gabor Boritt, "Lincoln's Opposition to the Mexican War," *Journal of the Illinois State Historical Society* 67 (1974): 79–100; compare, for example, the comments of the *Register* on January 21 and March 10, 1848, in Mitgang, *A Press Report*, 55 and 57, with the same paper on October 27, 1848, in *Collected Works*, 2: 11–13. Nor, finally, is it true Lincoln retired from politics between 1849 and 1854, in the sense of having abandoned involvement in it altogether. He held no elective office but remained important in party affairs throughout the state. More recently, Burlingame, *Inner World*, 1–19, argues to not much effect that Lincoln went through a "mid-life crisis" in this period.

2. *Collected Works*, 1: 420–22; Frank, *Lincoln as a Lawyer*, 105–110. Lincoln never entirely abandoned his fondness for interrogatories, though he learned to use them more effectively, for example, in the 1858 debates with Douglas. It is also worth noting that the use of interrogatories was quite common in this period and reflected the legal cast of politics.

3. *Collected Works*, 1: 427, 446, 447; compare 1: 457–58, 1: 473–74.

4. Ibid., 1: 451–52.

5. Boritt, "Lincoln's Opposition to the Mexican War," 79–100.

6. *Collected Works*, 1: 430–31.

7. Ibid., 1: 439.

8. *Collected Works*, 1: 465. The connection between narcissistic injury and depression is well developed in self psychology. See Kohut, *Analysis of the Self*, 17, 18n, 117–18; the discussion of Mr. C, 249–50; Mr. K, 257–59; and Miss F, 284. See also Kohut, *Restoration of the Self*, 281, and *Psychology of the Self*, ed. Arnold Goldberg, 263–96 (case of Mr. E).

9. *Collected Works*, 2: 320, 260. I am indebted to a conversation with Arthur Zilversmith, February 12, 1980, for a clarification of Lincoln's early attitudes on slavery and race.

10. *Collected Works*, 1: 260.

11. Herndon and Weik, *Life of Lincoln*, 64, has Lincoln vowing in 1830, after witnessing the slave trade in New Orleans, to hit slavery hard if he ever had the chance. However, Herndon's source was John Hanks, who according to Lincoln himself was not with him on that trip; see *Collected Works*, 4: 62; and Benjamin Quarles, *Lincoln and the Negro* (New York: Oxford University Press, 1962), 18.

12. *Collected Works,* 1: 74–75.

13. Ibid., 1: 279, 347–348.

14. Ibid., 1: 458.

15. Quarles, *Lincoln and the Negro,* 29–30, points out that Lincoln's record on slavery as a congressman was not altogether consistent. However, Quarles acknowledges that Lincoln's seemingly proslavery votes could well have been only parliamentary maneuvers. Compare Paul Findley, *A. Lincoln: The Crucible of Congress* (New York: Crown Publishers, 1979), 13–43.

16. *Collected Works,* 2: 20n.

17. Ibid., 1: 484, 382; compare 1: 337f.

18. Ibid., 1: 480–90, 395–398.

19. The best monograph on this subject is Donald W. Riddle, *Lincoln Runs for Congress* (New Brunswick, N.J.: Rutgers University Press, 1948).

20. *Collected Works,* 1: 350, 363.

21. Ibid., 1: 354, 349, 350, 351, 352, 353, 355, 356, 359–60, 365–66.

22. Ibid., 1: 453–454, 449, 452, 453, 463, 467–68.

23. Ibid., 1: 503.

24. Ibid., 2: 1–5, 6–11.

25. George W. Fredrickson, "A Man but Not a Brother: Abraham Lincoln and Racial Equality," *Journal of Southern History* 41 (1875), 41.

26. Ibid., 2: 132, 1: 268–69, 2: 82–91, 2: 121–132, 5: 340–41.

27. Ibid., 2: 124.

28. Ibid., 1: 507.

29. Ibid., 2: 14, 25, 29–30, 49. See, for background, Thomas Ewing, "Lincoln and the General Land Office, 1849," *Journal of the Illinois Historical Society* 25 (1932): 138–53.

30. *Collected Works,* 2: 45.

31. Ibid., 2: 40–41, 43, 44–45, 49.

32. Ibid., 2: 43–44.

33. Ibid., 2: 48–49, 49–50, 50–51, 53–54, 57, 61, 65; Herndon and Weik, *Life of Lincoln,* 246–247.

34. *Collected Works,* 3: 6; see also 2: 472, 3: 213; Neely, "Lincoln and the Mexican War," 24.

35. Donald, *Lincoln,* 119–141, closely parallels my narrative; Thomas, *Lincoln,* 125, characterizes Lincoln's role in Congress as diligent but unspectacular; Findley, *Crucible of Congress,* 216, says, "Lincoln came home from Congress politically strong"; Gabor Boritt, *Lincoln and the Economics of the American Dream* (Memphis: Memphis State University Press, 1978), 135, 142, 150, is somewhat ambiguous.

36. Herndon and Weik, *Life of Lincoln,* 246; note also Herndon to Jesse Weik, February 11, 1887, Hertz, *Hidden Lincoln,* 172.

37. *Collected Works,* 2: 461–62.

38. Herndon and Weik, *Life of Lincoln,* 325; Don E. Fehrenbacher, *Prelude to Greatness: Lincoln in the 1850s* (Stanford: Stanford University Press, 1962), 72 (Hebrew prophet quote) and 73, summarizing the historiography of the myth.

39. Christopher Breiseth, "Lincoln, Douglas, and Springfield in the 1858 Campaign," in Davis et al., *Public and Private Lincoln,* 101–20.

40. *Collected Works,* 2: 320.

41. Ibid., 2: 255, 492, 482, 501.

42. Ibid., 2: 273, 266, 349–52.

43. Ibid., 2: 437–42; Quarles, *Lincoln and the Negro,* 35; Boritt, *Lincoln and the Economics of the American Dream;* Eric Foner, *Free Soil, Free Labor, Free Men: The Ideology of the Republican Party before the Civil War* (New York: Oxford University Press, 1970), 45; Quarles, *Lincoln and the Negro,* 30–38.

44. The issue of Lincoln and race has been hotly debated since Lerone Bennett, "Was Abe Lincoln a White Supremacist?" *Ebony* 23 (1968): 35–38, 40, 42. Herbert Mitgang replied to Bennett quickly and self-assuredly, "Was Lincoln Just a Honkie?" *New York Times Magazine* (February 11, 1968): 34–35, 100–107. In fact, quite a lot of scholarship preceded Bennett's 1968 article. See, for example, Edward Magdol, "Owen Lovejoy's Role in the Campaign of 1858," *Journal of the Illinois Historical Society* 59 (1959): 403–16; and especially Quarles, *Lincoln and the Negro* (1962), and Arvarh E. Strickland, "The Illinois Background of Lincoln's Attitude toward Slavery and the Negro," *Journal of the Illinois Historical Society* 55 (1963): 474–94. See also Leon Litwack, *North of Slavery: The Negro in the Free States, 1790–1860* (Chicago: University of Chicago Press, 1961); and Martin Duberman, ed., *The Antislavery Vanguard: New Essays on the Abolitionists* (Princeton: Princeton University Press, 1965). Since 1968 a number of important works have appeared on this issue. The best general study is Foner, *Free Soil;* a careful analysis is Fredrickson, "A Man but Not a Brother." Lerone Bennett has expanded his 1968 article into a book-length study, *Forced Into Glory: Abraham Lincoln's Dream* (New York: Johnson Publishing Co., 2000), that adds little to the argument.

45. *Collected Works,* 3: 145–46; see also 2: 405, 498.

46. *Collected Works,* 2: 256, 250, 405–406; Kenneth M. Stampp, *The Imperiled Union: Essays on the Background of the Civil War* (New York: Oxford University Press, 1980), 128.

47. Frederick Douglass, "Oration in Memory of Abraham Lincoln, Delivered at the Unveiling of the Freedmen's Monument in Memory of Abraham Lincoln in Lincoln Park, Washington, D.C., April 14, 1876," *The Life and Writings of Frederick Douglass,* 8 vols. (New York: International Publishers, 1955), 4: 312. Compare Breiseth, "Lincoln and Frederick Douglass: Another Debate," *Journal of the Illinois State Historical Society* 68 (1975): 9–16.

48. Fredrickson, "A Man but Not a Brother," 50, makes this point, repeating, without credit, Harry V. Jaffa, *Crisis of the House Divided: An Interpretation of the Lincoln-Douglas Debates* (Seattle: University of Washington Press, 1959), 61; *Collected Works,* 2: 132, 255–256, 298–99; *Day by Day,* 2: 114.

49. *Collected Works,* 2: 274.

50. Ibid., 2: 222, 264.

51. Ibid., 2: 230.

52. See also ibid., 2: 242, 244.

53. Herndon and Weik, *Life of Lincoln,* 343.

54. James Gourley's statement to Herndon [1865–1866], Wilson and Davis, *Herndon's Informants,* 451–453.

55. *Collected Works,* 1: 315.

56. Beveridge, *Lincoln,* 2: 575, 318.

Chapter 8

1. Francis B. Carpenter, *Six Months at the White House with Abraham Lincoln: The Story of a Picture* (New York: Hurd and Houghton, 1867), 18, 30, 82, 217; Lamon, *Life of Lincoln*, 464, 470, 475; de Chambrun, *Impressions*, 21–22; Mitgang, *A Press Report*, 378; *Collected Works*, 1: 265.

2. Whitney, *Life on the Circuit*, 51–52, 65; Herndon to Cyrus D. Poole, September 5, 1886, Hertz, *Hidden Lincoln*, 12; Herndon and Weik, *Life of Lincoln*, 473.

3. See my discussion of the sermons that morning, *Apocalypse: On the Psychology of Fundamentalism in America* (Boston: Beacon Press, 1994), 176–181.

4. *Collected Works*, 1: 59.

5. Ibid., 1: 78.

6. Lamon, *Life of Lincoln*, 476–77; Hay, *Lincoln and the Civil War*, 30; compare 182; Mitgang, *A Press Report*, 378; Carpenter, *Six Months*, 44–46.

7. *Collected Works*, 1: 268.

8. Ibid., 4: 64; Whitney, *Life on the Circuit*, 51. In a footnote the editor of Whitney's book, Paul M. Angle, contrasts Whitney's account with that of William A. Grimshaw, who encountered a resolute Lincoln on the day of his defeat to Douglas. Angle's purpose seems to be to cast doubt on the authenticity of Whitney's account, which seems gratuitous; it is quite possible Lincoln showed two different moods on the same day for political and/or personal reasons.

9. *Collected Works*, 1: 95, 289.

10. Orville Hickman Browning, *The Diary of Orville Hickman Browning*, 2 vols. (Springfield: Illinois State Historical Library, 1925), 1: 489; Hay, *Diaries*, 11.

11. *Collected Works*, 1: 8, 2: 81; Lamon, *Life of Lincoln*, 468; Carpenter, *Six Months*, 145.

12. Fehrenbacher, *Prelude to Greatness*, 19–47; Donald, "A. Lincoln, Politician," *Lincoln Reconsidered*, 57–81, 88; *Collected Works*, 4: 64.

13. Hay, *Diaries*, 76, 11, 29, 66, 69, 77, 179, 204, 125.

14. Ibid., 76.

15. Trueblood, *Theologian*, 9.

16. Heinz Kohut first formulated these criteria in "Forms and Transformations of Narcissism," in *Search for the Self*, 1: 427–60. See also the discussion of Mr. M in *Restoration of the Self*, 1–62; and of Mr. E in *Psychology of the Self*, 263–96. Such criteria without theoretical foundation are necessarily arbitrary; see, for example, Martin A. Sweeney, "The Personality of Lincoln the War President," *Social Studies* 65 (1974): 164–67.

17. Carpenter, *Six Months*, 148–49; Herndon and Weik, *Life of Lincoln*, 244.

18. Burlingame, *Inner World*, 147–235, and on 374 in his index, lists nearly 75 examples of Lincoln's supposed anger in general.

19. Herndon and Weik, *Life of Lincoln*, 238–39; *Collected Works*, 2: 10–11.

20. For more on their relationship, see my "The Lives of William Herndon," *Journal of the Abraham Lincoln Association* 14 (1993), especially 9–11.

21. De Chambrun, *Impressions*, 82.

22. Carpenter, *Six Months*, 149–150, 278; Herndon and Weik, *Life of Lincoln*, 249–250; Lamon, *Life of Lincoln*, 478–79.

23. Basler, *Touchstone for Greatness,* 21; David C. Mearns, *The Lincoln Papers: The Story of the Collection with Selections to July 4, 1861,* 2 vols. (New York: Doubleday, 1948) 1: 169; Carpenter, *Six Months,* 80–81; Donald, *Lincoln Reconsidered,* 70; Herndon and Weik, *Life of Lincoln,* 94; Findley, *Crucible of Congress,* 67.

24. Herndon fragment, n.d., Hertz, *Hidden Lincoln,* 398–99; *Collected Works,* 8: 420.

25. *Collected Works,* 1: 510; Herndon and Weik, *Life of Lincoln,* 94.

26. Donald, *Lincoln Reconsidered,* 115–16; Herndon and Weik, *Life of Lincoln,* 256; Mitgang, *A Press Report,* 17–18, 26, 71; *Collected Works,* 1: 508, 516.

27. Hay, *Diaries,* 68, 79–80.

28. Carpenter, *Six Months,* 150; de Chambrun, *Impressions,* 100; Herndon to Jesse Weik, February 21, 1891, and December 22, 1888, and to C. O. Poole, January 5, 1886, Hertz, *Hidden Lincoln,* 263, 231, 124; Herndon and Weik, *Life of Lincoln,* 473; Lamon, *Life of Lincoln,* 478–79; Mitgang, *A Press Report,* 378; Lord Byron, *Don Juan,* canto 4, stanza 4; Whitney, *Life on the Circuit,* 146–47.

29. Turner and Turner, *Mary Todd Lincoln,* 293, 299; Mitgang, *A Press Report,* 35; S. A. Crawford to Herndon, January 4, 1886, Hertz, *Hidden Lincoln,* 285–87.

30. Donald, *Lincoln Reconsidered,* 70–71; Carpenter, *Six Months,* 33; Whitney, *Life on the Circuit,* 119; *Collected Works,* 3: 254; compare 8: 96.

31. Burlingame, *Inner World,* 88n.42, is at his best in discussing the letter.

32. *Collected Works,* 8: 116–17.

33. Ibid., 8: 332–33.

34. Herndon and Weik, *Life of Lincoln,* 258; Whitney, *Life on the Circuit,* 121–22.

35. *Collected Works,* 2: 390, 4: 62; Luther E. Robinson, *Abraham Lincoln as a Man of Letters* (New York: G. P. Putnam's Sons, 1923) 20; Daniel K. Lodge, *Abraham Lincoln: Master of Words* (New York: Appleton & Co., 1924), 7; Herndon to Jesse Weik, October 21, 1885, Hertz, *Hidden Lincoln,* 95; James T. Hickey, "Three R's in Lincoln's Education: Rogers, Riggin & Rankin," *Journal of the Illinois State Historical Society* 52 (1959): 195–207; William Greene to Herndon, May 30, 1865, Wilson and Davis, *Herndon's Informants,* 17–21.

36. Roy P. Basler, "Abraham Lincoln's Rhetoric," *American Literature* 11 (1939): 170–71; compare Basler, *Touchstone for Greatness,* 56, and Randall, *Lincoln the President,* 1: 3.

37. Trueblood, *Theologian,* 49, 56; Basler, "Lincoln's Rhetoric," 173; Sandburg, *The Prairie Years,* 1: 416.

38. Herndon to Jesse Weik, October 21, 1885, Hertz, *Hidden Lincoln,* 95; Basler, "Lincoln's Rhetoric," 173; Garry Wills, *Lincoln at Gettysburg: The Words that Remade America* (New York: Simon & Schuster, 1992); William K. Wimsatt and Cleanth Brooks, *Literary Criticisms: A Short History* (New York: Vintage Books, 1972), 74.

39. John G. Nicolay and John Hay, *Abraham Lincoln: A History,* 10 vols. (New York: Century, 1890), 3: 343–44; *Collected Works,* 1: 111.

40. Don E. Fehrenbacher, "Lincoln and the Weight of Responsibility," *Journal of the Illinois State Historical Society* 68 (1975): 48; Hay, *Diaries,* 138, 139; David C. Mearns, *Largely Lincoln* (New York: St. Martin's Press, 1961), 126–2; *Collected Works,* 6: 392; Lamon, *Life of Lincoln,* 477–78; Carpenter, *Six Months,* 49–52.

41. De Chambrun, *Impressions,* 83; *Collected Works,* 6: 392.

42. Fehrenbacher, "Lincoln and the Weight of Responsibility," 53.

43. George B. Forgie, *Patricide in the House Divided: A Psychological Interpretation of Lincoln and His Age* (New York: Norton, 1979), 243–50.

44. Basler, *A Touchstone for Greatness,* 206.

45. Ibid., 225; Wilson, *Patriotic Gore,* 106. For an odd, if interesting, approach to these issues, see A. Bronson Feldman, "Lincoln: The Creation of a Cult," *The Unconscious in History* (New York: Philosophical Library, 1959).

Acknowledgments

First books, even revised ones, require undue encouragement from friends and colleagues. It is unlikely that I can adequately thank everyone who has contributed to whatever insight this book brings to the study of Lincoln. Often those most helpful have disagreed with my conclusions, sometimes passionately. But each in different ways helped me make my points infinitely more clear.

For Geoffrey C. Ward to write the Foreword to this new edition brings me special pleasure, as he was the first to read this book's earliest incarnation 25 years ago as a rough version of what is now Chapter 2. His written comments then nearly equaled the length of my short paper. He insisted I was onto something that needed elaboration, and subsequently, as a book began to emerge, he read every word, added innumerable insights, corrected errors, and, in many conversations, nudged me along. No footnote can document that kind of assistance.

As work proceeded, I began an extended conversation with Christopher N. Breiseth, a colleague in history at Sangamon State University, in Springfield, and later president of Wilkes University. He got it all even before it made sense to me. He listened and provoked and read and listened some more. He always asked the crucial question, and he shared unsparingly his ideas from his own area of scholarship—Lincoln and race. Often his casual asides became my orienting ideas. The concept for Chapter 7, as I remember, began during a conversation in a noisy cafeteria over spilled coffee.

Sometime in the mid-1970s, Richard Current, one of a handful of recognized authorities on Lincoln, became interested in my work. His role in shaping ideas was incomparable. He seldom left a page without rewriting whole sections of murky prose, and he never hesitated to share his own knowledge or to let me know decisively when I was off base.

Roy Basler, the editor of Lincoln's *Collected Works* and a distinguished scholar, also proved to be an enormously helpful reader. More than most, Roy disagreed with many of my conclusions. But his caveats directed me toward greater clarity. I always assumed that anyone of Roy Basler's stature who took that much time to disagree affirmed something essentially valuable in my work. He was especially helpful with what are now Chapters 1, 2, 3, and 4.

A number of other friends and colleagues from years past went through the original manuscript with care and devotion. Thomas A. Kohut offered a wide range of helpful comments. Jack Nolan improved the style immeasurably. John Y. Simon read drafts of two early chapters, caught some egregious errors in the final version, and offered kind words of support. Lawrence J. Friedman also read two early chapters and made extensive comments on the completed manuscript that proved helpful. Harold Holzer caught numerous errors, large and small. Larry Shiner read the manuscript carefully and then prodded me to conclude. Marilyn Immel listened to pieces of my Lincoln work for years and read the final manuscript in a quizzical but supportive way. Judy Everson and Mike Lennon improved the text at many points. Both also helped me find a title.

Despite later disputes between us, I also want to thank Stephen B. Oates for his careful reading of the original manuscript. Bruce Mazlish, as well, helped me in many ways.

Most of my students' eyes glazed over whenever I started in on Lincoln again. But two—Mark Johnson and Cliff Wilson—listened carefully and read the final manuscript critically. The rest endured.

Many others have read parts of this book during its long birth. All have helped a great deal. These include Mark Neely, Gabor Boritt, Robert Brugger, Stanley H. Cath, Norman Naimark, Ernest Wolf, Fred Weinstein, James E. Hurt, Frank J. Williams, Daniel Offer, Neil Harris, George Fredrickson, George B. Forgie, Cullom Davis, William Gilmore, Becky Veach, Ralph Stone, Richard Johnston, John Demos, and Kathleen Dalton.

From 1974 to 1977 I directed a project funded by the National Endowment for the Humanities to develop interpretive materials for the Lincoln sites in Springfield. That project proved an education in itself. Most of the scholars who served as advisers for that project already have been thanked for their later involvement in my own work. But I also want to extend my sincere thanks to Don Fehrenbacher, who taught me a great deal about Lincoln. I also want to thank Gerd Stern, our producer, whose search for Lincoln paralleled my own. One important result of the project was to make me intimately familiar with the physical sites of the Lincoln story. An understanding of those sites could only have come from the sustained help and friendship of many people in Springfield who helped me come to know Lincoln: Sally and Paul Schanbacher, Carolyn and Bob Oxtoby, Edith and Jim Meyers, Al Banton, Molly Becker, and Calista Herndon.

Presenting some of my Lincoln work to the Seattle Psychoanalytic Institute in 1973 also proved useful. I would also like to thank my classmates (and Jerome Kavka) at the Chicago Institute for Psychoanalysis who once listened to four hours of Lincoln, and had much to contribute. The late Mel Prosen, associate chairman of the Department of Psychiatry at Rush Medical School in Chicago, and my co-leader of the psychohistory seminar, heard much of Lincoln and graciously shared his intimate knowledge of psychoanalytic theory.

Many libraries and their always helpful staffs have assisted me. But one—the Illinois State Historical Library in Springfield—deserves very special mention. James T. Hickey shared his extensive knowledge of Lincoln and allowed me to read the letters of Robert Todd Lincoln. Cheryl Schnirring, Roger Bridges, Dan Holt, and Laurel Bowen were always available and helpful. I also want to thank many in the Illinois Department of Conservation, especially John Patterson, for help at many points. Ruth Friedman, a graduate student at Sangamon State, generously shared some of her research on the eighth judicial circuit. Another student, Terry Otten, shared his work and helped introduce me to the records at Jacksonville State Hospital.

Three research assistants at quite different stages of this book deserve special mention. In the beginning, Becky Veach tracked down countless references and gathered materials. Then, as I was completing the final draft and finishing off footnotes, Melinda Kwedar proved invaluable. More recently, Bob Johnson, a CUNY Ph.D. student and a lawyer, helped immensely with research materials for my revisions of Chapter 6.

I gained much from my semester-long dialogue with James Oakes in our Ph.D. course on "Lincoln and the Civil War" at the Graduate Center of the City University of New York in the spring of 2000. This new edition draws heavily on that experience; indeed, it would be unimaginable without it.

Notwithstanding all this expert advice, any errors of fact or interpretation that remain are, alas, my sole responsibility.

I am not forgetting the dedication of the 1982 edition of this book to my first wife, Carol, but it seems as life moves on this transformed study should be for the grandchildren: Trevor, Jay, and Carolyn.

Charles B. Strozier, Brooklyn, July 2000

Index

Index

H

Hackett, James H., 251

Halsted, Oliver S., 122

Hampton, Moses, 238

Hanks, Dennis: on AL, 18, 24, 31; daughter of, 142; joins Thomas's household, 7, 22; marries Elizabeth Johnston, 26; on Mary, 94; on move to Indiana, 22; on Nancy, 10, 11; on Thomas, 12, 14, 17, 18; turkey story and, 30, 265n64

Hanks, John, 10, 24, 63

Hanks, Lucy (grandmother), 3, 4, 7

Hanks, Nancy. *See* Lincoln, Nancy Hanks

Hanks, Sophie, 7

Hanna, John, 164

Hardin, John J., 59, 197

Harris, Ruth, 128–129

Hatch, Ozias M., 103

Hay, John: on ambition, 47; on early days of Civil War, 231; on humor, 233–234, 241; on Mary, 119; Robert and, xviii, 165, 166

Hazel, Caleb, 21

Heal, Mrs. George C., 156

Hearn, George A., 130

Helm, Emilie Todd, 94, 115, 117, 128

Henning, Fanny, 56, 60, 61–63, 64

Henry, Anson G., 59; AL's death and, 130–131; Mary and, 123, 135; on Mary and Julia Trumbull, 99–100

Herndon, William: accuracy of, 51; on AL's absences, 145, 148–149; on AL as father, 155, 157; AL's treatment of, 55–56; on AL and women, 63, 272n74; on ambition, 47; boards with Speed, 55; on education, 246–247; house divided speech and, 207–209; on humor, 236–237, 241, 242; on intensity, 26; on Mary, xix, 69, 99, 109, 114, 157–158; Mary and, 103–107, 142, 246; Mexican War and, 185–188; paternity theory of, 7–9; on personality, 225; practices law with AL, 174–175; Robert and, 166, 167, 169; on Thomas, 12–13, 15, 262n28; visits Sarah, 27–28; writes *Life of Lincoln,* xvii–xxi; on youth, xvi

Herndon's Informants (Wilson and Davis), xx

Hill, Samuel, 39

Holland, Josiah G., 13, 101

"House divided" speech, 206–208, 217–220, 222–223; motivation for, 208–209, 211–217

Humphreys, Elizabeth. *See* Todd, Elizabeth Humphreys

Hurst, Charles R., 55

I

Iles, Elijah, 37

Illegitimacy: AL's view of, 7, 8–9; in American life, 6; of Nancy, 3–6, 9

Illinois: AL serves in legislature of, 191–193, 196–197; eighth circuit in, 177; Thomas owns property in, 14; *see also* Charleston, Ill.; New Salem, Ill.; Springfield, Ill.

Illinois Central Railroad, 180–181

Illinois Internal Improvement Act, 40

Indiana, 22, 33–34

Inner World, The (Burlingame), 236

Interrogatories, 184–188, 282n2

J

Jayne, Julia, 93, 243

Johnson, Robert J., 270n50

Johnston, Elizabeth (stepsister), 26

Johnston, John D. (stepbrother), 14, 26, 71, 72–73; requests loan, 70

Johnston, Matilda (stepsister), 26–27, 263n56

Johnston, Sarah Bush. *See* Lincoln, Sarah Bush Johnston

Judd, Adeline, 113

Judd, Norman, 121

Merriman, E. H., 92
Mexican War, 183, 184–188, 282n1
Miner, Noyes W., 121, 137, 156
Moore, C. H., 180
Morrison, James L. D., 202, 203

N

Nativist movement, 117–118
New Salem Debating Society, 36, 266n1
New Salem, Ill., 36–39
Nicolay, John G., xviii, 165, 166, 233
Normality, defined by Freud, 41
Norris, Elizabeth L., 89, 93, 97, 98

O

Offutt, Denton, 31, 37
Oregon Territory, secretaryship of, 204–205
Orne, Sally, 133
Owens, Mary (later Mary Vineyard), 31, 226, 229; AL's courtship of, 12, 42–44, 228

P

Panic of 1837, 75, 76
Parker, Eliza. See Todd, Eliza Parker
Pekin agreement, 196–197
"Perpetuation of Our Political Institutions, The." See Lyceum Speech
Phillips, Wendell, 174
Plato, 80
Poetry, by Lincoln, 33–34
Polk, James A., 184–188
Popular sovereignty, 209, 216–217
Postmaster, AL as, 38
Preston, William B., 203
Prostitutes, AL's reported visits to, 63, 272n74
Psychohistory, xii, xv, 259n1

R

Railroads: Illinois Central, 180–181; popular sovereignty and, 216–217; Rock Island, 182
Randall, James G., xv–xvi
Randall, Ruth Painter: on engage-ment, 46; on Hay, 119; on marriage, 101; on Mary and Herndon, 106; on Mary's personality, 92, 97; on Speed, 56, 270n56
Real, Mrs. George C., 107
Reavis, Isham, 149
"Rebecca Letters," 93, 243, 249
Religion, 85, 87, 195–196
Riney, Zachariah, 21
Robertson, George, 223
Rock Island Bridge case, 182
Romine, John, 24–25
Rosette, John E., 247
Rutledge, Ann, 41–42, 104, 226, 228

S

Sandburg, Carl: Herndon material and, xx; on Nancy, 5, 9; on Sarah, 28
Sangamo Journal: AL works for, 39; Lyceum Speech published in, 78
Schouler, William, 201
Schurz, Carl, 241
Scripps, John L., xvi–xvii
Second Inaugural Address, 85–86, 246
Seward, William, 250
Shakespeare, William, 251–254
Shearer, Hannah, 112, 116, 117, 120, 125, 143
Shields, James, 93, 243–244
Shutes, Milton, 51
Sickles, Dan, 122
Simon, John Y., 78
Simon, Paul, 40
Slavery: AL's law practice and, 174; AL's positions on, 85–86, 189–192, 193, 209, 211–213, 215–223, 282n11; Clay and, 200; federal vs. local authority and, 83; Mary on AL's position on, 117; panic of 1837 and, 75; Taylor's election and, 198–199; Thomas opposes, 22; in Washington, D.C., 183, 188–189, 191–195